Concepts and Dialogues across Shifting Spaces in Intercultural Business

Concepts and Dialogues across Shifting Spaces in Intercultural Business

Edited by

Clara Sarmento

Cambridge Scholars Publishing

Concepts and Dialogues across Shifting Spaces in Intercultural Business

Edited by Clara Sarmento

This book first published 2022

Cambridge Scholars Publishing

Lady Stephenson Library, Newcastle upon Tyne, NE6 2PA, UK

British Library Cataloguing in Publication Data
A catalogue record for this book is available from the British Library

ISBN (10): 1-5275-7725-2
ISBN (13): 978-1-5275-7725-1

TABLE OF CONTENTS

INTRODUCTION

Concepts and Dialogues across Shifting Spaces in Intercultural Business explores western and non-western, northern and southern epistemologies (Santos and Meneses, 2010), both conventional and alternative, in order to withstand independent, sustainable and critical methodologies for intercultural business. By articulating concepts, theories, structures, performances and aesthetics, across different cultures and communication channels, the networks of cultural codes and practices emerge and are critically observed, thus blurring conceptual frontiers and challenging customary criteria of legitimation.

This book includes contributions that focus on expressions of contemporary mutability, on contexts, interpretations, identities, ideologies and subjectivities inherent to the development of relations between business companies, nations and communities. The volume also explores how the promotion, marketing and branding of cultural heritage has led to the development of thriving economic strategies, e.g. through tourism and the creative industries. Widespread mobility, along with the growing interest for cultural heritage (see the case of cultural tourism) and the desire for authentic experiences, have encouraged the contact between different cultures, i.e., have fostered intercultural flows. The challenge of this view resides precisely on how culture-based initiatives can be used to boost the creation of business opportunities and enhance added value to the economy.

Throughout the contemporary global market, the many languages of intercultural communication play a key role in building successful business ventures. The use of context analysis methodologies, as well as the measurement of cultural variables in a business environment, enhance intercultural understanding, in line with the new paths of the world economy. Intercultural issues are present in all territories and every business is somehow the subject and the object of intercultural exchanges, needing both to integrate and to be integrated. This world in constant mutation, that seems to live under a kaleidoscopic dynamic, requires business agents who are interculturally competent. This means that those business agents are: a) able to communicate with partners from other cultures in a way that earns their respect and trust; b) equipped to encourage cooperation and productivity across borders; c) capable of adapting their technical, professional and personal skills to local conditions and constraints; d) adjustable and generally at ease with/in different cultures.

In this book, intercultural studies reach well beyond the mere catalogue of alleged national characteristics and the standard approach to the negative implications of cultural differences. Instead, these chapters focus on the sharing of knowledge between cultures, making the most of both their similarities and differences, within the diverse framework of global business. Culture is addressed as a profitable commodity, as an asset for any ambitious company willing to expand, as a tool and object of business and economic growth. In this perspective, interdisciplinary knowledge about the theories and practices of intercultural studies assumes a perspective of self- and hetero-knowledge, a critical perspective that is also aware of the new routes of economic expansion. This approach pays as much attention to the centres from which the cultural matrices once emanated as to the contemporary postcolonial peripheries (or new centres), bearing in mind that centre and periphery are nowadays interchangeable concepts in constant renegotiation.

The many purposes of the chapters here compiled include analysing the relationship between culture, communication, society, economy, and political context; the ability to assess, adapt and (trans)create information across cultural borders; the implementation of differentiated business strategies based on non-standard cultural knowledge; the challenges of communicating between different business cultures; the development of culturally aware, ethical and sustainable business; the understanding of local practices, values and regulations, their opportunities and obstacles within the global business environment.

Concepts and Dialogues across Shifting Spaces in Intercultural Business opens with a reflection on intercultural negotiations between Japan and the United States of America. Based upon interviews and surveys conducted among Japanese and American business agents, with a wide experience in transactions between those two countries, "Intercultural Negotiations between Japanese and American Businesspeople: Conducting mutually beneficial business" examines the differing cultural values implicit in the responses obtained and the lessons drawn from experience. Successful businesspeople carefully plan before a meeting, take a deep insight into changing business alliances and power relations, and focus on fulfilling the other party's needs. Also, they expand their behavioral repertoire by incorporating one another's strengths, such as American analytical ways of thinking and Japanese holistic ways of thinking, thus achieving intercultural competence.

Along with experience, education and learning are also key words for interculturally effective business innovation and sustainable development. However, the Covid-19 crisis has led us to rethink the ways in which we relate to each other and understand economic, social, and environmental development. Education for sustainability, based on the acquisition of both entrepreneurial and citizenship skills, allows us to promote the creation of innovative business and social projects. "A New Insight into Business Innovation and Sustainable Development: The role of education" argues that intercultural competence does not fragment knowledge but, instead, supports the connection between different domains of science and business, in a globalized reality where all human beings are more and more confronted with similar challenges. Therefore, in order to reach a truly inclusive education, intercultural principles must always be present.

The two following chapters explore the growing need for intercultural competence in two different professional and business contexts. Intercultural competence implies the practice of effective communication skills as much as the awareness of cultural and linguistic diversity. Within linguistic diversity – and the respective impact on intercultural communication skills – one must include speech-language pathologies and their therapies. "Intercultural Competence, Communication and Education: The speech-language pathologist/therapist's (SLP/T) intervention" discusses how these professionals' role is crucial for improving human communication, increasing cultural know-how, and diversifying the profession by developing intercultural procedures. In another field, "Marketing Mix for Sustainable Cultural Industries" explores the set of variables that must be considered by companies when formulating their intercultural communication, marketing and commercialization strategies. Specifically, the cultural and creative industries – due to their growing impact over economy, culture, environment and society – should implement strategies that guarantee a balance of these four factors, in order to promote the sustainable development of the territory. At the same time, as the significance of the creative economy continues to grow, vital synergies with tourism are emerging, with a considerable potential for the development of new products, experiences and markets (OECD, 2014). These new links are driving a shift from conventional models of cultural tourism to new models of creative tourism based on tangible and intangible heritage and contemporary creativity.

Tourism is one of the biggest vehicles for intercultural communication nowadays. But instead of seeking a utopian communion between hosts and guests from different cultures, tourism should recognize that difference is actually an opportunity to promote and create value out of cultural variety. Experiencing difference is a fundamental motivation for tourism as an intercultural practice, for the satisfaction of clients, and for sustainable innovation led by culturally-aware managers and promoters. The next chapters approach the topic of tourism as a global intercultural business, resorting to notions of identity, power, heritage, discourse, representation and territory, among other concepts employed by intercultural studies.

Analyzing tourism as a global cultural phenomenon means not only thinking about it in terms of the world's economy, but also regarding the transformation of geographic spaces into significant places, within the ever-polemic concept of globalization, often understood as a manifestation of western dominance. "Tourism as Intercultural Business: Locating concepts and questioning identities" addresses matters of ethics, power and cultural hegemony, while considering the opportunities and challenges of tourism as an intercultural business. Opportunities include the engagement of local communities in the protection of cultural heritage, as well as the enhancement of sustainable tourism, with an impact on employment, poverty reduction, environmental protection and the general preservation of authenticity in culture and traditions. By recognizing the value of different sections of the community, cultural resources and traditions that could otherwise be seen as ordinary become exceptional. And the exceptional is what tourists seek, as opposed to the commonplace routine of everyday life.

It is evident that tourism is a fundamental sector of the global economy, but the Covid-19 pandemic has reverted this whole situation. Therefore, discussions about the different types of value involved in tourism-related goods and services have to be carried out within the context of the current 'viral society'. "The Value of Products and Services in Tourism: The case of viral society" understands this unprecedented emerging paradigm of virulent social formations in terms of societal processes, such as the consecutive confinements, in different spaces and times. The value of goods and services is here discussed in articulation with the analysis of various historical types of value, the role of information and knowledge about consumption, the current conjuncture, the (re)production of new social mobilities, and the informative-textual value of products and services in the tourism industry, before concluding with the hypothesis of an alternative mode of de-confinement through 'social remobilities'.

Cultural heritage plays an essential role in the cooperation between regions and countries and in the creation of new types of business in the sector of tourism. Cultural entrepreneurship accounts for a growing percentage of countries' GDPs and labour force, and plays a leading role in retaining local populations, preserving cultural heritage and contributing to cultural understanding. "Using Cultural Heritage to Create Business Opportunities: Successful cases from France, Germany and Spain" analyses case-studies from three European countries that seem to embody what could be described as the process of branding cultural identity. In these examples, the symbolic value of culture is commodified, more or less standardised, in order to meet the general demand for some degree of authenticity, identity or alterity, with the potential to attract tourism. Local communities are at the heart of these case studies, combining static and simple stereotypes with complex and heterogeneous identities. Oktoberfest, Puy du Fou and Tomatina may be considered symbolic icons of German, French and Spanish cultures, respectively, but in reality they are mere illustrations of a regional segment of those cultures. Nevertheless, as those products appear to condense a standard cultural representation, they have been commodified and successfully marketed as tourist assets for an international diverse audience.

The chapters "Translating the Culture of the Ribeira Sacra's Viticultural Business: An intercultural dialogue" and "Underwater Cultural Heritage as a Blue Tourism Driver: A pilot project from littoral Alentejo, Portugal" analyse other examples of thriving business opportunities in heritage-related cultural tourism. Although the wine business is centuries-old, in recent times harvesting grapes and many other practices related to wine production in general have become trendy activities in tourism. "Translating the Culture of the Ribeira Sacra's Viticultural Business" combines the business of wine, translation studies and cultural transfer in advertising, in order to perform a deep analysis of the bilingual Spanish-English online catalogue of the Ribeira Sacra (Galicia, Spain) region. The sea and the coastline areas are also driving forces of economy. For this reason, coastal and maritime tourism, also called Blue Tourism, is part of the EU's blue growth strategy and constitutes one of the most important sectors of the blue economy, being the largest in terms of employment and accounting for one third of the economy linked to the sea. Within the frame of the United Nations' decade of ocean science for sustainable development, "Underwater Cultural Heritage as a Blue Tourism Driver" explores an on-going pilot project developed in littoral Alentejo, on the Southwest coast of Portugal, as an alternative approach to using underwater cultural heritage as a driver for blue tourism, sea sustainability and public awareness.

All these case studies prove that, in the contemporary business context, companies have no chance but to remain open to an intercultural dialogue with partners and clients from all over the globe and from the most diverse – and often unexpected – sectors. In order to accomplish this goal successfully, strong communication skills accompanied by a deep cultural understanding are the key. "Bridging the Gap: The importance of interculturality in business relations" discusses how business agents must stop looking at cultural differences as an obstacle and should start seeing them as competitive advantages instead.

Developing intercultural practices and skills in business implies a special attention to national and international legal regulations, as much as to ethical values in general, from universal human rights to the values and traditions that regulate the everyday life of a specific community. The challenges of intercultural dialogue and the need for companies to comply with human rights are highlighted in "Intercultural Dialogue in Business: Mutual benefits and human rights". Although religion and politics often constrain a culture's codes of conduct, the image of a company that invests in social and environmental projects, and that respects intercultural diversity and human rights, is always positively affected. As large corporations increasingly play a political role in the global agenda, respect for human rights and a true intercultural focus provide a competitive advantage in the international marketplace.

"Audit Performance and Independence: A cultural approach between Latin and Nordic countries" discusses the many ways in which the cultural framework commonly associated with a country may impact on the development and performance of any business. To reach this goal, corporate governance is used as an example of good practices that may help organisations prevent fraud, considered from the perspective of financial engineering. Financial frauds have undermined the public opinion's trust in the auditor as well as the general confidence in business companies, and have also shown the lack of independence of the different players at stake, including top managers, auditors and accounting professionals. As an immediate consequence, international institutions issued ethical and professional guidelines for the reinforcement of the organisations' internal control. However, institutions responsible for the supervision of auditors and listed companies, such as the Portuguese Stock Commission, suffered a significant amount of pressure and underwent serious conflicts of interests. This chapter considers examples not only from Portugal but also from Nordic countries such as Norway, Sweden and Finland, because ethical differences are commonly associated with the cultural traits of each country, and this has an impact on the prerequisite of independence that characterizes auditing worldwide.

Relying solely on the role of institutional investors as the only agents capable of promoting an evolution in the paradigm of business may not always be effective. The role of private law is also crucial in order to enhance the development of the international business environment, especially as far as the demand for corporate purpose is concerned. "The New Paradigm of the Corporation: A comparative approach between law and business" describes how a significant movement sustaining a change in the understanding of corporate purpose has emerged worldwide, over the last few years. The movement involves academics, CEOs and policy makers from many different countries and rests upon the idea of purpose. It argues – against Friedman's doctrine of maximization of shareholders' value as the sole intent of a company – that the purpose of a company should consider the interests of those who interact with it, such as creditors, suppliers, workers, customers and society as a whole. Therefore, and in line with other chapters in this book, "The new paradigm of the corporation" sustains that the purpose of a business company should include social and intercultural concerns as well.

The chapters collected in *Concepts and Dialogues across Shifting Spaces in Intercultural Business* seek to understand the international context under a theoretical and empirical methodology in line with the demands of a diverse and inclusive worldwide market. The understanding of culture – both one's own and the 'other's' culture – contributes to the construction of sustainable, socially responsible companies, capable of being integrated into (and of integrating) the multiple cultures of the global diaspora. By combining intercultural studies with research areas such as economics, communication, politics, history, management, and law, this book allows for a better understanding of the complex environment that underlies the 21st century business world.

Concepts and Dialogues across Shifting Spaces in Intercultural Business is the result of the research conducted by the guest-editor at the Centre for Intercultural Studies (www.iscap.ipp.pt/cei) of ISCAP, the Business School of the Polytechnic of Porto – P.PORTO. This book also results from the wide international network and the ground-breaking educational practices developed along the years at the Master's Program in Intercultural Studies for Business of ISCAP-P.PORTO. The guest-editor dedicates this book to her students at ISCAP-P.PORTO, for their courage, resilience and unyielding commitment to work during the pandemic crisis.

Clara Sarmento
Porto, September 2021

References

OECD (2014), *Tourism and the Creative Economy*, OECD Studies on Tourism, OECD Publishing, Paris, https://doi.org/10.1787/9789264207875-en.

SANTOS, Boaventura Sousa; MENESES, Maria Paula (2010), *Epistemologias do Sul*, 2nd edition. Coimbra: Almedina.

CHAPTER 1

INTERCULTURAL NEGOTIATION BETWEEN JAPANESE AND AMERICAN BUSINESSPEOPLE: CONDUCTING MUTUALLY BENEFICIAL BUSINESS

JUNKO KOBAYASHI AND LINDA VISWAT

KANSAI GAIDAI UNIVERSITY-OTEMON GAKUIN UNIVERSITY

1. Introduction

Business is becoming more and more global at an astonishing speed, and negotiation plays an integral role, not only in business transactions with other companies, but also in business procedures within a company. Negotiation is commonly defined as the process by which people with conflicting interests produce certain outcomes through dialog (Sakuma 2011, 13). However, it is never an easy job to integrate conflicting interests and bring negotiation to a successful completion, especially in intercultural negotiation, a very complex activity involving many cultural and situational factors. Particularly important cultural differences to understand in negotiation are collectivism versus individualism, hierarchy versus egalitarianism and high-context cultures versus low-context cultures (Brett 2007; Chaney and Martin 2014; Gesteland 2012; Lustig and Koester 2010). In the individualism-collectivism dimension, cultures differ in the extent to which individual autonomy is regarded favorably or unfavorably. In the hierarchy-egalitarianism taxonomy, cultures differ in the degree to which they view status inequalities as just or unjust. In high- and low-context cultures, cultures differ in the extent to which they depend on the context in communication and in the extent to which they regard implicit messages as preferable. Situational factors include power relations between sellers and buyers, enlarging and shrinking markets and the number of competitors.

Power relations are constantly changing by the degree of dependence on the other party (Fukuda 2012; Sakuma 2011; Neale and Lys 2016).

Then, what kinds of problems have Japanese and American businesspeople encountered when negotiating with American or Japanese counterparts? The purpose of this paper is to explore how Japanese and American businesspeople have dealt with differing cultural values and power relations in negotiation and what they have learned from their experience so that they can obtain mutually beneficial results.

2. Methodology

For the above purpose, surveys of Japanese and American businesspeople who have experience in transactions with American or Japanese counterparts were conducted either through interviews or questionnaires. Respondents had a choice of answering questions either verbally or in writing. The researchers asked for more detailed explanations when necessary.

The respondents were 30 Japanese and 21 Americans whose age ranged from their twenties to their seventies. 46 of the respondents were male and 5 were female.

They were asked whether they had negotiation experience. If the answer was in the affirmative, they were asked to describe their experiences, and respond as to whether they were satisfied with the outcome of their negotiations. If the answer was negative, they were asked to give reasons. Lastly, they were asked to feel free to give advice on successful negotiation.

Data was analyzed using the KJ method in order to increase credibility and reliability. The KJ method developed by Kawakita Jiro (1967, 1970) provides a means for organizing qualitative data by combining separate concepts through card-making, grouping, naming and chart-making. It aims to create factors by synthesizing various data or ideas.

3. Survey results

The results of the surveys indicated that with M & A and business alliances, a lot of people had intercultural negotiation experience and they recognized the need to understand the other party's cultural values and conduct market research. Also, many respondents emphasized the importance of advance preparation (Malhotra and Bazerman 2007; Neale and Lys 2016; Watkins 1999).

3.1. Negotiation within a workplace

The following is negotiation within a company. The purpose of negotiation within a company is mainly to proceed with projects efficiently and partly to ask for a raise and demand continued employment.

3.1.1. Showing respect for differing cultural values

Within a workplace, advance preparation for launching projects efficiently means to understand the other party's cultural values and show respect for those values. An American with experience working as a manager in a newly acquired company focused on Japanese employees' loyalty to their company and their collective attitude (Sakuma 1994; Samovar and Porter 2001) in order to ease Japanese employees' anxiety. "The company had been successful prior to being acquired. We told the employees that we wanted to learn from the company's prior success;" and "I adopted Japanese customs. Along with every other employee, I had my desk within the department. I put my street shoes in the locker every morning and wore slippers in the office. I had lunch every day with my colleagues and never hesitated to have what was being served in the cafeteria."

On the other hand, Japanese people who were appointed as managers in newly acquired companies respected American employees' freedom and valued their individualism (Ferraro 1998; Stewart and Bennett 1991). "When I teach American workers how to use a new machine, they are usually given a month to master the operation, but in the next stage, some workers can't use it efficiently. When they can't achieve a certain quota, I have them choose to either come to the workplace early the next morning or work overtime that day;" and "I give notice to the employees who make mistakes by recommending: Use this site. However, if employees still make many mistakes, I have them redo it at their convenience."

3.1.2. Utilizing differing cultural values

With regard to utilizing differing cultural values, examples are closely related to Japanese holistic and American analytical views (Sakuma 1994; Suzuki 2017). An American project leader working at a Japanese company stated that he was pleased with the Japanese management of valuing human resources based on Japanese holistic ways of thinking. “They try to have employees who aren’t very capable relocate to a different department or reeducate them.” He continued to mention that when he worked at an American company before, the toughest job as a project leader was to decide which subordinates he should dismiss.

On the other hand, a Japanese person who was appointed as manager of an American branch office stated that he adopted the merit system based on American analytical ways of thinking. “In a department of quality control, I have decided to indicate figures regarding how many products each employee checked and how many defects the employee detected and have some efficient workers get a raise.” In the past when he had passed performance reviews on to his subordinates, a few people voiced complaints. That is why he decided to present the figures in order to prevent potential grievances.

3.1.3. Establishing cooperative human relations and grasping local needs

With respect to projects focused on finding new markets abroad, a number of people pointed out that it is indispensable to grasp local needs (Gesteland 2012; Kisaki 2020; Tanihara 2011) by establishing cooperative human relations with local colleagues. Specific examples are companies dealing in washing machines and lawn mowers. “We learned from American colleagues that Americans can’t dry clothes outside and we have valued the function of clothes dryers;” and “Plenty of Americans own big gardens, and American colleagues made us recognize the need to develop lawn mowers which are appropriate to the big gardens.” After understanding the local needs, the engineers discussed how to develop machines which are sensitive to local needs.

Also, in the field of software, both Japanese and Americans agreed on the need for collaboration. “Japanese value storylines in anime while Americans pursue excitement. While cherishing the original plots, we collaborate with Americans on how to add the flavor of excitement;” and “If characters in anime are only Asians, Americans feel strange. When I suggested that some characters should be Caucasians, Hispanics and Africans, my suggestion was welcomed.” Since then, the anime producers have discussed many times how to create better works.

3.1.4 Complaints toward the other party

In contrast with the above successful examples, some negotiations ended up having no effect. American complaints about Japanese people concern insufficient explanations for promoting projects and giving feedback. "Many Japanese say at meetings, 'This is a problem here,' and do not offer any possible fix. Japanese tend to be more cautious and not say anything unless they are pretty sure what they say will work;" "Japanese people often say, 'This is the way it is because this is the way we have always done it' and it is not a good reason for anything;" and "Japanese bosses tend to just pass sheets of performance reviews to their subordinates. No feedback is given on a daily basis."

On the other hand, Japanese complaints toward Americans are failures to observe project deadlines and a tendency to overrate their abilities. "Many Americans don't observe project deadlines. We have to make sure in the middle of projects, 'How is your project coming along?';" and "When declining an American request for raise, we have to make the reason clear. For instance, 'Your performance was fantastic, but you had conflicts with your colleagues. Unless you change your attitude, you can't get a raise.';" and "Americans tend to claim the group achievements as their own, so we have to be cautious about our judgment."

3.1.5 Understanding incompatible cultural differences

We have to become aware that some cultural values are incompatible, and therefore they can't be fused. What Japanese and Americans who have experience in working at both Japanese and American companies noted were their attitudes toward taking risks and the degree of making compromises. "At meetings in a Japanese company, when an employee tried something new, a boss avoided taking risks by collecting data. Even if an American employee insisted that it is worth a try, the boss responded that he would need permission from the head office;" and "Japanese managers provided lots of input and had strong views on what they wanted. However, they were willing to compromise based on what was good for the division. American managers were less involved in the details, but they were also less willing to accept an organization that was optimized for the division."

3.2. Negotiation with other companies

In negotiation with other companies, two main purposes were identified: promoting joint projects efficiently and setting the prices of products. In both cases, businesspeople emphasized advance preparation as a key requirement.

3.2.1. Showing respect for differing cultural values

Like negotiation within a workplace, both Japanese and American businesspeople stated that they should do research on the other party's corporate philosophies and cultural values beforehand in order to show respect for other companies or differing cultural values. While market prices fluctuate, businesspeople often have fairly limited freedom in negotiations over the prices of products. Many businesspeople mentioned that whether they can negotiate smoothly depends on human relations with the other party. American businesspeople who succeeded in transactions with Japanese companies shared their experiences. "Before negotiation, I carefully read the corporate philosophies of Japanese companies and talked about the philosophies;" and "I had read many books on Japan, especially how Japan had achieved remarkable success after World War II in such a short period of time, and raised the theme. My knowledge seemed to impress Japanese businesspeople." He added that his predecessor talked about American football, which didn't make sense to Japanese. Consequently, the negotiation didn't move forward.

On the other hand, Japanese businesspeople who achieved success in the transactions with American companies complimented the American company's initiative and American attitude of being willing to take risks (Foster 1992; Lewicki, Saunders, and Barry 2006). "Your company has done up-to-date research on how to cope with new kinds of viruses in remarkably changing IT industry;" and "Developing new products always involves risks, and we admire your courageous decisions without worrying too much about risks."

3.2.2. Advance survey of market price and the prices of competitors

When setting the prices of products, businesspeople paid attention to the world situation and the prices of competitors. A Japanese businessperson who conducted transactions with raw materials emphasized the need to constantly check the fluctuation of market price. "The price of raw materials goes up and down radically depending on world situation, especially the political climate in oil producing nations, and I have to pursue an appropriate price each time." Another Japanese businessperson who had rich negotiation experience focused on the prices of competitors. "In a global community we have to agree on a price after taking our competitors' prices into account, so we always keep an eye on the competitors' prices and the product reviews in the market."

3.2.3. Recognizing who has the authority to decide

Whether the purpose of negotiation is the promotion of projects or the price of products, what is equally important is to recognize who has the authority to decide (Chaney and Martin 2014; Sakuma 1994; Tanihara 2005). American businesspeople learned from their past failures. "A Japanese who is a fluent speaker of English does not necessarily have the authority to decide. In fact, he is just working as an interpreter, and we have to find out who has the power;" and "At the end of the negotiation, I was told, 'We'll report on the content of today's meetings to the head office.' I thought that it was a waste of time. We should have demanded beforehand that a person with decision-making power should be delegated." A Japanese person with rich business experience also mentioned, "I found out that in the United States just an order taker is not welcomed. Since then, I have asked my boss in advance to entrust decision-making power to me."

On the other hand, Japanese businesspeople learned from their past failures. "American employees only know their own jobs. Even when I asked their colleague, they just answered, 'I don't know.' When a person in charge was expected to take a long vacation, I should have asked beforehand who I should contact during that period;" and "Americans often change jobs. Even when we exchanged a contract with an American in charge, the person left the office later. I should have specified the whole content of the contract."

3.2.4. Dealing with communication problems

Businesspeople who understood some differences in communication styles recognized the need to adjust their communication styles to the other culture (Ferraro 1998; Samovar and Porter 2001; Takemura 2020). American businesspeople who faced communication problems shared their experiences. "Japanese people often say, 'It will be difficult.' I found out that it means 'No.' Since then, I have decided to ask, 'What is the less difficult way?'; and "Listen to what is said and what is left unsaid. Don't overload people with information just because you can't feel comfortable in silence. Wait for questions. Through the questions, you would sometimes have to figure out what is the most important issue." They realized that in Japanese culture, the interlocutor often has to figure out the implied crucial piece of information (Hall 1977).

On the other hand, Japanese businesspeople insisted that contracts should include items on breach of contract. "In transactions with non-Japanese companies, oral agreements have no effect. Since I found out that they often failed to fulfill the agreements, we have decided to include some items. For instance, when companies failed to make payments on appointed dates, they should pay back the money with interest;" and "When I order clothes from Hispanic-American companies, we seldom get the clothes on time. We have decided to specify the contractual penalties. If they send the clothes two weeks later than the appointed dates, they have to give us 10% discount, and if they are even later, the order will be cancelled."

3.2.5. Grasping the expectations of other companies

Japanese businesspeople with rich experience in conducting transactions with American companies mentioned the need to grasp the expectations of other companies: "Some American clients insist that they would like high-quality machines, but the definition of high-quality machines differs from culture to culture. Japanese clients are more demanding while American clients in general would like adequate machines at a low price;" and "Some ethnic groups, although they claim that they need quality machines, actually give priority to the price of machines, not quality."

3.3. No negotiation experience

Around 20 percent of respondents had no negotiation experience. Their reasons were classified into three groups: (1) They are pleased with the corporate philosophy of their present company; (2) The working environment of their present company is better than that of a previous company; and (3) Placing a price on products is based on market price. The specific examples of the corporate philosophy are: "The corporate philosophy, *kaizen* (continuous improvement) is similar to my family culture;" and "The company has strong social responsibility including environmental problems." With regard to the specific examples of the working environment, "The present company recognized my expertise more highly than the previous company;" "When I worked as a salesperson before, I was told by my boss to sell the company products by any means. In the present company, however, I can sell the company products to people who really need them;" and "The present company has health benefits and I feel secure."

4. Discussion

The above results demonstrated that advance preparation is important in intercultural negotiation whether it is conducted within a company or with other companies. If businesspeople have some knowledge of what Japanese and American businesspeople learned from their experiences, they can apply the knowledge to various negotiation situations in order to show respect for the other party.

4.1. Showing respect for differing cultural values

One point of principled negotiation involves separating individuals from a problem (Fisher, Ury, and Patton, 1991). In reality, however, it is extremely difficult to implement. Businesspeople in a disadvantageous situation have difficulty repressing their emotions, so a practical policy on the part of businesspeople in an advantageous position is to offer the other party a site where they can control their emotions. The above examples proved that it would be effective if an American manager mentions Japanese employees' loyalty to their company and follows collective actions or if a Japanese manager offers American subordinates options and values American individualism.

4.2. Incorporating one another's strengths

The above results also indicated that we can make effective use of human resources and minimize employees' complaints by incorporating one another's strengths. The American project leader became aware of Japanese holistic ways of thinking and succeeded in establishing mutually beneficial relations by reevaluating his subordinates' abilities and relocating them to different divisions, for example, from a sales department to a back office. On the other hand, the Japanese managers adopted American analytical ways of thinking with accurate figures in performance reviews and established better relations. Americans often change jobs, and salaries in their previous workplaces are important. As a result, Japanese managers have decided to indicate figures in order to prevent potential problems and also to motivate their subordinates.

4.3. Establishing complementary relations

Both Japanese and American businesspeople mentioned that projects worked out well after establishing cooperative human relations and grasping local needs. They have established complementary relations by recognizing Japanese high-quality machines and American proficiency of introducing products to the audience. In anime also, they have succeeded in raising box office sales remarkably by combining the merits from both cultures.

4.4. What Japanese and Americans can learn from each other's complaints

The complaints pointed out by both Japanese and Americans are closely interconnected. Japanese people don't give detailed explanations about projects, so Americans may not observe the project deadlines. If a Japanese person adds explanations such as "This is an important project, so if you achieve success within the deadline, you may deserve a raise," American employees may become highly motivated. If a Japanese mentions some solutions after explaining some merits of conventional ways and some risks concerning the new ideas in the case of failure, it will help Americans understand that Japanese value groupism; that is, they don't want to cause trouble to other members of the group. If they discuss the problem at a meeting, they may find ways to reduce risks.

As for Japanese managers' insufficient feedback, it is important for Japanese managers to understand that Americans expect communication on a daily basis. While Japanese culture takes working diligently for granted, Americans often need words for recognizing hard work and for encouragement. American businesspeople gave frank comments. "When I was working at an American company, I was often praised by my boss, 'Thank you for your hard work.' In a Japanese company, however, I'm seldom told by my boss;" and "American bosses speak to me casually. For instance, when I dealt with mortgages and asked for my clients' bank statements, some clients got angry by saying, 'Why is the bank statement necessary?' However, my boss helped me calm down by saying, 'Don't worry. It's their problem.'" If Japanese managers communicate with their subordinates on a daily basis and casually mention benchmarks for rating their job performance, Americans will be less likely to overrate their jobs.

We can expect to improve human relations by adopting merits from the other culture. Japanese people can learn from the American contractual society and include items in contracts to demonstrate that employees who can't perform to the required standard will be dismissed. On the other hand, Americans can learn from Japanese holistic ways of thinking and can ease their stress by reevaluating their subordinates' abilities from multiple viewpoints. If they have to dismiss their subordinates because of the recession of their company, they can write a letter of recommendation, for example, they might mention that their subordinates can do a good job in a back office even though their sales activities are mediocre.

4.5. Ascertaining the true intent of other companies

It is also important to ascertain the true intent of other companies (Chaney and Martin 2014; Gesteland 2012) by asking questions because "the more questions you ask, the more difficult it becomes for the other party to come up with consistent answers—unless they are telling the truth" (Malhotra and Bazerman 2007, 205). Japanese businesspeople stated that businesspeople should not take non-Japanese clients' statements at face value. "Some non-Japanese clients purport to want to establish long-term relations only so as to make a contract advantageous to them, so we have to detect if they really hope for it;" and "Depending on the financial condition of the other company, they may demand a further discount. Businesspeople shouldn't make much compromise at the first transaction while taking the possible change into consideration." When some non-Japanese companies make an offer to resume transactions with Japanese companies because the Japanese companies have quality products, Japanese companies should make a contract favorable to themselves by pointing out the other party's previous unilateral breach of contract.

4.6. Unexpected results

The survey results also demonstrated that with regard to one cultural dimension on vertical and egalitarian societies which has been regarded as significant (Brett 2007; Lustig and Koester 2010), there is actually little difference between Japanese and American cultures. This is probably because power relations are important in any negotiation. The remarks of American businesspeople reflected this position. "Automotive companies have strong purchasing functions and routinely pressure suppliers to deliver annual cost reductions. We had to implement internal productivity measures to reduce the cost per part, and also think about what additional services and solutions could be sold to the automotive company (sourcing, design and new materials) to add additional margin;" and "I can ask my boss questions, but I can't argue back to the boss. If I do, I may be made the target of dismissal." On the other hand, Japanese businesspeople described the situation as follows: "When I agree with my boss's opinion, I can express it right away. If I don't agree with it, I will keep silent which implies hesitation. My boss can become aware of my reluctant attitude."

5. Conclusion

As the above results demonstrated, successful businesspeople take initiative in understanding differing cultural values and devising ways to show respect for them. Also, they expand their behavioral repertoire by incorporating one another's strengths such as American analytical thinking or Japanese holistic thinking. Further, they establish complementary relations when their cultural values are not compatible. Nowadays M & A and business alliances are frequently implemented, and power relations are constantly changing. We can't predict which company will be under the control of another company, so it is indispensable for every single businessperson to understand differing cultural values and rapid changes in the business world.

Also, the results indicated that feelings of satisfaction are relative. Some people can feel satisfied by contrasting the present working environment with that of a previous workplace. If we understand this, we can vicariously experience how others feel and acknowledge their dissatisfaction calmly.

No one can predict what will happen in the future, so it will be all the more important to cooperate with one another in a variety of ways. In such a period of uncertainty, companies that can understand the other party's cultural values and implement mutually beneficial ideas are more likely to continue to prosper in difficult circumstances.

Acknowledgments

We would like to express our deep gratitude to Japanese and American businesspeople who willingly participated in our surveys despite their tight schedules, especially those people who gave detailed comments on our follow-up questions. We also would like to express appreciation to Cambridge Scholars Publishing for inviting us to join the project, and to

Editor Clara Sarmento for offering us warm support.

References

Brett, Jeanne, M. 2007. *Negotiating globally* (2nd ed.). San Francisco: Jossey-Base.

Chaney, Lillian, H., and Martin, Jeanette, S. 2014. *Intercultural business communication*. Boston: Pearson.

Ferraro, Gary, P. 1998. *The cultural dimension of international business* (3rd ed). New Jersey: Prentice Hall.

Fisher, Roger, Ury, William, and Patton, Bruce. 1991. *Getting to yes: Negotiation agreement without giving in* (2nd ed.). NY: Penguin Books.

Foster, Dean, A. 1992. *Bargaining across borders: How to negotiate business successfully anywhere in the world*. NY: McGraw-Hill.

Fukuda, Takeshi. 2012. *Koushouryoku wo kitaeru hon* [Improving ability to negotiate]. Translated by the authors. Tokyo: Mikasashobou.

Gesteland, Richard, R. 2012. *Cross-cultural business behavior: A guide for global management*. Copenhagen: Copenhagen Business School Press.

Hall, Edward, T. 1977. *Beyond culture*. NY: Anchor.

Kawakita, Jiro. 1967. *Hassouhou* [Clues to creativity]. Translated by the authors. Tokyo: Chukoushinsho.

Kawakita, Jiro. 1970. *Zokuhassouhou* [The second series of clues to creativity]. Translated by the authors. Tokyo: Chukoushinsho.

Kisaki, Kenji. 2020. *Purodusu no kihon* [Foundations of producing]. Translated by the authors. Tokyo: Shueisha.

Lewicki, Roy, J., Saunders, David, M., and Barry, Bruce. 2006. *Negotiation* (5th ed.). Boston: McGraw Hill.

Lustig, Myron, and Koester, Jolene. 2010. *Intercultural competence: Interpersonal communication across cultures* (6th ed.). Boston: Allyn and Bacon.

Malhotra, Deepak, and Bazerman, Max, H. 2007. *Negotiation genius.* NY: Bantam.

Neale, Margaret A. and Lys, Thomas Z. 2016. *Getting (more of) what you want.* London: People Books.

Sakuma, Masaru. 1994. *Kokusaibijinesu to koushouryoku* [International business and ability to negotiate]. Translated by the authors. Tokyo: NHK Books.

Sakuma, Masaru. 2011. *Koshouryoku nyuumon* [An introduction to ability to negotiate] (4th ed.). Translated by the authors. Tokyo: Nihonkeizaishinbun.

Samovar, Larry, A., and Porter, Richard, E. 2001. *Communication between cultures*. Belmont: Wadsworth.

Stewart, Edward, C., and Bennett, Milton, J. 1991. *American cultural patterns* (rev. ed.) Yarmouth: Intercultural Press.

Suzuki, Daisetsu. 2017. *Toyotekina mikata* [Eastern ways of thinking]. Translated by the authors. Tokyo: Iwanami.

Takemura, Kazuhiro. 2020. *Koshono hiketsu* [Tips for negotiations]. Translated by the authors. Tokyo: Jiyukokumin.

Tanihara, Makoto. 2005. *Kosho settokuno gijyutsu* [Skills to negotiate and persuade]. Translated by the authors. Tokyo: Dobunkan.

Tanihara, Makoto. 2011. *Bijinesu koushou* [Business negotiations]. Translated by the authors. Tokyo: Gentousha.

Watkins, Michael. 1999. "Negotiating in a complex world". *Negotiation Journal,* No.15: 229-270.

CHAPTER 2

A NEW INSIGHT INTO BUSINESS INNOVATION AND SUSTAINABLE DEVELOPMENT: THE ROLE OF EDUCATION

LUÍSA BRAVO LAMAS AND MARCO LAMAS
CENTRE FOR INTERCULTURAL STUDIES (CEI)
ISCAP – P.PORTO, POLYTECHNIC OF PORTO

The challenges of globalisation

Human life has always undergone great changes over time. In the last decades, these changes have occurred due to the relentless search for improvement in quality of life and to the innovations introduced in health, technology, economics, and communication, reaching all areas that involve human behaviour. Globalisation has imposed profound changes that have completely altered everyday life around the globe. It is easy to buy products manufactured in distant countries, which in turn resort to raw materials from other continents. The various steps of a product, from production and distribution to final consumption, have contributed to a great increase in pollution and the unrestrained use of natural resources, jeopardizing the sustainability of the species' survival. This phenomenon cannot be considered only from an environmental and economic point of view, since "Globalization is political, technological and cultural, as well as economic. It has been influenced above all by developments in systems of communication, dating back only to the late 1960's" (Giddens, 1999, p. 2).

Globalization cannot be considered as an incident, but rather as an effective change in our lives, that requires new forms of relationship (Giddens, 2001). We need to value knowledge in order to eliminate poverty and free ourselves from ignorance, but this must be accompanied by a dialogue between reason and the subject, bringing us closer and protecting us against the totalitarian and individualistic temptations that destroy humankind

(Touraine, 1994). Therefore, we must take into account not only the consequences of the capitalist economic model, but also of the individualistic policies that have been carried out by different states, excluding and discriminating residents from other countries and imposing a political and cultural hegemony that fragments and destroys societies (Giddens, 2001; Touraine, 1994).

Globalisation has widened the gap between the richest and the poorest, within countries and between countries. These differences, despite being clearly visible through the different reports and recommendations produced by international organizations, have not changed the course of events. Fundamental rights are not guaranteed to the entire population of the world, despite the Universal Declaration of Human Rights (UN, 1948), that committed the signatory states to promote the universal and effective respect for human rights and fundamental freedoms, considering that "all human beings are born free and equal in dignity and rights".

Following the proposal by Santos (2002), states all over the world must work jointly and democratically, respecting the role of international and non-governmental organizations, solving together problems that they are not able to solve by themselves. The idea of completely independent and autonomous states is as illusory as the idea of totally independent and autonomous individuals (Cortina, 2011; Menezes, 2005). Just as we need each other in order to survive, in the same way, states need other states. This mutual dependence exists not only at the economic and political level, but also at the social level, which necessarily involves the valorisation of interculturality.

We have to commit ourselves to a better future, demanding more from each other, in order to deal with the globalised world that has changed our lives and endangered the survival of humankind. There is a global need for new "forms of world interdependence" and "planetary consciousness", as Giddens argues:

> Globalisation—which is a process of uneven development that fragments as it coordinates—introduces new forms of world interdependence, in which, once again, there are no "others." These create novel forms of risk and danger at the same time as they promote far-reaching possibilities of global security. (1996, p. 175)

The moment we are going through demands different solutions, which require new business models, new roles for states, and greater cooperation and solidarity, in order to reach sustainable development. This is only possible through global citizenship, based on a better coexistence, where interculturality and diversity replace any type of discrimination. We believe that education is the key for this change.

The COVID-19 pandemic

With the rapid spread of COVID-19, travels stopped, stores, businesses and schools closed, and only health services and essential services kept on functioning. The images of desert streets in cities all over the world caused widespread anxiety, leading people to think that nothing would ever be the same again.

But the economy could not stop, as it would jeopardize the survival of populations, and so activities were resumed. The use of digital platforms increased rapidly, teleworking became the norm, meetings started to be held online, and the same happened with teaching. Government officials were left with the arduous task of reconciling economic activity and curbing the number of infected people, while scientific research was devoted to discovering a vaccine and an effective treatment for the virus.

The pandemic, contrary to what one might think, did not change consumption and human behaviour in general. The United in Science 2020 Report compiled by the World Meteorological Organization shows that "Overall emissions reductions in 2020 will lead to a small reduction in the annual increase of the atmospheric concentrations of long-lived greenhouse gases" (2020, p. 2).

On the other hand, although we all feel caught up in this pandemic context, the way of experiencing it is clearly unequal. Rich countries are concerned about the spread of the virus within their territorial limits, closing borders when it suits them, trying to stop the pandemic in "their spaces", acquiring vaccines for "their residents", and closing foreign trade. While poor countries are simply trying to survive with fewer vaccines. Inequalities have clearly been increasing, not only between countries but also among citizens residing in the same country. Unemployment has increased with the bankruptcy of companies that are less technologically prepared and have less cash management capacity, mostly SMEs (Small and Medium-sized Enterprises), as mentioned by Bartik et al:

> On average, the businesses reported having reduced their active employment by 39% since January. The decline was particularly sharp in the Mid-

> Atlantic region (which includes New York City), where 54% of firms were closed and employment was down by 47%. (2020, p. 17656)

In addition to size, another factor that has affected the economy is related to the sectors of activity, namely those that are affected by legal provisions, timetable constraints or even by the closure of commercial establishments. Conversely, we see other sectors and entrepreneurs that are adapting and thriving with the situation, namely online commerce, real estate, personal services, and any kind of business with low face-to-face interaction. Consequently, poverty worsens considerably and, with it, less noble sentiments plague the world population, trying to find culprits who, as a result, are excluded, marginalized and rejected.

A recent briefing note on COVID-19 by Mckinsey (2021) predicts that, by the end of this pandemic, COVID-19 would have cost between 16 and 36 trillion dollars. But this will not be the only impact of the pandemic, as the experts' panel involved in the study states that:

> In the next two decades, competition for global influence is likely to reach its highest level since the Cold War. Current tensions are most apparent in the unfolding competition between China and the United States, the homes of 76 of the world's 100 most valuable companies (McKinsey, 2021, parag. 5)

There have been, however, some exceptions that prove that solidarity has not disappeared, and that the search for paths leading to the common good of humankind continues to exist among states and people. The role of some prominent figures is fundamental in the appeal to the solidarity and change that we must undertake for a better future. Among those figures, we highlight the words of Pope Francis. Following the WHO declaration of the pandemic in March 2020, the highest representative of the Catholic Church joined virtually citizens from all around the world in a prayer in the deserted St. Peter's Square, declaring that we are all on the same boat, and that no one is safe alone (Pope Francis, 2020).

The Director General of the World Health Organization, Dr Tedros Adhanom Ghebreyesus, also calls for the need to find joint answers, such as waving patents, even temporarily and without loss for the companies:

> These are significant steps but we cannot rest until everyone has access, and we need to ensure sustainable vaccine supply chains for the long-term that are vastly bigger than what we have now. This will become even more important if we have to vaccinate people with boosters or reformulate vaccines to tackle variants. Waving patents temporarily won't mean

innovators miss out. Like during the HIV crisis or in a war, companies will be paid royalties for the products they manufacture (Ghebreyesus, parag. 10, 2021).

Business and Sustainable Development

Globalisation, climate changes, and the current pandemic context may jeopardize the survival of humanity, and the solution lies in a change in our behaviour. According to Santos (2020), we cannot remain within the same paradigm of understanding and acting:

> I am talking about the fact that the virus is a co-creation of humans and nature, a co-creation that is a product of the way in which men have interfered with natural processes, especially since the 16th century. This long-time span coincides with that of modern capitalism, colonialism and patriarchy. (p. 26)

Mazuccato (2021) follows the same line of thought, stating that capitalism no longer had answers, even before COVID-19, for the problems and challenges facing the world, in particular the climate crisis, stressing that: “From global heating to biodiversity loss, human activity is eroding the conditions necessary for social and environmental stability” (p. 26).

The United Nations adopted in 2015 the Sustainable Development Goals (SDGs), as a universal strategy to end poverty, protect the planet, guarantee that the 17 fundamental SDGs are achieved by 2030, and that “no one will be left behind”. This commitment reinforces that these 17 SDGs “are integrated and indivisible and balance the three dimensions of sustainable development: the economic, social and environmental” (UN, 2015, preamble). This Agenda for Sustainable Development establishes goals, fixes targets, and includes areas of critical importance for humanity and the planet, such as people, planet, prosperity, peace, and partnership (UN, 2015).

The role of governments is important in order to ensure, through the use of law, that companies respect the changes that must be undertaken to reduce the global warming that affects the planet as a whole, and that people change the way they consume, avoiding goods produced from non-renewable materials, and reducing consumption in general. This ambitious agenda was designed not just with environmental concerns in mind, but also, and even more, in order to end poverty, hunger, and discrimination against women and girls; reduce inequalities; provide health care, better education, decent work, social protection, and job opportunities in general. These purposes will be easier to implement if each and every one actively participates in the exercise of their citizenship for the guarantee of human rights and for the common good of the world's population.

Sustainable Development, very much debated nowadays, is not a new concept. Already in 1983, the United Nations gave sustainable development the necessary prominence, through the resolution 38/161 of 19 December, which created a special commission with the objective of developing a report on the environment, with a view to the world from the year 2000 onwards. This report already included strategic proposals for sustainable development, resulting in the creation of the World Commission on Environment and Development (WCED). The concept, as presented in the aforementioned report, suggests that we must satisfy present needs without compromising the needs of future generations. The report assumes that, for this to happen, we must safeguard the basic needs of the poor around the world, because, if this does not happen and if poverty continues to be endemic, there will be serious environmental consequences (UN, 1987, p. 24).

It is therefore mandatory to adopt a new perspective on the economic development of companies and countries, a perspective that should be focused not only on the economy, but also on the environment and society. This should be the purpose of politicians and leaders of large companies alike, as Leitão sustains: "A new sustainable economic model designed for the Earth – and not exclusively for the market –, with an essential respect for ecological principles and capable of bringing its benefits to all the people" (2015, p. 152, our translation).

Circular economy, one of the possible solutions for a sustainable development is, as referred by the Ellen MacArthur Foundation (2017), "based on the principles of designing out waste and pollution, keeping products and materials in use, and regenerating natural systems". Thus, circular economy is based upon a model that provides a new way of looking at economic development, which is in line with nature. Circular economy allows business agents to design new management practices and innovative business models, capable of ensuring sustainability for both companies and the environment.

The European Commission, in line with the need to invest in the circular economy, adopted, in March 2020, as part of the New Green Deal, the new Circular Economy Action Plan (CEAP), that seeks a reduction in the consumption of natural resources, as well as the creation of jobs and the desired goal of climate neutrality by 2050 (European Commission, 2020). For this, legislative and non-legislative measures have been established in order to reach the following sustainable principles:

- improving product durability, reusability, upgradability and reparability, addressing the presence of hazardous chemicals in products, and increasing their energy and resource efficiency;
- increasing recycled content in products, while ensuring their performance and safety;
- enabling remanufacturing and high-quality recycling;
- reducing carbon and environmental footprints;
- restricting single-use and countering premature obsolescence;
- introducing a ban on the destruction of unsold durable goods;
- incentivising product-as-a-service or other models where producers keep the ownership of the product or the responsibility for its performance throughout its lifecycle;
- mobilising the potential of digitalisation of product information, including solutions such as digital passports, tagging and watermarks;
- rewarding products based on their different sustainability performance, including by linking high performance levels to incentives. (European Commission, 2020, p. 4)

Both our society and the world economy have been largely organized, as it has been possible to see, in a capitalist model that does not provide the necessary answers for the countless challenges we face. Instead, this model is increasingly using the finite resources available in the planet and enlarging the social and economic differences between countries and among citizens of the same country. It is crucial to implement the necessary actions to attain the SDGs and the transition to a circular economy, but this will only be achieved by innovating in country and business governance.

Business Innovation through social intrapreneurship and corporate social responsibility

Taking into account globalisation, the pandemic situation, the need to ensure sustainable development, the economic and social crises that are happening at an ever faster pace (also a consequence of globalisation and COVID-19), as well as the rapid evolution of technology and the constant changes in the customers' needs, desires, and the problems they want to solve, one specific solution emerges: changing the way we think and manage business, from its creation to its expansion and transformation .

Business leaders must undertake a positive attitude and search for solutions, recognizing that, nowadays, entrepreneurship is the engine that drives the economy of many nations, promoting employability, giving rise to new industries, and constituting a source of innovation that can be a starting point for the renewal of organizations, institutions and perhaps even of entire countries (Lamas, 2012). It is mandatory, however, to rethink entrepreneurship in its essence, what it means and what it represents, and also how we can promote it. We need to transform threats into opportunities, taking advantage of globalisation, of the increasing importance of internationalization and interculturality, of the evolution of technology, and of the growing awareness of consumers. Only in this way will we be able to create a favourable environment for companies, particularly startups, so that they can simultaneously succeed and contribute to sustainable development. (Cerqueira et al, 2021).

One of the solutions for business innovation lies in social intrapreneurship. It should be noted that, like the concepts of entrepreneurship and social innovation, intrapreneurship is also a fashionable concept, which is good, as it allows to put the subject "on the table" for discussion, raise public awareness and, even more important, create conditions for its implementation. However, because it is so widely used, the concept of social intrapreneurship sometimes generates confusion and decontextualization. It is important to point out from the outset that social intrapreneurship is a "win-win" situation, as it has a positive impact on the community where organizations are located, but also on the organizations themselves.

Starting by organizations, they are facing, as we have already had the opportunity to see, challenging times. They have been living this situation for years, because of all the factors described previously in this chapter; but they have also been facing changes at a global scale, in technology, customers, environment, and competition. Uncertainty, which is a constant in our lives, has increased considerably over the last two years, since the appearance of the first case of COVID-19 in China, a local problem that quickly became global, and originated a pandemic within only a few months.

Intrapreneurship provides substance for the reinvention of companies, not only regarding their products and/or services but also in the way they deal with management, marketing, finance and especially with people. Traditional organizational structures, which define hierarchies, communication, and the division of labour within companies, have failed to respond to changes and, in some cases, became obsolete. Some companies, according to Alexander Ostwervalder (2017), support the need to create a new role parallel to the CEO (Chief Executive Officer), that of the chief entrepreneur, which allows organizations to promote an environment that fosters change management, creativity and innovation. This generates teams with autonomy, decision-making capacity, and their own budgets, thus eliminating bureaucracy, rigid procedures and processes, and deeply-rooted "sacred cows".

Regardless of whether or not we include the figure of the chief entrepreneur, when companies succeed in changing their organizational structures, they also reach the opportunity to adopt a different strategy, based on an agile business model, driven by hypotheses (which often goes through test and error), and focused on customers. Companies become capable of achieving co-creation (i.e. develop products and/or services with the collaboration of customers), making faster decisions, giving autonomy and decision-making capacity to employees, and admitting the failures that will certainly occur along the way. Therefore, companies grow into being able to promote their social component much more effectively, identifying and solving social problems.

More than words, we must be supported by data. Yunus Social Business, an organization focused on social business, describes the advantages of combining intrapreneurship with social responsibility, thus reaching social intrapreneurship. Yunus developed a study whose object were several social intrapreneurship initiatives promoted by companies in Europe and the United States, in order to understand their direct impact on these companies. The study was developed in partnership with Porticus, Schwab Foundation, INSEAD and the Hoffmann Global Institute for Business & Society. The results were released in January 2020 at the World Economic Forum and clearly demonstrate that this is the path companies must follow in order to promote intrapreneurship, in particular social intrapreneurship (Yunus Social Business, 2020).

The advantages of social intrapreneurship are evident both internally and externally: 87% of employees agreed that they felt more loyal to the company due to its social purpose; externally, 82% of those who responded said they were willing to pay more for a sustainable product, and 92.7% said that the environmental impact of the company was a relevant factor. More than 85% replied that an intrapreneurship program allowed the company to differentiate itself from competitors, and more than 86% stated that it allowed the company to be more innovative. Finally, more than 75% of respondents said that the company could leverage its corporate knowledge when trying to respond to social problems and support social causes (Yunus Social Business, 2020). There is no doubt that intrapreneurship creates internal advantages that can be transformed into competitive advantages and, of course, external advantages, by solving real problems, thereby contributing to achieving the objectives of sustainable development in its economic, social, and environmental aspects.

Along with the concept of social intrapreneurship, another concept that has been increasingly valued is that of corporate social responsibility, the two being closely related. There is a growing consensus as to the role it plays, namely regarding its operationalization, which stems from the need to think about the company's mission, integrating, from the outset, its contribution to society. This perspective will generate, as mentioned before, benefits both internally (economic) and externally (social and environmental) (Azevedo et al, S/D).

Companies need to reinvent the way they design their business models, but they also need to deal with management, marketing, finance and, especially, people, while using social intrapreneurship and corporate social responsibility. And here we must address another relevant concept that is "purpose". Nowadays, there are higher education institutions that include in their offer not only courses, but even master's or executive programs on "purpose". Mazzucato (2021) goes further and argues that states should also concretely define their mission and purpose, because the only way to solve the problems that we are currently facing is to innovate, not only in terms of technology, but also in the social, organizational and political domains. And, in order to do so, according to Mazzucato, "the 'mission-oriented' approach – partnerships between the public and private sectors aimed at solving key societal problems – is desperately needed" (2021, p. 22).

It is true that the starting point of a company influences the way in which it creates and delivers value and thus guarantees its sustainability. The definition of mission and purpose is an investment of time and reflection, and should not be created as an obligation, something to include only on a website or business plan (Bourbon & Lamas, M., 2021). Mission and purpose must clearly convey the reasons for the company's existence, what its purpose is, what it intends to achieve, and how it intends to contribute to society. For this, regardless of the sector of activity in which the company operates, it is essential to understand who the company will work for, what its segmentation is, and thus understand what customers really value, not forgetting, as already shown, their social and environmental concerns. It is essential that there is a consonance of values, which highlights the relevance of the company's mission and purpose.

This notion of purpose is also sustained by Simon Sinek (2011), when he states that "people don't buy WHAT you do, they buy WHY you do it" (p. 46), resorting to his concept of "golden circle". The "golden circle" conveys evidence of how companies can achieve more results if they never forget to start any project by asking "Why?" and "What is our purpose?". Companies must therefore start from the assumption that they are creating something not only to guarantee their survival or earn money, but also to create value for society. This will certainly be a differentiating factor in relation to competition, something fundamental in the increasingly competitive market in which we live. And as Sinek (2011) mentions:

> A company is a culture. A group of people brought together around a common set of values and beliefs. It's not products or services that bind a company together. It's not size and might that make a company strong, it's the culture—the strong sense of beliefs and values that everyone, from the CEO to the receptionist, all share. (p. 99)

Still, from the point of view of purpose, and bearing in mind the impact that organizations aspire to cause internally and externally, Michalowicz (2020), influenced by the work of psychologist Abraham Maslow and his theory of the hierarchy of needs (physiology, safety, social, esteem, self-fulfilment), argues that organizations, just like each one of us, are equally influenced by a pyramid. He adapted this pyramid model to organizations, also defining five levels: a) sales, without them there is no business; b) profit, more important than sales is what guarantees survival and growth; c) order, which allows for a structured management of the company; d) impact for all stakeholders; e) legacy, the lasting impact on society. According to this theory, the main objective of a company should be to ensure a balance at all levels, recognizing that they are all interconnected.

In this globalised world in constant change, with growing competition and permanent challenges, companies must be prepared to make decisions quickly and on a daily basis. A new perspective on the design of business models (based on mission and purpose) and on the management of companies, along with principles of flexibility, proximity, internationalization, openness, and relationship with different cultures (interculturality), are fundamental for success (Cerqueira et al, 2021).

The role of Education and Interculturality

> We need science, solidarity and solutions to tackle both the COVID-19 pandemic and the climate crisis. I urge leaders to heed the facts contained in this report, unite behind the science and take urgent climate action to set a path towards a safer, more sustainable future for all (WMO, 2021, Foreword).

We take up the words of the Secretary General of the United Nations, António Guterres, in his preface to the United in Science 2020 report, regarding the importance of science, and in particular of education, which is called to fulfil its fundamental role in sustainable development. It is important to rethink the way we deal with each other and the environment, moving towards an economic model that suits the needs of the world's population and the planet's sustainability. Education for global citizenship is the way forward to respond to the pandemic and to achieve sustainable development, a goal to which we must all be committed. Migrants, as part of the single community of humankind, play a decisive role in sharing sustainable traditional practices, that have been relegated by capitalism. These practices can be used and adapted to the budding economic model of circular economy, where interculturality emerges as the best way to coexist with other cultures.

UNESCO, according to Qian Tang, Assistant Director-General for Education, has been promoting education for a sustainable development since 1992, a policy that is now stronger and more necessary than ever, due to climate changes. To achieve the related SDGs, a shift in values, behaviour and new skills is required (UNESCO, 2017):

> The new 2030 Agenda for Sustainable Development clearly reflects this vision of the importance of an appropriate educational response. Education is explicitly formulated as a stand-alone goal – Sustainable Development Goal 4. Numerous education related targets and indicators are also contained within other Sustainable Development Goals (SDGs). Education is both a goal in itself and a means for attaining all the other SDGs. It is not only an integral part of sustainable development, but also a key enabler for it. That is why education represents an essential strategy in the pursuit of the SDGs (UNESCO, 2017, Foreword).

As mentioned before, in order to meet the 2030 Agenda, supported by the SDGs, we must use the knowledge that has been constructed over time for the sake of sustainable development and behaviour change. This call for action focuses on a joint mission, with the contribution of governments, economic agents, educators and, fundamentally, people from the whole planet. Intercultural work will allow us to get the most of the knowledge originated from intercultural exchanges, which will certainly lead to a better future. This can be done through business and education partnerships, as suggested by the SDGs, but also in common daily interactions. The change towards a new economic model will bring about benefits for the whole world population. It is then extremely important that the combined work of institutions and citizens effectively responds to the new and pressing challenges of globalisation, backed by a better relationship with nature. The "glocal" must be understood and lived by all, under a prevailing global approach to local actions, facilitated by interdependent networks that may ultimately provide the wellbeing of the local and global community (Lamas, 2019).

We consider education for global citizenship to be an important axis in this conception, that integrates the four pillars – learning to be, learning to know, learning to live together, learning to do – mentioned by the UNESCO report (Delors, 1996). By focusing on the preparation of individuals to become effective transforming agents, education becomes a web where each one collaborates in the creation of a better, more just society, guided by the values of democracy, solidarity, peace, equality, and respect for the environment (Lamas, 2019). This implies a true exercise of citizenship in the classroom, both in the knowledge building process and in the development of the skills needed for a truly democratic participation, where we include education for entrepreneurship.

Education for sustainable development needs to be worked on since early childhood, so that every human being may become an active citizen, conscious of their role in the community. To this end, we underline the importance that should be given to education for entrepreneurship, namely in the development of entrepreneurial skills, such as creativity, initiative, teamwork, learning-by-doing, motivation, perseverance, and resource mobilization, among other skills that promote cultural, social or environmental initiative (Luís et al, 2018).

To make this happen, it is necessary to involve students, not only in specific courses but also, and even more important, in activities and projects from different scientific domains, under a transdisciplinary approach and within a complex and demanding context. Because this is the reality that they will find later in their working lives, in their community, in companies, organizations, and in the different countries where they will be working (Luís et al, 2018). As Lans et al. (2008) argue, whenever skills are applied in context, experiential learning happens, leading to reflection and to more committed contributions and interactions.

Education creates opportunities for students, challenging them in their own diversity, so that they may discover their capabilities and use them to solve real problems in their communities. At the same time, an effective education promotes students' personal, academic, and professional development. But in order to do so, education needs to keep up with the new demands of global economy, society, environment, and culture. Caride (2005) argues that, given the uncertainty that the future holds, we must bet on a critical education, that fosters comprehensive objectives, towards the fair, equitable, solidary, integral and sustainable development of communities.

We realize then that the role of education in this new insight into business innovation and sustainable development is aligned with the seven complex lessons in education for the future, that Morin endorses (1999). An education that does not fragment knowledge but, instead, supports the connection between different domains of science, in a reality where all human beings are confronted with the same problems, whose resolution depends on what people want for the future of the planetary community. In this truly inclusive education, interculturality must always be present.

References

Azevedo, C., Filipa, C., & Melro, A. (n/d). Empreendedorismo Social Corporativo: Conceitos e Práticas. I*ES: Social Business School*. https://www.ies-sbs.org/media/filer_public/81/04/8104a309-470c-4aca-9c1f-2704c4750197/empreendedorismo_social_corporativo_vciem_revisto_20150924.pdf

Bartik, A. W., Bertrand, M., Cullen, Z., Glaeser, E., Luca, M. & Stanton, C. (2020). The impact of COVID-19 on small business outcomes and expectations. *PNAS*, 117(30), 17656–17666. https://www.pnas.org/content/pnas/117/30/17656.full.pdf

Bourbon, R., & Lamas, M. (2021). Modelos de Negócio e Internacionalização: O caso da Jump Willy. Portuguese Journal of Finance, Management and Accounting, 7(13), 47-69. http://u3isjournal.isvouga.pt/index.php/PJFM

Caride, J. A. (2005). In the Name of Environmental Education: words and things in the complex territory of education–environment–development relations. *Policy Futures in Education,* 3(3), 260-270. http://educacionysustentabilidad.tecsuma.cl/wp-content/uploads/2011/11/EAS-MUNDO-07-Caride-2005-In-the-name-of-Env-Ed.pdf

Cerqueira, C., Lamas, M., & Baranovskiy, S. (2021). Interculturality Role in Startups Internationalization: Eligent Club's Virtual Accelerator Program Case. *E-Revista de Estudos Interculturais do CEI–ISCAP*, 3(9), 1-22. https://doi.org/10.34630/erei.v3i9.4217

Cortina, A. (2011). Los valores de una ciudadania activa. Em B. Toro, & Tallone, *Educación, valores y ciudadanía: Metas educativas 2021: La educacíon que queremos para la generación de los bicentenários* (pp. 95-107). Madrid: OEI e Fundación SM Joaquín Turina. Obtido em 25 de Outubro de 2016, de https://oei.int/oficinas/secretaria-general?id=7

Delors, J. (1996). *Learning: the treasure within; report to UNESCO of the International Commission on Education for the Twenty-first Century*. UNESCO. https://unesdoc.unesco.org/ark:/48223/pf0000109590

Ellen Macarthur Foundation (2017). *What is Circular Economy*. Ellen MacArthur foundation. https://www.ellenmacarthurfoundation.org/circular-economy/what-is-the-circular-economy

European Commission (2020). *Communication from the Commission to the European Parliament, the Council, the European Economic and Social Committee and the Committee of the Regions: A new Circular Economy Action Plan For a cleaner and more competitive Europe*. Brussels, 11.3.2020 COM (2020) 98 final. https://eur-lex.europa.eu/resource.html?uri=cellar:9903b325-6388-11ea-b735-01aa75ed71a1.0017.02/DOC_1&format=PDF

Ghebreyesus, T., A. (2021, March 5th). Waive Covid vaccine patents to put world on war footing. The Guardian. https://www.theguardian.com/commentisfree/2021/mar/05/vaccination-covid-vaccines-rich-nations

Giddens, A. (1996). *The Consequences of Modernity (6th ed.)*. Polity Press.

Giddens, A. (1999, April 7th). *Globalisation* [Lecture notes]. Reith lectures 1999: Runaway World. http://downloads.bbc.co.uk/rmhttp/radio4/transcripts/1999_reith1.pdf

Giddens, A. (2001). *Modernidade e Identidade Pessoal*. Celta Editora.

Lamas, L. B. (2019). *A Educação para a Cidadania em Portugal: Incidências das políticas educativas nas práticas escolares no concelho de Vila Nova de Gaia* [Doctoral dissertation, Universidade Santiago de Compostela]. Minerva. http://hdl.handle.net/10347/19877

Lamas, M. (2012). *Educação e Empreendedorismo: Uma análise teórica e etnográfica da relação* [Doctoral dissertation, Universidade Santiago de Compostela]. Minerva. http://hdl.handle.net/10347/6174

Lans, T. et al. (2008). Entrepreneurship Education and Training in a Small Business Context; Insights from Competence-based Approach. *Journal of Enterprising Culture*, 16 (4), 363 – 383.

Leitão, A. (Setembro, 2015). Economia circular: uma nova filosofia de gestão para o séc. XXI. Portuguese Journal of Finance, Management and Accounting, Vol 1, Nº 2, pp. 149-171. http://u3isjournal.isvouga.pt/index.php/PJFMA/article/view/114

Luís, A., Lamas, L., B., & Lamas, M. (2018). Subsídios das competências empreendedoras na Educação para a Cidadania na Universidade Metodista Unida de Moçambique. Em: *Actas do Fórum Internacional África, Cooperação, Educação e Desenvolvimento (II FIACED)*, pp. 74-94. ISCED Douro. Penafiel, Portugal. http://fiaced.iscedouro.pt/assets/files/II_FIACED_livro_atas_2018.pdf

Mazzucato, M. (2021). *Mission Economy: A Moonshot guide to changing capitalism*. Penguin Books.

McKinsey Company. (2021, July). *COVID-19: Briefing note #64*. https://www.mckinsey.com/business-functions/risk/our-insights/covid-19-implications-for-business

Menezes, I. (2005). A educação para a cidadania como dimensão transversal do currículo escolar. Em C. Carvalho, F. Sousa & J. Pintassilgo. *De que falamos quando falamos de Cidadania?* (pp. 13-19). Porto Editora

Michalowicz, M. (2020). Fix this next: Make the vital change that will level up your business. Penguin.

Morin, E. (1999). *Os sete saberes para a educação*. Instituto Piaget.

ONU (1948). Declaração Universal, from 10 December 1948, n.º 57/79, 9 March. *Diário da República: I série n.º 57 (1978)*. https://dre.pt/declaracao-universal-dos-direitos-humanos

Osterwalder, A. (2017, March 17th). Why Every Company Needs A Chief Entrepreneur. *Strategyser*. https://www.strategyzer.com/blog/why-every-company-needs-a-chief-entrepreneur

Pope Francis. (2020, March 27th). Vatican. *Extraordinary moment of prayer presided over by Pope Francis*. https://www.vatican.va/content/francesco/pt/homilies/2020/documents/papa-francesco_20200327_omelia-epidemia.html

Santos, B. S. (2002). *Pela mão de Alice: O social e o político na pós-modernidade* (8ª ed). Edições Afrontamento.

Santos, B. S. (2020). Metaphors in progress, *Seminar*, 733, p. 22-26. http://www.boaventuradesousasantos.pt/media/2070_Metaphors%20in%20progress_Sept2020.pdf

Sinek, S. (2011). *Start with why: How great leaders inspire everyone to take action*. Penguin Books.

Touraine, A. (1994). *Crítica da Modernidade*. Instituto Piaget.
UN. (1948). *Universal Declaration of Human Rights*. https://www.un.org/en/about-us/universal-declaration-of-human-rights
UN. (1983). Resolution, from 19 December 1983, nº 38/161. https://undocs.org/pdf?symbol=en/A/RES/38/161
UN. (1987). *Report on the World Comission on Environment and Development*. https://www.un.org/ga/search/view_doc.asp?symbol=A/42/427&Lang=E
UN. (2015). Transforming our world: the 2030 Agenda for Sustainable Development. https://www.un.org/ga/search/view_doc.asp?symbol=A/RES/70/1&Lang=E
UNESCO. (2017). *Education for Sustainable Development Goals Learning Objectives*. https://www.unesco.de/sites/default/files/2018-08/unesco_education_for_sustainable_development_goals.pdf
WHO. (2020, March 11th). *WHO characterizes COVID-19 as a pandemic* [Video]. Streaming Service. https://www.youtube.com/watch?v=sbT6AANFOm4
WMO. (2021). *The United in Science 2020 Report* https://library.wmo.int/doc_num.php?explnum_id=10361
Yunus Social Business. (2020). *Business as unusual*. https://www.yunussb.com/business-as-unusualfbclid=IwAR1nAd0eDFobiWkW2Vb9xvNZxeT6w5XmgKiyooZQQiXqB0rYxGRmBbbnk4

CHAPTER 3

INTERCULTURAL COMPETENCE, COMMUNICATION AND EDUCATION: THE SPEECH-LANGUAGE PATHOLOGIST/THERAPIST'S (SLP/T) INTERVENTION

JOANA ROCHA, SUSANA VAZ FREITAS AND RITA ALEGRIA

FERNANDO PESSOA UNIVERSITY

1. Introduction

A Speech-Language Pathologist/Therapist (SLP/T) is the professional responsible for the prevention, assessment, diagnosis, and treatment of speech, language, communication, and swallowing disorders in children and adults (American Speech-Language-Hearing 2016). According to this definition it can be said that communication is the primary subject of the SLP/T profession (Farrugia-Bernard 2018).

The end result of the responses and adjustments of someone to a communication disorder are associated with the confidence and empathy established with the SLP/T. This is a major responsibility for these professionals. Based on this statement, it was found that the attitudes and actions of the SLP/T could result in an effective clinical outcome and intervention efficacy (Fourie 2009).

The assessment of communication disorders implies a detailed linguistic-communicative analysis, while the judgment of the impact of communicative disorders on the person's life involves a thorough analysis of personal, subjective and psychosocial issues. SLP/Ts are competent in assessing linguistic and communicative variables and designing therapeutic intervention plans appropriate to each case. Most SLP/Ts' clients have overlapping linguistic-communicative disorders and emotional and psychological problems (American Speech-Language-Hearing 2016).

Communication can be described as the ability to send and receive different types of messages (Hulit, Fahey, and Howard 2014) and can be conceptualised as a key element of intercultural competence (Kim 2009; Spitzberg and Changnon 2009). Consequently SLP/Ts should have a solid understanding of intercultural relationships. Communication is a fundamental aspect in people's everyday functioning life and it plays a significant and unique role in intercultural speech, as it constitutes a decisive factor in terms of managing significant relationships in intercultural contexts (Pilarska 2015). Communication signifies a fundamental human need and a basic human right and should receive major consideration (Sen 2015).

Communication abilities include verbal and non-verbal skills that facilitate people's independence (Roulstone and Lindsay 2012). The communication process is considered functional when all the different processes (e.g., speech, language, hearing) are efficient, and whichever disorder that may occur in these processes can result in a communication disorder (Jijo et al. 2019). In fact, the process of communication is not always easy for every human being. People who use forms of communication that are not common in their communities, such as sign language, braille, augmentative and alternative communication, or dialects may find some obstacles (McLeod 2018).

Communication disorders are reported as having a high prevalence and considered a substantial educational and public health problem (Law, J. et al. 2000; McLeod and McKinnon 2007; Overby and Baft-Neff 2017; Pinborough-Zimmerman, J., Satterfield et al. 2007).

A study stated that individuals with communication disorders could be economically deprived or more commonly found to be jobless (Ruben 2000). In this same investigation, researchers reported that communication disorders in the USA would be considered a major public health issue in the future (Ruben 2000). So it is crucial to improve cultural competency, especially in health professionals, in order to reduce health discrepancies and enhance health effects (Hawala-Druy and Hill 2012).

The number of multilingual communicators is rising around the world due to the endlessly growing rates of globalisation and immigration (Chaber

2016). Some studies have shown that SLP/Ts that intervene in intercultural contexts and linguistically diverse settings must make changes and efforts in order to deliver equitable services (Barratt, Khoza-Shangase, and Msimang 2012).

With the expansion of globalisation, every professional activity (including health and education professions, as well as business activities) requires specific skills that enable fluent and clear communication with individuals from different cultures (Dang 2016). In this context, interculturalism is essential in the real world in many different domains, such as social, political, economic, geographical, and international relations (Hussain 2018).

The primary aim of this chapter is to illustrate up-to-date international applications of intercultural practices in speech-language pathology/therapy services and also to discuss the importance of intercultural competence and communication in health and education professionals.

2. Intercultural competence and communication

Competences are defined as a rational set of skills, knowledge and attitudes as well as evident outputs that are considered vital to a professional performance (L. M. Jeffrey and Brunton 2011; Mulder 2014).

Intercultural (or multicultural) communication is referred to as the communication that occurs between two culturally diverse individuals (Ganapathi 2019). Intercultural communication skills involve the capacity to understand and use language competently to communicate, an adequate behavioural flexibility to different situations, the ability to interact with others using adequate conversational skills, and also possessing good social skills (Jandt 2017). The prerequisites needed for a correct communication are: (1) linguistic knowledge (semantic, phonology, and syntax); (2) knowledge of actions, events, and objects; and (3) social knowledge (Penn 1999).

Globalisation, increasing emigration, the development of the transportation infrastructure, urbanisation, the continuous upgrading of information technologies, international occupations, study exchange programs, interdependent economies, foreign travel, political alliances and global peace threats are bringing together people of different cultures with an unprecedented regularity and urgency (Samovar et al. 2017). In this way intercultural communication competency has emerged because of the recent societal diversity in the world. The key solution for an efficient intercultural exchange is the ability to be open-minded, the capacity to assimilate and accept new cultural inputs, avoid stereotypes and consider the differences. Intercultural encounters can be supported in well-developed intercultural communication competences and correspond to constant learning about other cultures. This can contribute to a more tolerant and a respectful world (Ilie 2019).

Khatib, Tabari, and Mohammadi (2016) stated that languages are considered culturally determined and are thought to be closely connected (Khatib, Tabari, and Mohammadi 2016). Fuller and Wardhaugh (2017) reported various scenarios that can explain the relation between language and culture: (1) the social system may influence or determine linguistic behaviour; (2) the linguistic behaviour may impact or dictate the social worldview; (3) there is a bidirectional influence between language and society; (4) no relationship was found between linguistic behaviour and social structure (Fuller, M., Heijne-Penninga, M., Kamans, E., van Vuuren, M., de Jong 2017).

The intercultural communication competence refers to a specific attribute that supports an effective intercultural communication, such as attitudes (e.g., respect, openness, consideration for the perspectives of other people and active listening), knowledge (e.g., cultural self-awareness, culture-specific knowledge, and sociolinguistic awareness) and skills (e.g., listening, evaluating, interpreting, observing, analysing, and relating). Deardoff (2011) also defined internal outcomes such as flexibility, empathy and adaptability and external outcomes that will lead to efficient intercultural communication behaviours (Deardorff 2011).

In order to be highly efficient, professionals that specifically deal with communication (in health or education settings) have to acknowledge the importance of the social setting and cultural conventions – including the differences in nonverbal communication – that are associated with different cultures.

3. Intercultural communication in health and education professionals

Health professionals consider that an effective communication established with their patients/clients has the possibility of resulting in positive health outcomes. However, it is not clear across health professionals what it really means to have an effective communication competence (Spitzberg

2013). In fact, health communication can be described as an interpersonal communication activity that is focussed on humanising and enhancing the population's health level (Nutbeam 1998). Communication competence comprises behaviours, non-verbal and verbal forms and attitudes that enhance the therapeutic adherence and the patients' confidence, which reflects positively on the therapeutic bond (Silverman, Kurtz, and Draper 2016).

The professional's communication competences are improved in clinical practice. Communication competence in health professionals strengthens therapeutic relationships and, consecutively, achieves a better adherence and health outcomes in patients/clients. The therapeutic relationship is a fundamental characteristic that exists in most health professions, especially those that adopt person-centred approaches (Fourie 2009). The research review confirms that most of the patients' judgments about the professionals' competences do not derive from the technical competences analyses, but are mainly supported by the socio-emotional components of the bond established between patient and professional (DiMatteo, Prince, and Taranta 1979). The relationship has to be enriched with some prerequisites that will maximise the health results: determination, firmness, trust, understanding and empathy. These can be summarised into a communication ideal containing three components: positivity, assertiveness and clarity (Belim and De Almeida 2018). Empathy is considered an essential component of the clinician-client relationship, but health professionals strive to achieve a balance between empathy and clinical distance. Studies suggest that professionals with high levels of empathy have less burnout and more job satisfaction (Larson, E. B., & Yao 2005). In the same way, empathy is also related to higher patient satisfaction (D. Jeffrey 2016). People's therapeutic adherence in health care is thought to be influenced by several economic, cultural and social factors (Wilkinson and Marmot 2003).

Education professionals were studied by Bayramali (2019), who stated that the goal of the teacher is to use various technologies of learning activities that will fully realise one of the main tasks of education – the formation of a personality, owning a number of communicative skills and abilities, capable of productively building interaction with other people, skilfully applying all sorts of communication techniques. The need to use communicative technologies in the study of social disciplines is also determined by the set of specialities at the school, for which the mastering of communication skills is an integral part of professional competence (Bayramali 2019).

Intercultural communication competence is a type of communication stated as "the fifth skill," following that of listening, speaking, reading and writing, which assists the individual's capacity to answer in different cultural settings (Kramsch 2003). It requires language skills and attributes as well as cultural knowledge, that helps the professional to actively interact in multiple cultural contexts (Hammer and Bennett 1998). In educational settings, the on-going increase of international students arriving to educational institutions may impact a demand in sociocultural and academic challenges, specifically in settings where intercultural differences can result in conflicts (Ragoonaden, Sivia, and Baxan 2015). In addition, it is stated that teachers have little or no training to work in classrooms with culturally diverse students and consequently have a smaller amount of contact with the concepts of intercultural education (Johnston and Wiltse 2004; Kea, Campbell-Whatley, and Richards 2006; Shariff 2008). Villegas and Lucas (2002; 2007) reported a set of parameters that characterises the culturally accessible teacher: (1) sociocultural consciousness; (2) affirming attitudes towards students of culturally diverse backgrounds; (3) commitment to act as agents of change; (4) constructive views of learning; (5) learning about students; (6) culturally responsive teaching practices (Ana María Villegas and Lucas 2002; Ana Maria Villegas and Lucas 2007). Barletta Manjarrés (2009) refers to these qualities as a culturally supportive pedagogical approach that acknowledges teachers with chances of acquiring pluricultural, plurilingual and intercultural abilities (Ladson-Billings 2014). Intercultural education should overcome the common idea of competence (i.e., attitudes, skills and knowledge), in order to include the promotion of critical consciousness of the world and a dedication to social relevant topics (Kumagai and Lypson 2009).

According to Bennett (1986) there are five important pedagogical orientations for acting in intercultural settings: nonverbal communication, verbal communication, social values, intellectual modes and orientation modes (Bennett 1986). Ethics, interculturalism and humanism in education denotes the necessity for the professional training of teachers for addressing human needs (Kumagai and Lypson 2009). The intercultural communication competence includes the adaptation of early acquired communication competences, as well as the specific prerequisites of intercultural competence (Berardo and Deardorff 2012): communicate in a second language; use communication technologies; an awareness of gender issues and equal opportunities; valuing and respect for people of different cultures; good interpersonal and interaction skills; ability to work in an intercultural context; adapt easily to new situations; work in a multinational team; knowledge about different cultures and customs; and ability to demonstrate tolerance, cultural sensitivity and awareness.

Communication leaders exhibit six major competences: strategic decision-making capability, self-dynamics, relationship building, communication knowledge management capability, team collaboration and ethical orientation. These competences impact professional outcomes, and the organisational context (Fuller et al. 2018). Health and educational organisations concur that professionals should be prepared to face the communication challenges of a complex and uncertain future (Fuller et al. 2018). Cultural competence and diversity are one of the main focuses of the health and education policy. Connecting and engaging with patients/clients, students, or others is essential (Morjikian and Bellack 2005).

4. The role of the Speech-Language Pathologist/Therapist (SLP/T) in intercultural communication

The intercultural competence of the SLP/T is a continuing process that implicates not only self-awareness but also a humble approach in which SLP/Ts identify all the aspects unknown about the cultures and languages of their patients, families and communities, in the pursuit of a culture-specific knowledge (Taiebine and Doukkali 2018).

Professional competence requires that SLP/Ts consider in their practice the linguistic and cultural characteristics of their patients and the distinctive values of each client and their families, in order to achieve an assessment and intervention as effective as possible (American Speech-Language-Hearing 2004). Clinical approaches, evaluation protocols and therapy that may be considered suitable for one individual may not be relevant for another (ASHA 2017), so the SLP/T should always take into account the distinctive influence of a patient linguistic and cultural background in the selection of clinical approaches:

> Culture and cultural diversity can incorporate a variety of factors, including but not limited to age, disability, ethnicity, gender identity (encompasses gender expression), national origin (encompasses related aspects e.g., ancestry, culture, language, dialect, citizenship, and immigration status), race, religion, sex, sexual orientation, and veteran status. (ASHA 2017)

SLP/Ts have to demonstrate a relevant level of cultural competence in research, teaching and therapy aspects of the scope of speech-language pathology/therapy (Horton-Ikard et al. 2009). SLP/T professionals have been facing an important challenge in encountering the needs of patients and families that came from distinctive backgrounds (culturally and religiously), specifically those that have suffered from severe poverty and war (Mathisen et al. 2015). According to these authors, SLP/Ts as well as other health professionals should include holistic assessments and interventions as part of their clinical practice. The SLP/T assessment of diverse populations request that this professional considers the diversity of languages and cultures (McLeod 2014).

The narrow knowledge and understanding that SLP/Ts possess about their patients' culture and language contexts is considered a challenge because the language and cultural environment of patients and their families is substantial for the SLP/T assessment and intervention, considering that they both influence the interpretation of assessment data, particularly if the SLP/T considers his particular worldview as the only foundation in this process (McLeod et al. 2013; Mdlalo, Flack, and Joubert 2016).

McNeilly (2019) reported in her study the problems that SLP/Ts are confronted with when intervening with children that are learning a new language (McNeilly 2019). This study explores the challenges that SLP/Ts face in their assessment procedures, the strategies used and the diverse options of intervention. SLP/Ts must develop skills and knowledge to proficiently assess the language profile and necessities of bilingual children and their families. This implies the selection of adequate procedures of assessment, to work as a team with interpreters (in case the SLP/T is not proficient in the language), and to understand and differentiate a communication disorder that is independent of the fact that the child has not yet acquired English skills (Thordardottir 2011).

Language and speech disorders occur when they are different from the norm. However, each language and speech is inserted in the culture of each person and that implies that what is considered a disorder in one may not be disordered in another. This also implies an emergent need to discriminate between a real speech and/or language disorder from an individual's cultural idiosyncrasies (Ndung'u and Kinyua 2009).

This means that the SLP/T should be culturally conscious of and recognise cultural variability between her/himself and the patient, and act with ethical responsibility, in other words, the SLP/T should be an intercultural counsellor (Randolph and Bradshaw 2018). Therefore, a culturally competent SLP/T has to distinguish between what are dialects and what are considered language disorders and routinely self-assess his/her cultural understanding (Oetting, Gregory, and Rivière 2016).

Corinne, Williams, and McLeod (2012) conducted a study to characterise perspectives and experiences of multilingualism in 128 Australian SLP/Ts. They verified that 48.4% of SLP/Ts had a low proficiency in a language(s) other than English but only 9.4% of SLP/Ts reported that they were especially skilled in another language. SLP/Ts reported having evaluated children's speech (50.5%) and/or language (34.2%) without the support of translators. The principal language used in their clinical practice was English. The SLP/Ts pointed out the limited resources they had to accurately differentiate between a speech/language disorder *versus* difference (Williams and McLeod 2012).

Chaber (2016) in her review concluded that SLP/Ts should never recommend the disregarding of their children's home language in regard to language intervention, particularly children with specific language disorders. In the results presented by this author, none of the studies mentioned showed that a monolingual method is positively comparable to a bilingual approach. SLP/Ts' practice should rely on evidence-based research regarding the efficacy of a specific language intervention approach, regardless of whether it is delivered bilingually or not (Chaber 2016).

Linguistically diverse populations have raised some discussion about SLP/Ts' intervention regarding the existence of specific barriers, such as: lack of assessments in diverse languages, lack of language interpreters, lack of awareness of their clients' culture, and lack of knowledge of developmental milestones in clients' language (Kadyamusuma 2016). As a consequence, SLP/Ts in the United States have been inadvertently causing a disproportional rate of Native Americans and African American children in special education, because of biased assessment procedures. Increasing intercultural competence is fundamental to promote equity in assessment for all children (Farrugia-Bernard 2018).

5. Conclusion

Intercultural communication is a fundamental skill for any professional at present in a multicultural world. Intercultural business contexts must include health and educational settings. The best way to understand intercultural business communication is to deeply absorb all the information and culture involved in a specific subject or situation. Some business schools include experiential learning for business education so that their students may learn communication skills experiencing the culture (Cross 2000).

Given this fact, it is important that all professionals understand the relevance of communication and what is implied when this capacity is weakened. People with difficulties in communicating are susceptible to violations of their human rights (e.g., Marshall and Barrett 2018). So, according to this, every person must support others' right to effectively communicate. Each individual has the power to fight for people's right to communicate, so that equality, justice and human dignity can be achieved (McLeod 2018). Every professional has a vital role in preventing people's vulnerability to exclusion and exploitation, and in fostering awareness of human rights abuse derived from communication difficulties.

On the other hand, it is imperative to understand the role of the SLP/T as the professional that is responsible for human communication disorders and the great attention from scholars and policymakers that this subject requires.

References

American Speech-Language-Hearing. 2004. "Preferred Practice Patterns for the Profession of Speech-Language Pathology."

American Speech-Language-Hearing, Association. 2016. "Scope of Practice in Speech-Language Pathology."

ASHA, American Speech-Language-Hearing Association. 2017. "Issues in Ethics: Cultural and Linguistic Competence."

Barratt, Joanne, Katijah Khoza-Shangase, and Kwandinjabulo Msimang. 2012. "Speech-Language Assessment in a Linguistically Diverse Setting: Preliminary Exploration of the Possible Impact of Informal 'Solutions' within the South African Context." *South African Journal of Communication Disorders* 59 (1): 34–44.

Bayramali, R. 2019. "Forming Communicative Competence of Technical Higher Education Institution Students by Innovative Means." *Eastern European Scientific Journal*, no. 1.

Belim, C, and C V De Almeida. 2018. "Communication Competencies Are the Key! A Model of Communication for the Health Professional to Optimize the Health Literacy—Assertiveness, Clear Language and Positivity." *Journal of Health Communication* 3 (3): 31.

Bennett, Christine I. 1986. *Comprehensive Multicultural Education: Theory and Practice*. Allyn and Bacon Boston.

Berardo, Kate, and Darla K Deardorff. 2012. *Building Cultural Competence: Innovative Activities and Models*. Stylus Publishing, LLC.

Chaber, Alexandra. 2016. "M. Cl. Sc SLP Candidate University of Western Ontario: School of Communication Sciences and Disorders This Critical Review Examines Whether or Not a Bilingual Language Intervention Yields Better Outcomes Compared to a Monolingual Approach in Bilingual Chi."

Cross, Elsie Y. 2000. *Managing Diversity--the Courage to Lead*. Greenwood Publishing Group.

Dang, Linh. 2016. "Intercultural Communication: Differences between Western and Asian Perspective."

Deardorff, Darla K. 2011. "Assessing Intercultural Competence." *New Directions for Institutional Research* 2011 (149): 65.

DiMatteo, M Robin, Louise M Prince, and Angelo Taranta. 1979. "Patients' Percentions of Physicians' Behavior." *Journal of Community Health* 4 (4): 280–90.

Farrugia-Bernard, Audrey M. 2018. "Speech-Language Pathologists as Determiners of the Human Right to Diversity in Communication for School Children in the US." *International Journal of Speech-Language Pathology* 20 (1): 170–73.

Fourie, Robert J. 2009. "Qualitative Study of the Therapeutic Relationship in Speech and Language Therapy: Perspectives of Adults with Acquired Communication and Swallowing Disorders." *International Journal of Language & Communication Disorders* 44 (6): 979–99.

Fuller, M., Heijne-Penninga, M., Kamans, E., van Vuuren, M., de Jong, M. 2017. "Identifying Competence Characteristics for Excellent Communication Professionals A Work Field Perspective." *Journal of Communications Management* 22 (2): 233–52.

Fuller, Melissa, Marjolein Heijne-Penninga, Elanor Kamans, Mark van Vuuren, Menno de Jong, and Marca Wolfensberger. 2018. "Identifying Competence Characteristics for Excellent Communication Professionals." *Journal of Communication Management*.

Ganapathi, Nalina. 2019. "The Need for Intercultural Communication Skills in the Multicultural Settings." *Symbiosis Centre for Management Studies*.

Hammer, Mitchell R, and Milton J Bennett. 1998. *The Intercultural Development Inventory (IDI) Manual*. Intercultural Communication Institute Portland, OR.

Hawala-Druy, Souzan, and Mary H Hill. 2012. "Interdisciplinary: Cultural Competency and Culturally Congruent Education for Millennials in

Health Professions." *Nurse Education Today* 32 (7): 772–78.

Horton-Ikard, RaMonda, Maria L Munoz, Shurita Thomas-Tate, and Yolanda Keller-Bell. 2009. "Establishing a Pedagogical Framework for the Multicultural Course in Communication Sciences and Disorders." *American Journal of Speech-Language Pathology*.

Hulit, Lloyd M, Kathleen R Fahey, and Merle R Howard. 2014. *Born to Talk: An Introduction to Speech and Language Development*. Pearson Higher Ed.

Hussain, Shafaat. 2018. "Managing Communication Challenges in Multicultural Organizations." *International Journal of Media, Journalism and Mass Communications (IJMJMC)* 4 (2): 44–49.

Ilie, Oana-Antonia. 2019. "The Intercultural Competence. Developing Effective Intercultural Communication Skills." In *International Conference KNOWLEDGE-BASED ORGANIZATION*, 25:264–68. Sciendo.

Jandt, Fred E. 2017. *An Introduction to Intercultural Communication: Identities in a Global Community*. Sage Publications.

Jeffrey, D. 2016. "Clarifying Empathy: The First Step to More Humane Clinical Care." *British Journal of General Practice* 66 (643): e143–45.

Jeffrey, Lynn Maud, and Margaret Ann Brunton. 2011. "Developing a Framework for Communication Management Competencies." *Journal of Vocational Education & Training* 63 (1): 57–75.

Jijo, Pottackal Mathai, Konadath Sreeraj, K Sandhya, M Preethi, and Pujar Rashmi. 2019. "Prevalence and Causes of Communication Disorders-A Retrospective Study from Northern Karnataka." *Clinical Epidemiology and Global Health*.

Johnston, Ingrid, and Lynne Wiltse. 2004. "Re-Mapping Literary Worlds: Postcolonial Pedagogy in Practice." *Alberta Journal of Educational Research* 50 (3): 327.

Kadyamusuma, M R. 2016. "Limitations to Practicing as a Bilingual Speech-Language Pathologist in the United States." *Journal of Speech Pathology & Therapy* 1 (2): e103.

Kea, Cathy, Gloria D Campbell-Whatley, and Heraldo V Richards. 2006. "Becoming Culturally Responsive Educators: Rethinking Teacher Education Pedagogy." *National Center for Culturally Responsive Educational Systems*, 1–15.

Khatib, Mohammad, Bizhan Hekmatshoar Tabari, and Mohammad Javad Mohammadi. 2016. "Tracing Native Culture in Iranian Students Academic Writing: Focus on Acknowledgements." *International Journal of English Language and Literature Studies* 5 (1): 46–54.

Kim, Young Yun. 2009. "The Identity Factor in Intercultural Competence." *The Sage Handbook of Intercultural Competence* 1: 53–65.

Kramsch, Claire. 2003. "Teaching Language along the Cultural Faultline." *Culture as the Core: Perspectives on Culture in Second Language Learning*, 19–35.

Kumagai, Arno K, and Monica L Lypson. 2009. "Beyond Cultural Competence: Critical Consciousness, Social Justice, and Multicultural Education." *Academic Medicine* 84 (6): 782–87.

Ladson-Billings, Gloria. 2014. "Culturally Relevant Pedagogy 2.0: Aka the Remix." *Harvard Educational Review* 84 (1): 74–84.

Larson, E. B., & Yao, X. 2005. "Clinical Empathy as Emotional Labor in the Patient-Physician Relationship." *JAMA* 293 (9): 1100–1106.

Law, J., J. Boyle, F. Harris, A. Harkness, and C. Nye. 2000. "Prevalence and Natural History of Primary Speech and Language Delay: Findings from a Systematic Review of the Literature." *International Journal of Language and Communication Disorders* 35 (2): 165–88.

Marshall, Julie, and Helen Barrett. 2018. "Human Rights of Refugee-Survivors of Sexual and Gender-Based Violence with Communication Disability." *International Journal of Speech-Language Pathology* 20 (1): 44–49.

Mathisen, Bernice, Lindsay B Carey, Christa L Carey-Sargeant, Gwendalyn Webb, CaraJane Millar, and Lilli Krikheli. 2015. "Religion, Spirituality and Speech-Language Pathology: A Viewpoint for Ensuring Patient-Centred Holistic Care." *Journal of Religion and Health* 54 (6): 2309–23.

McLeod, Sharynne. 2014. "Resourcing Speech-Language Pathologists to Work with Multilingual Children." *International Journal of Speech-Language Pathology* 16 (3): 208–18.

—. 2018. "Communication Rights: Fundamental Human Rights for All." *International Journal of Speech-Language Pathology* 20 (1): 3–11.

McLeod, Sharynne, and David H McKinnon. 2007. "Prevalence of Communication Disorders Compared with Other Learning Needs in 14 500 Primary and Secondary School Students." *International Journal of Language & Communication Disorders* 42 (S1): 37–59.

McLeod, Sharynne, Sarah Verdon, Caroline Bowen, and International Expert Panel on Multilingual Children's Speech. 2013. "International Aspirations for Speech-Language Pathologists' Practice with Multilingual Children with Speech Sound Disorders: Development of a Position Paper." *Journal of Communication Disorders* 46 (4): 375–87.

McNeilly, Lemmietta G. 2019. "Strategies Utilized by Speech-Language Pathologists to Effectively Address the Communication Needs of

Migrant School-Age Children." *Folia Phoniatrica et Logopaedica* 71 (2–3): 127–34.

Mdlalo, Thandeka, Penelope Flack, and Robin Joubert. 2016. "Are South African Speech-Language Therapists Adequately Equipped to Assess English Additional Language (EAL) Speakers Who Are from an Indigenous Linguistic and Cultural Background? A Profile and Exploration of the Current Situation." *South African Journal of Communication Disorders* 63 (1): 1–5.

Morjikian, Robin, and Janis Bellack. 2005. "The RWJ Executive Nurse Fellows Program, Part 1: Leading Change." *Jona: The Journal of Nursing Administration* 35 (10): 431–38.

Mulder, M. 2014. "Conceptions of Professional Competence." In *International Handbook of Research in Professional and Practice-Based Learning*, edited by Dordrecht. Springer, 107–37.

Ndung'u, Ruth, and Mathew Kinyua. 2009. "Cultural Perspectives in Language and Speech Disorders." *Disability Studies Quarterly* 29 (4).

Nutbeam, Don. 1998. "Health Promotion Glossary." *Health Promotion International* 13 (4): 349–64.

Oetting, Janna B, Kyomi D Gregory, and Andrew M Rivière. 2016. "Changing How Speech-Language Pathologists Think and Talk about Dialect Variation." *Perspectives of the ASHA Special Interest Groups* 1 (16): 28–37.

Overby, Megan S, and Annette Baft-Neff. 2017. "Perceptions of Telepractice Pedagogy in Speech-Language Pathology: A Quantitative Analysis." *Journal of Telemedicine and Telecare* 23 (5): 550–57.

Penn, C. 1999. "Pragmatic Assessment and Therapy for Persons with Brain Damage: What Have Clinicians Gleaned in Two Decades?" *Brain Lang* 68 (3): 535–52.

Pilarska, Justyna. 2015. "Interpersonal Skills in Dealing with Multiculturalism: Bosnian Borderland Case." *European Journal of Social Science Education and Research* 2 (4): 337–48.

Pinborough-Zimmerman, J., Satterfield, R., J. Miller, D. Bilder, S. Hossain, and W. McMahon. 2007. "Communication Disorders: Prevalence and Comorbid Intellectual Disability, Autism, and Emotional/Behavioral Disorders." *American Journal of Speech-Language Pathology*.

Ragoonaden, Karen O, Awneet Sivia, and Victorina Baxan. 2015. "Teaching for Diversity in Teacher Education: Transformative Frameworks." *Canadian Journal for the Scholarship of Teaching and Learning* 6 (3): 6.

Randolph, Crystal C, and Janet L Bradshaw. 2018. "An Exploratory Study of Speech-Language Pathologists' Perceptions of Multicultural Counseling in Communication Sciences and Disorders." *Teaching and Learning in Communication Sciences & Disorders* 2 (3): 1.

Roulstone, S, and G Lindsay. 2012. "The Perspectives of Children and Young People Who Have Speech, Language and Communication Needs, and Their Parents-Better Communication Research Programme." Retrieved 05/03/12, from https://www.education.gov.uk/publications ….

Ruben, Robert J. 2000. "Redefining the Survival of the Fittest: Communication Disorders in the 21st Century." *The Laryngoscope* 110 (2): 241.

Samovar, Larry A, Richard E Porter, Edwin R McDaniel, and Carolyn Sexton Roy. 2017. *Communication between Cultures*. Nelson Education.

Sen, A Fulya. 2015. "Communication and Human Rights." *Procedia-Social and Behavioral Sciences* 174: 2813–17.

Shariff, Farha D. 2008. "The Liminality of Culture: Second Generation South Asian Canadian Identity and the Potential for Postcolonial Texts." *Journal of Teaching and Learning* 5 (2).

Silverman, Jonathan, Suzanne Kurtz, and Juliet Draper. 2016. *Skills for Communicating with Patients*. crc press.

Spitzberg, Brian H. 2013. "(Re) Introducing Communication Competence to the Health Professions." *Journal of Public Health Research* 2 (3).

Spitzberg, Brian H, and Gabrielle Changnon. 2009. "Conceptualizing Intercultural Competence." *The SAGE Handbook of Intercultural Competence*, 2–52.

Taiebine, Mohamed, and Abdelhakim Doukkali. 2018. "Reflection in the Implementation of Intercultural Communication Skills in Speech and Language Pathology Classes in Morocco." *American Journal of Educational Science* 4 (4): 122–26.

Thordardottir, E. 2011. "Bilingualism: Normal Development and Clinical Intervention." In *CASLPA 2011 Conference, Montreal, Canada*, 27–30.

Villegas, Ana Maria, and Tamara Lucas. 2007. "The Culturally Responsive Teacher." *Educational Leadership* 64 (6): 28.

Villegas, Ana María, and Tamara Lucas. 2002. "Preparing Culturally Responsive Teachers: Rethinking the Curriculum." *Journal of Teacher Education* 53 (1): 20–32.

Wilkinson, Richard G, and Michael Marmot. 2003. *Social Determinants of Health: The Solid Facts*. World Health Organization.

Williams, Corinne J, and Sharynne McLeod. 2012. "Speech-Language Pathologists' Assessment and Intervention Practices with Multilingual Children." *International Journal of Speech-Language Pathology* 14 (3): 292–305.

CHAPTER 4

MARKETING MIX FOR SUSTAINABLE CULTURAL INDUSTRIES

BÁRBARA SANTOS AND OSCAR BERNARDES
ISCAP – P.PORTO, POLYTECHNIC OF PORTO

Introduction

The cultural and creative industries produce goods and services by combining artistic value and economic potential (Yang & Černevičiūtė, 2017), while promoting the sustainable development of territories and their cultures. The cultural industry is involved in the commercialization, creation, and production of cultural content (Lima, 2007), and the creative industry involves artistic, scientific, and economic creativity (Hanson, 2012). Therefore, the creative and innovative process is at the base of the cultural and creative industries. Artistic creativity encompasses imagination in activities related to text, images, and sound; Scientific creativity is directed towards problem-solving; and Economic creativity is directed towards innovation in an organizational context (e.g., technology, practices, marketing) and constitutes a competitive advantage (Hanson, 2012). In this sense, each product or service must have an innovative characteristic.

The cultural and creative industries represent a subset of the creative economy, which involves community art, culture and commercial activity. Consequently, the combination of these activities contributes and associates the three objectives of sustainability: Economic, Environmental, and Social (Oyekunle, 2014).

The marketing mix for sustainable cultural industries is an innovative tool that promotes the sustainability of companies and, consequently, their offerings. From the perspective of the cultural and creative industries, these offers need to have a cultural and creative element. Tourism, for example, is an industry that promotes cultural experiences. This sector consists of several components, from tourist agents to local commerce, and has a strong environmental and social impact on the surrounding community (Oliveira, 2015). Our chapter aims to relate sustainability to the cultural and creative industries. In this way, we were able to combine the economic (business) factor with the cultural and creative factor and illustrate the importance of sustainable marketing for the creative and cultural industries. Therefore, we will present a literature review of sustainable marketing and its mix and possible links to the cultural sector, taking as an example the activity of tourism, and conceiving a marketing mix associated with culture and sustainability. The marketing tools for sustainable cultural industries must be adapted to the needs of each company and/or each sector. As a result, we will approach marketing for sustainable cultural industries as part of economic-cultural creativity.

Sustainable Marketing

Sustainable marketing is an important part of building a relationship between the company and the customer, based on values such as trust and public interest. Taking into consideration the existing environmental and social concerns of society in general, companies now demonstrate greater responsibility in the exercise of their activity. This responsibility is present in the sustainable marketing process (Seretny & Seretny, 2012).

The concept of sustainable marketing began to be developed in the 1970s (Eneizan, Wahab, & Sharif, 2016), having emerged in a more ecological perspective of marketing, so that companies could incorporate their environmental concerns in product development (Kardos, Gabor, & Cristache, 2019). At the end of the 1980s and the 1990s, the need to understand the role of marketing in society (Kardos et al., 2019) and the new demands of consumers, in the search for environmentally responsible products (Eneizan et al., 2016) led to the emergence of sustainable[1] marketing, also known as green/ecological marketing (Kai, He, & Wang, 2012).

Society has shown a greater concern for sustainable development, therefore corporate responsibility has begun to be questioned, which has led to the implementation of sustainable practices in the exercise of economic activity (Kardos et al., 2019). In this way, with sustainable marketing, the company provides environmentally and socially responsible products that are profitable, thus answering the questions of sustainable development (Rahdari,

[1] Term adopted throughout the chapter.

Sepasi, & Moradi, 2016) and society's claims (Mombeuil, Fotiadis, & Wang, 2019).

Sustainable marketing strategies contribute to organizational sustainability and the achievement of sustainable development objectives, so the company's financial success must go hand in hand with its surroundings. In the business field, all stakeholders matter without prejudice to any of the parts.

Sustainable marketing, when applied, has an impact at the level of the three sustainability factors, so that the company is seeing an increase in profitability, being able to reach more customers (Thevanes & Weerasinghe, 2019) and gain competitive advantage (Eneizan et al., 2016). The company also manages to reduce the negative impact on the environment, by supporting eco-innovation and saving water and energy, reducing the use of paper and plastic and greenhouse gas emissions (Durmaz & Yasar, 2016). These factors contribute to reducing pollution, improving health and rationalizing the waste management system by reducing paper and plastic. The company also promotes ecological behavior and guarantees the satisfaction of its stakeholders, having a positive impact on the social factor (Durmaz & Yasar, 2016).

Sustainable marketing is also known as the marketing that seeks to meet the needs of current customers, without compromising the needs of the next generation of customers (Seretny & Seretny, 2012). With the reduction of the negative impact on the social and natural environment, future generations will have no scarcity of resources or negative effects on their daily life. In this way, customers' well-being and the environment are protected. According to Rastogi and Pant (2019) the adoption of sustainable marketing has had positive effects such as the increase in demand and consumption for ecological products, including food products, which reduces consumption and demand for processed products, the reduction in the use of plastic bags in purchases, the choice of biological fertilizers for the soil, and the recycling of industrial products.

In this way, the company, in addition to creating a relationship with the consumer, also establishes a relationship with society and the environment (George & Salim, 2019). Greater social and environmental awareness is promoted through a change in behavior in the external and internal environment. The production processes and methods used are rethought and reformulated in the direction of greater sustainability. Sustainable marketing thus contributes to organizational sustainability (Thevanes & Weerasinghe, 2019).

Sustainable marketing is based on the components of traditional marketing: Product; Price; Place and Distribution (Eneizan et al., 2016), and encompasses the entire management process of the company, therefore it must be present in all strategic planning (Pomering, 2017). To this mix is added a determinant in the success of companies: people (Warrink, Akhunjonov, & Obrenovic, 2018), also in the sense of sustainability.

Marketing Mix for sustainable cultural industries

Companies must rethink and reassess the materials and processes used, from product design to packaging, sales strategy, place of production, price, and distribution channels (Kotler, 2011). These factors are also valid for tourism, since all business activities that produce tourism goods and services are inherent to this sector (Neves, 2012). The consumer (e.g., tourist) is also referred to as being part of sustainable marketing (Mahmoud, 2019), as it is included in its objectives.

The marketing mix for sustainable cultural industries must be reformulated in the direction of sustainability, so both the product, the price, the distribution, and promotion must be rethought. Of these factors, the consumer is more sensitive to price and promotion (Dangelico & Vocalelli, 2017).

The marketing mix for sustainable cultural industries represents the set of variables that must be considered by intercultural services in the formulation of their marketing/commercialization strategies due to their direct impact on the economy, culture, environment, and society (Figure 1).

Therefore, one must seek a balance between these four factors for promoting better local development and not just the most influential variables (price and promotion). The company aims to reach the consumer, obtain profit, preserve the environment and society, and contribute to the environmental culture, therefore the marketing mix for sustainable cultural industries is designed accordingly.

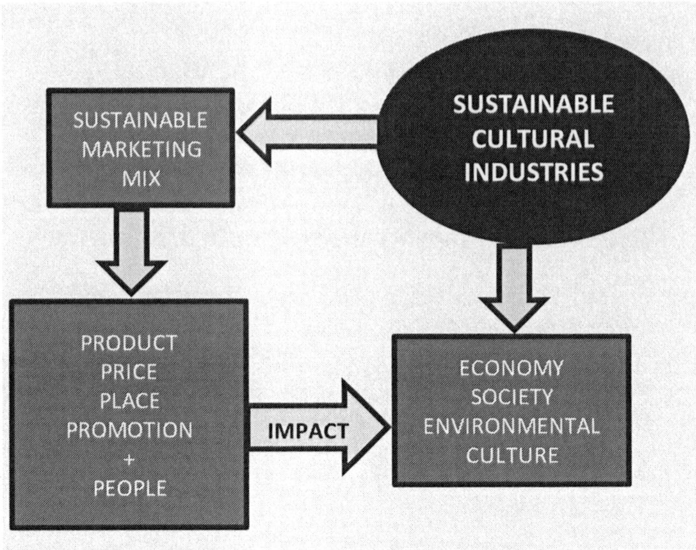

Figure 1: Relationship between sustainable marketing mix and the sustainable cultural industries. Source: Created by the authors.

Product

The product, from the perspective of sustainable marketing, is generally designated as a green product, or sustainable, or ecological or environmentally friendly, such terminations are used by professionals to attract and inform creative & cultural customers (Mahmoud, 2019). These products are designed so that the negative impact on the environment is reduced, not only during their design, but throughout their life cycle (Mahmoud, 2019; Solaiman, Osman, Suberi, & Ab, 2015). Sustainable products must have characteristics that minimize the negative impact on the environment during their production and after their use (Dangelico & Vocalelli, 2017; Taghian, Polonsky, & Souza, 2016). In the tourism industry, handicrafts, cultural events (Rodrigues, 2017), accommodation, gastronomy, leisure, and other activities that are cultural, social, or artistic, are considered as products/services (Neves, 2012).

A product is not sustainable only because of the result, but because of all the factors that are inherent to it, such as the materials and the methods used, the packaging (Mahmoud, 2019), the design, the installation, the instructions, the quality (Taghian et al., 2016), and the labels (Chairunnisa, Fahmi, &

Jahroh, 2019), among others. In cultural and creative industries, for example, in packaging products, recycled materials can be used instead of plastic. These are products designed to protect the environment by reducing the use of energy and resources (Ottman, Stafford, & Hartman, 2006).

Sustainability should be considered in the process, regardless of whether it is about developing a new product or improving an existing one (Taghian et al., 2016). In the case of an existing cultural and creative product, it is a question of rethinking and modifying all the associated elements, whereas in a new product it is a question of using the most sustainable process from the beginning. These products may have functional characteristics like those of traditional products or include new characteristics depending on what the consumer wants (Taghian et al., 2016). This approach makes it possible for companies not only to reach their current customers but also to attract new customers.

Price

The cost of purchasing a sustainable product is called premium price and reflects what the consumer has paid to obtain a product with environmentally responsible characteristics (Dangelico & Vocalelli, 2017) that represent an added value for customers (Davari & Strutton, 2014; Mahmoud, 2019). This added value in the tourism industry can, for example, be a rewarding cultural experience for the consumer.

In the product price, several aspects are taken into consideration, such as competition (Taghian et al., 2016), production costs, equipment, materials used, quality (Dangelico & Vocalelli, 2017), the value that the consumer is willing to give (Chairunnisa et al., 2019), the investment made in innovation (Dangelico & Vocalelli, 2017), possible costs of modifying the entire production process for a new and sustainable process (Agustini, Athanasius, & Retnawati, 2019), performance improvements, superior designs and new functions. These factors imply additional costs for the company, with an expected return (Davari & Strutton, 2014), so the price of a sustainable product is higher than the price of traditional products (Chairunnisa et al., 2019).

The price is stipulated taking into consideration all the elements inherent to the design process, and the fact that it is an environmentally responsible product implies a higher cost for its acquisition. Although the price may be higher, some customers prefer a sustainable alternative to the traditional one regardless of the purchase cost (Mahmoud, 2019). For others, the price is a decisive factor. Consumers are all different and when purchasing a product, they prefer different elements. Price must be accessible and competitive, which is the most difficult element of sustainable marketing (Agustini et al., 2019).

The product's sustainability can, however, make it more economical in the long-term (Peattie, 2001), so although it is expensive, its acquisition can bring greater compensation. Due to its characteristics, the sustainable product has a longer useful life compared to the traditional product (Singh & Pandey, 2012), so that the consumer, when purchasing the product, obtains greater savings, as its replacement is not necessary during a large period of time. Therefore, when purchasing a cultural and creative sustainable product it is necessary to take into consideration not only the price but also the durability of the product. This factor, as well as performance, packaging, and/or design, can be an additional benefit for the customer (Singh & Pandey, 2012).

Place

The place is a point of sale where products for purchase are displayed, and it can be physical and/or virtual (Mahmoud, 2019). While some authors argue that it is a place that leads consumers to a "cleaner" environment (Chairunnisa et al., 2019), other authors understand that the product must be in a place that reaches all customers (Dangelico & Vocalelli, 2017; Davari & Strutton, 2014; Singh & Pandey, 2012). According to this last point of view, the cultural and creative industries can reach any consumer, with or without ecological concerns, which could be an asset. For example, when planning an event, factors such as energy, pollution, and all other factors that are included must be taken into consideration. In this case, the product on display would be the event and/or show offered to the consumer.

This factor encompasses the management of various activities such as distribution and reverse logistics (Dangelico & Vocalelli, 2017). Distribution is an important element that must take place as planned without harming the consumer's needs (Chairunnisa et al., 2019) and must be a cleaner option. For the company to maintain the sustainability standard, it must ensure that distribution is also sustainable (Mahmoud, 2019), in order to avoid creating a negative impact on the environment (Singh & Pandey, 2012). The product must be supplied to the consumer without a negative impact on the environment. While distribution takes the product to the consumer, reverse logistics implies the opposite.

Reverse logistics involves recycling, remanufacturing, and recycling the products that are returned, thus contributing to minimizing the negative impact on the environment (Dangelico & Vocalelli, 2017). Consequently, through reverse logistics, the company manages to optimize its resources, as it can save time and costs, and thus obtain a greater profit (Dangelico & Vocalelli, 2017). Although it appears to be a process with benefits for all, it is also a process that needs to be regulated (Singh & Pandey, 2012), thus constituting a difficulty.

Promotion

Promotion is a strategic tool used to promote a company's products and/or services (Agustini et al., 2019). The promotional means used involve advertising, advertisements, sales promotion, communicating at the point of sale (Agustini et al., 2019; Chairunnisa et al., 2019; Taghian et al., 2016), and any other promotional activity.

Regardless of the means used, the promotion aims to sensitize the consumer to choose more sustainable products (Agustini et al., 2019; Mahmoud, 2019). However, this promotion must be in accordance with the standards adopted by the company. Therefore, all business activity must consider environmental awareness, otherwise, consumers can "leave" the company. Promotion can either involve a creative product and/or cultural service, or it can reflect only the environmental awareness of the business entity or instill the consumer in adopting a healthy lifestyle (Taghian et al., 2016).

When promoting sustainable creative products and/or cultural services, it is imperative that there is information from the environmental point of view that is more "responsible" and not confusing for the consumer (Taghian et al., 2016), which leads to eco-labels and their importance. Eco-labels are an important promotion tool because they illustrate the company's environmental awareness and serve as a guarantee to consumers (Dangelico & Vocalelli, 2017) that this is, in fact, an "environmentally friendly" product (Solaiman et al., 2015). It is also a differentiating factor between sustainable products and conventional products (Solaiman et al., 2015).

People

Employees are an integral part of the company, so in carrying out their actions they must convey the desired image. In the field of sustainability, for this to happen, the company must educate (Pomering, 2017) their employees to adopt more sustainable behaviors (Warrink et al., 2018). In this way, employees remain aligned with the company's ideals and promote the adoption of the same behavior among customers.

However, the company must take in consideration the employee’s nature and needs. Through a set of internal actions such as integration, communication, safety in the workplace, healthcare, among others, the relationship between the company and the employee is reinforced (Rudawska, Frąckiewicz, & Wiścicka-Fernando, 2016). The cultural and creative industries must also invest in the professional growth and development of their employees, through training courses (Khan, 2014) and promoting ethical behavior (Warrink et al., 2018). Through these incentives, employees remain motivated and satisfied, so the level of productivity and creativity increases (Rudawska et al., 2016).

In this sense, the cultural and creative industries must treat their employees with ethics and responsibility (Warrink et al., 2018). The image that the employee, in (in)direct contact, transmits to customers can influence the purchase (Khorsheed, Abdulla, Othman, Mohammed, & Sadq, 2020; Warrink et al., 2018) . Employee behavior can have an influence on the consumer, just like the way the company treats its employees can have a negative effect. The company's image depends on the working conditions offered and the way employees are treated (Khorsheed et al., 2020).

Conclusion

The tourism sector has a direct relationship with the local community (Costa, 2011) so this activity should be developed with more responsibility, as any negative/positive effect generated affects the local population more directly. Therefore, and due to the implication that the sector has in its environment, there must be a balance in its practice.

The tourism sector, in the perspective of sustainability, implies a balance at the economic, social, environmental, and cultural level (Costa, 2011). Thus, in addition to being an economic activity, tourism is also a cultural activity with environmental and social consequences for the local community. The various cultural and creative agents involved must adopt more sustainable measures, so that negative effects are minimized. The marketing mix for sustainable cultural industries acts as an innovative tool, capable of creating and/or developing new methods of action and increased responsibility in terms of sustainability. Each cultural and creative industry must adapt this tool to its needs, as the lines of activity and respective products differ. Thus, the marketing mix for sustainable cultural industries must be adapted and developed considering the offer of a specific company and the impact of the respective activity on the environment.

The marketing mix for sustainable cultural industries also works as a deontology tool, so local entities, by adopting it, are contributing directly to more sustainable behaviors and influencing consumers in the same direction (indirect level). Companies involved in cultural activities thus contribute to the differentiation and growth of the region and, consequently, to sustainable development. We can then conclude that tourism, as a sector of cultural and creative industries in general, should resort to the marketing mix for sustainable cultural industries, in order to emphasize economic, cultural, environmental, and social balance, as well as to direct the impact of its economic activities towards the harmonious development of the territory.

References

Agustini, M. H., Athanasius, S. S., & Retnawati, B. B. (2019). Identification of green marketing strategies : perspective of a developing country. *Innovative Marketing*, 15(4), 42–56. https://doi.org/10.21511/im.15(4).2019.04

Chairunnisa, S. S., Fahmi, I., & Jahroh, S. (2019). How important is green marketing mix for consumer? Lesson from the body shop. *Journal of Management*, 23(2), 321–337. https://doi.org/10.24912/jm.v23i2.504

Costa, I. E. da. (2011). *O marketing turístico sustentável na perspetiva das comunidades locais: O pólo de desenvolvimento turístico da Serra da Estrela*. Instituto Universitário de Lisboa.

Dangelico, R. M., & Vocalelli, D. (2017). "Green marketing": An analysis of definitions, strategy steps, and tools through a systematic review of the literature. *Journal of Cleaner Production*, 165, 1263–1279. https://doi.org/10.1016/j.jclepro.2017.07.184

Davari, A., & Strutton, D. (2014). Marketing mix strategies for closing the gap between green consumers ' pro-environmental beliefs and behaviors. *Journal of Strategic Marketing*, 22(7), 563–586. https://doi.org/10.1080/0965254X.2014.914059

Durmaz, Y., & Yasar, H. V. (2016). Green marketing and benefits to business. *Business and Management Studies*, 2 (May), 64–71. https://doi.org/10.11114/bms.v2i2.1624

Eneizan, B. M., Wahab, K. A., & Sharif, Z. M. (2016). Prior research on green marketing and green marketing strategy : Critical analysis. *Singaporean Journal of Business Economics, and Management Studies*,

5 (March 2018), 1–26. https://doi.org/10.12816/0033265

George, S., & Salim, A. (2019). Demystifying the environmental perspectives on sustainable marketing in Saudi Arabia. *Journal of Advanced Research in Dynamical and Control Systems*, 11(8 Special Issue), 2193–2202.

Hanson, D. (2012). Indústria creativas. *Sistemas & Gestão*, 7, 222–238. https://doi.org/10.7177/sg.2012.v7.n2.a7

Kai, H., He, H., & Wang, W. Y. C. (2012). Green marketing and its impact on supply chain management in industrial markets. *Industrial Marketing Management*, 41(4), 557–562. https://doi.org/10.1016/j.indmarman.2012.04.002

Kardos, M., Gabor, M. R., & Cristache, N. (2019). Green marketing's roles in sustainability and ecopreneurship. Case study : green packaging's impact on romanian young consumers' environmental responsibility. *Sustainability*, 11(1), 1–13. https://doi.org/10.3390/su11030873

Khorsheed, R. K., Abdulla, D. F., Othman, B. A., Mohammed, H. O., & Sadq, Z. M. (2020). The role of services marketing mix 7P ' s on achieving competitive advantages (the case of Paitaxt Technical Institute in Kurdistan Region of Iraq). *TEST Engineering & Management*, (June), 15947–15971.

Kotler, P. (2011). Reinventing marketing to manage. *Journal of Marketing*, 75(July), 132–135. https://doi.org/10.159/jmkg.75.4.132.

Lima, C. L. C. (2007). Políticas culturais para o desenvolvimento: O debate sobre as indústrias culturais e criativas. In *Terceiro Encontro de Estudos Multidisciplninares em Cultura*. Salvador.

Mahmoud, T. O. (2019). Green marketing : A marketing mix concept. *International Journal of Eletrical, Eletronics and Computers*, 4(January), 20–26. https://doi.org/10.22161/eec.4.1.3

Mombeuil, C., Fotiadis, A. K., & Wang, Z. (2019). The pandora ' s box of corporate social irresponsibility : An exploratory study within a failed State context. *Journal of Cleaner Production*, 234, 1306–1321. https://doi.org/10.1016/j.jclepro.2019.06.262

Neves, J. do R. O. (2012). *O papel dos eventos no reforço da Atractividade turística de Cabo Verde*. Escola Superior de Hotelaria e Turismo do Estoril.

Oliveira, V. F. C. (2015). *Modo de gestão para a sustentabilidade de destinos turísticos: Análise do caso de estudo de percursos da região de Sintra-Cascais*. Universidade de Lisboa.

Ottman, J. A., Stafford, E. R., & Hartman, C. L. (2006). Avoiding green marketing myopia: Ways to improve consumer appeal for environmentally preferable products. *Environment*, 48(5), 22–36.

https://doi.org/10.3200/ENVT.48.5.22-36

Oyekunle, O. A. (2014). Building the creative industries for sustainable economic development in South Africa. *International Journal of Sustainable Development*, 48–72. Retrieved from http://www.ssrn.com/link/OIDA-Intl-Journal-Sustainable-Dev.html

Peattie, K. (2001). Towards Sustainability: The third age of green marketing. *The Marketing Review*, 2, 129–146. https://doi.org/10.1362/1469347012569869

Pomering, A. (2017). Marketing for sustainability: Extending the conceptualisation of the marketing mix to drive value for individuals and society at large. *Australasian Marketing Journal*, 25(2), 157–165. https://doi.org/10.1016/j.ausmj.2017.04.011

Rahdari, A., Sepasi, S., & Moradi, M. (2016). Achieving sustainability through schumpeterian social entrepreneurship : The role of social enterprises. *Journal of Cleaner Production*, 137, 347–360. https://doi.org/10.1016/j.jclepro.2016.06.159

Rastogi, A. K., & Pant, L. K. (2019). A study on green marketing: its use and importance. *Journal of Global Economy*, 14(October 2018), 71–80.

Rodrigues, B. H. do R. (2017). *Turismo cultural e desenvolvimento . A rota das catedrais e o caso de Santarém*. Universidade de Coimbra.

Rudawska, E., Frąckiewicz, E., & Wiścicka-Fernando, M. (2016). Sustainable marketing mix -The basic assumptions 1. *Polityki Europejskie, Finanse i Marketing*, 15(December 2017), 130–137. https://doi.org/10.22630/PEFIM.2016.15.64.12

Seretny, M., & Seretny, A. (2012). Sustainable marketing -A new era in the responsible marketing development. *Foundations of Management*, 4(2), 63–76. https://doi.org/10.2478/fman-2013-0011

Singh, P. B., & Pandey, K. K. (2012). Green marketing : Policies and practices for sustainable development. *Journal of Management*, 5(1), 22–30.

Solaiman, M., Osman, A., Suberi, M., & Ab, B. (2015). Green marketing : A marketing mix point of view. *International Journal of Business and Technopreneurship*, 5(1), 87–98.

Taghian, M., Polonsky, M., & Souza, C. D. (2016). Green marketing strategies. In D. Sarkar, R. Datta, A. Mukherjee, & R. Hannigan (eds.), *An integrated approach to environmental management* (First, pp. 231–254). Nova Jersey: John Wiley & Sons, Inc.

Thevanes, N., & Weerasinghe, M. K. P. W. D. R. (2019). Contribution of green marketing in creating sustainable organization. In *15º International Conference on Business Management* (pp. 725–742).

Warrink, D., Akhunjonov, U., & Obrenovic, B. (2018). The marketing mix in a marketing 3.0 context. *International Journal of Innovation and Economic Development*, 4(4), 7–30. https://doi.org/10.18775/ijied.1849-7551-7020.2015.44.2001

Yang, J., & Černevičiūtė, J. (2017). Cultural and creative industries (CCI) and sustainable development: China's cultural industries clusters. *The International Journal Entrepreneurship and Sustainability Issues*, 5(6), 231–242. https://doi.org/10.9770/jesi.2017.5.2(6)

CHAPTER 5

TOURISM AS INTERCULTURAL BUSINESS: LOCATING CONCEPTS AND QUESTIONING IDENTITIES

CLARA SARMENTO
CENTRE FOR INTERCULTURAL STUDIES (CEI)
ISCAP – P.PORTO, POLYTECHNIC OF PORTO

Introduction

This chapter approaches the topic of tourism as a global intercultural business, resorting to notions of culture, identity, representation and territory, among other concepts used in intercultural studies[1]. Studying global tourism not only means thinking about it in terms of the world's economy, but also regarding issues of identity and difference, representation, heritage, history and transformation of geographic spaces into significant places. Exploring tourism as a world cultural phenomenon is a way of associating it with the ever-polemic concept of globalization, often understood as a manifestation of Western dominance. Thus, this chapter will also address matters of ethics, power and cultural hegemony. Indeed, international tourism increasingly offers a global formula, where local cultures are shown as a mere display of colourful leisure for wealthy visitors to enjoy. Culture is adapted and reduced to the impact of light entertainment and aesthetic appeal, as in the cases of *moliceiro* boat races in Portugal, *capoeira* martial art in Brazil, *mendhi* body art in Tunisia, *bindi* in India, or *tango* in Argentina.

---

[1] This chapter employs the concept of "intercultural" as a synonym for movement, communication, and encounter between cultures (Abdallah-Pretceille, 2006; Ibanez & Saenz, 2006; Sarmento, 2010, 2014, 2016; Dervin, Gajardo & Lavanchy, 2011; Holliday, 2011, 2013; Dervin & Gross, 2016; Imbert, 2014).

We shall begin by attempting to define what we actually understand as tourism. Tourism is a leisure activity that directly contrasts with the daily procedures of paid or unpaid organized labour. Tourism involves an outward movement, a journey to places where one 'stays' but does not 'live'. Tourists' stays are temporary, and always aimed at returning home to an organized work routine. Visited places are different from those places where work and everyday life happen. In fact, this difference is the key characteristic that turns such places into desirable holiday destinations. Activities carried out while one is 'away' take on a different note or intensity from activities undertaken while one is 'at home': as tourists, our outlook on the surrounding environment is much more intense than during the course of everyday life[2]. The tourists' experience differs from the daily experience, at least regarding one of the following aspects: location, activity, landscape and sensory experience (Urry, 2002). Whether advertising alters our perception of holidays as an intense experience in different places or triggers already nurtured holiday expectations remains unclear. Notwithstanding, while there are historical and sociological variants on what tourism is, it is possible to describe some common features related to the social practice of tourism in the 21st century, at least in Western economies whose societies have a clear and structured boundary between work and leisure. According to John Urry, in so-called modern societies, tourism is a legalized and organized leisure activity, which can be compared to its opposite facet, work, an activity that is also legalized and organized (2002: 2 et seq.).

The definition of tourism is seen as a part of the Western common sense. It is one of Raymond Williams' "structures of feeling" (1961, 1976) or Paul duGay's "significant practices" (1997, 2007), produced by and for society, from a wide range of discourses that allow us to represent and communicate ideas about work, leisure, exoticism, everyday life, distance, pleasure, freedom, obligations and responsibilities, among other concepts. However, societies where people cannot travel because of a lack of resources, due to warfare or political reasons, or because of job demands or lack of transport will hardly see tourism in a similar fashion.

---

[2] John Urry identified two observational models that can be aligned with the classic distinction between traveller and tourist: the romantic observation of the traveller and the collective observation of the tourist. Romantic observation requires solitude, privacy and a personal relationship with the object that is observed, whereas collective observation requires the constant presence of others, something that is critical to the creation of the carnival-like atmosphere of Disneyworld, for example (Urry, 2002).

1. Tourism: A brief overview of the business

Mass tourism has only become a trend in the last two hundred years, mainly in North America and Europe, then gradually across the world, or nearly all of it, although, in practice, visiting other cultures in order to have intense or different experiences is not a new thing. In Ancient Rome, road infrastructures allowed the privileged elite to travel for work or leisure. The pursuit of intense religious experiences – or a simple escape from a mundane life – remained entirely associated with the pilgrimages of the Middle Ages. From the 13th century, all over Europe, travellers would venture on long pilgrimages to religious places of their devotion, whilst staying in inns and monasteries along the way. In the 15th century, travellers could already go as far as the Holy Land, departing from Venice. In the 18th century, the Grand Tour established itself as a vehicle of cultural education for the sons of the British aristocracy. From the outset, this trip would be undertaken so that classical sites of Greece and Italy could be visited, including galleries, museums and monuments. In the 19th century, the sons and also the daughters of the *haute bourgeoisie* would also embark on the Grand Tour, which became a more sensory and aesthetic experience of contemplating the sublime, often by revelling in natural landscapes. In the same century, the American elite also began crossing the Atlantic in order to travel across Europe, to visit its historical, cultural and natural sites. Nevertheless, before the 20th century, all these examples of travel for pleasure and cultural enrichment could only be afforded by a wealthy and privileged few. Social tourism practices were only consolidated in the course of the 20th century, taking up 40% of the time available for leisure. Vacationing then became a fixture of a Western lifestyle. According to the United Nations World Tourism Organization (UNWTO), international tourism escalated from a little more than one million tourists in 1959 to over a billion in 2014.

A brief overview of late 20th century and first decades of the 21st century shows that Southeast Asia's growing economies such as Thailand, Malaysia and Singapore, have been particularly effective in attracting international visitors and generating jobs in the tourist sector. Many Eastern European countries, such as the Czech Republic, Hungary and Poland, have developed successful tourism sectors after the fall of communism in 1989. The richest countries still control the international tourism market. France, Spain, the US and Italy have remained on top of the list of the most sought-after tourist destinations, although their position has been threatened by the growth of tourism in the East. China is already the world's fourth largest tourist destination and was the country with the highest spending in this sector in 2019[3]. One of the reasons for the growth of tourism in Asia is the extraordinary development of Asian economies. Europeans are increasingly travelling to Oriental and Southeast Asian countries. Even within the same vast Asia-Pacific region, tourists from Singapore, South Korea, Japan, Australia and China tend to favour holiday destinations such as Indonesia, Malaysia, Thailand and the Philippines. This creates an intense tourist flow that bypasses Europe and the Americas.

Going against the stereotype of one-sided cultural, economic and political currents, a more befitting image of a decentralized network of alternate and multidirectional flows manifests itself. This network enhances the contingent nature of economics and politics, and suggests that nowaday's complex global systems may easily shift power between East and West. However, the rapid rise in the number of tourists travelling across the globe can either bring wealth and prosperity to a region or lead to human exploitation and environmental damage. Tourism may serve to impose a culture over other or to evade the laws and regulations of one's country of origin. In Thailand and Cambodia, for instance, tourist inflows from Japan, Europe and America have given rise to a lucrative sex tourism trade that exploits women and children within a context where legal and protective

[3] 2019 was another year of strong growth, although slower when compared to the exceptional rates of 2017 and 2018 (6% increase in both years). Demand was slower mainly in advanced economies and particularly in Europe. Uncertainty surrounding Brexit, geopolitical and trade tensions, and the global economic slowdown, weighed on growth. 2019 was also the year of major shifts in the sector with the collapse of Thomas Cook and of several low-cost airlines in Europe. However, all regions enjoyed an increase in arrivals. The Middle East (+8%) led this growth, followed by Asia and the Pacific (+5%). International arrivals in Europe and Africa (both +4%) increased in line with the world average, while the Americas saw a growth of 2%. However, in 2020, the world faced an unprecedented global health, social and economic emergency due to the COVID-19 pandemic. Travel and tourism were among the most affected sectors. In an unprecedented shock to the tourism sector, the COVID-19 pandemic cut international tourist arrivals in the first quarter of 2020 to a fraction of what they were a year before. Asia and the Pacific, the first region to suffer the impact of COVID-19, saw a 35% decrease in arrivals in the first quarter of 2020. The second-hardest hit was Europe with a 19% decline, followed by the Americas (-15%), Africa (-12%) and the Middle East (-11%). The general scenario of 2020 points to declines of 58% to 78% in international tourist arrivals, depending on the speed of the containment, the duration of travel restrictions and the re-opening of national borders. The plunge in international travel has put 100 to 120 million direct tourism jobs at risk. The impact for 2021 and the outlook for 2022 remain highly uncertain. (UNWTO, 2020a; 2020b).

mechanisms are rarely accessible. Conversely, tourism can also mean respect and appreciation for the culture that is visited, thus strengthening cultural exchanges between different peoples. Tourism can revive local cultures, promote the cultural heritage of a region, and lead to the reinvention of traditions and customs that have long been cast aside. According to Cohen and Kennedy, traditions that survive are those that have been reinvented, they are not the same as their original prototype (2000: 228). We shall now discuss some of the ways tourism is viewed as a social and cultural phenomenon, as well as a vehicle for the invention and reinvention of traditions.

2. Tourism as a social and cultural practice

In *The Elementary Forms of Religious Life* (1915), Emile Durkheim described how religious rites, sacred objects and beliefs could be distinguished from the objects and practices of daily life, which he called profane. Places of devotion and objects used in religious rites are addressed with a degree of respect that is in stark contrast with those other daily life objects and practices. The function of sacredness is to bring communities together and reinforce shared beliefs by means of ceremonies and rituals. Profane does not receive this exceptional treatment, but finds resonance in common sense and daily life experiences. In order to enter the realm of sacredness, one must renounce ordinary life and embrace the extraordinary. In pre-modern societies, religion worked as a sphere within the realm of extraordinariness. Some would experience extraordinariness through pilgrimage, whereas many others would experience it in local religious festivities, Holy days and their rituals. One must not forget that, in English, the term 'holiday' is derived from the combination of two words: 'Holy' and 'day'.

In 21st century Western societies, it is quite unlikely that religion can set the boundaries between what is commonplace and what is extraordinary. Instead, Harrison claims that holidays and travel are a means we resort to in order to seek extraordinary experiences, that is, to encounter sacredness (1995: 240). We visit tourist attractions to contemplate them with veneration; we expect that by vacationing, we will be suddenly carried away from our daily work routine into an extraordinary landscape of pleasure, from where we will arise and return regenerated. Before leaving, we make intense preparations for the holiday experience; when we return, we share objects, images and memories. Holidays and tourism are part of those social practices that have a specific function and meaning in modern societies, their cultural significance is shared and disseminated among most citizens of Western societies.

Although Durkheim's theories can be applied to the phenomenon of tourism, in reality, tourists are not worshippers nor do they frequent an exclusive place of devotion. Tourists collect experiences that can range from contemplating natural landscapes (such as the Natural Park of Peneda Gerês or the Alps) to a historical re-enactment (such as the Medieval Fairs of Santa Maria da Feira and Óbidos), from *in loco* observation of the way of life of indigenous populations (such as the Maoris or Sami) to EuroDisney's fairytale attractions. At Disney's theme parks, daily life conventions are suddenly lifted, whilst visitors engage in childlike behaviours that bring them closer to the need for the extraordinary in a secular world. Such as in the Middle Ages, contemporary tourists have become pilgrims and tourist attractions have turned into places of regeneration and authenticity, which is in fact often (though not always) illusory, ephemeral and artificial (Harrison, 1995: 240 et seq.).

However, not all tourists seek illusory experiences. On the contrary, they might deliberately seek an authentic experience, be it a historical re-enactment, an immersion into an indigenous culture or even in a specific workplace. For instance, Tokyo stock exchange can be visited by tourists, who can watch transactions, take a guided tour and play a stock trading simulation game, using news and corporate information in a virtual securities market. Historical re-enactments can portray with authenticity the life of slaves on a 19th century plantation field or some Old West rodeo. 21st century tourism involves more and more observation and/or participation in real life re-enactments, whether related to the past or present. John Urry reiterates that tourists are contemporary pilgrims searching for the authenticity of other times and other places, far from those times and places that make up their daily lives (2002: 9). This can be witnessed by the popularity of safaris in Africa, glamping in the desert or tours to the jungle tribes of the Amazon.

Social media, photography, digital technologies, glossy magazines and television bring to our homes images of tourist devotional places that trigger a wanderlust in us. These media ensure that tourists already know what they will visit long before they leave, what they should expect to see when they get there, and how they shall interpret a certain attraction. Tourists are encouraged to act as collectors, the bearers of a checklist of places to visit and things to do. Those who visit more places collect a greater amount of mementos, passport stamps, photographs and posts on social networks, thus acquiring a new social and even professional status, as social media travel influencers. Places that are visited or are to be visited are represented with a particular discourse that identifies and distinguishes them from others: Paris is represented as the City of Lights and romance; Spain as the land of passion and flamenco; the Maldives as a kind of tropical paradise; India as a haven of mysticism and spirituality; China as the bastion of the mysterious East; Brazil as an Eden of sensuality and joy. Attractions such as Niagara Falls, Stonehenge, the Eiffel Tower or Miami Beach are also culturally demarcated territories, shaped by common meanings, transformed by economy and technology, quite distant from their original meaning. According to John Urry, what we experience is based on pre-existing cultural images, where the physical object in itself has become nearly invisible (2002: 59).

In all these territories, those people who find jobs and earn their income in tourist development activities, embrace it with joy. Those who live in a tourist destination, but do not reap direct benefits from tourism, can somehow take pride in showing off their culture to visitors and thereby learning from them about other cultures. However, those who have been displaced from their homes and do not benefit from tourism financially can see visitors as invaders and may antagonize them. Moreover, visitors can demand high standards of lodging and services, in a clear contrast with the actual living conditions of local inhabitants. This intricate network of shared (often conflictual) meanings, different individual experiences, and political and business decisions, interwoven around the geographic space itself, gives rise to an invented territory that can be known as Algarve, Porto, Douro, Mustique, Bora Bora, Bali or Dubai.

3. Cultural territories and the identities of tourism

The seemingly homogeneous identity expressed in the term "tourist" only exists within its contingent relationship with the hosts that receive, accommodate and often tolerate tourists in their territories. One cannot be a tourist and a host at the same time, because being a tourist means in its core to be away from home or from their place of origin; being a tourist means not being a host. The concept of tourist as a homogeneous identity constructed by the mass travel industry has been challenged, as there is not a single type of tourist, but a wide range of identities associated with travel (Apostolopoulos, Leivadi & Yiannakis, 1996). A usual definition is that which distinguishes 'tourists' from 'travellers'. Travellers visit places whilst searching for authenticity, either by observing natural landscapes or by taking part in local culture. Tourists, on the other hand, seek fun in the company of other people with similar goals. In this construction of identities, tourists are generally associated with superficial, non-authentic experiences, provided by the mass travel industry, whereas travellers are identified with ancient pilgrims, seeking to understand and participate in the cultures they visit (Cohen, 1996: 90). Hence, the distinction created between tourists and travellers is translated into a permanent antagonism, in an identity logic based on mutually exclusive dichotomous pairs.

The spatial markers that build identities are equally important. For instance, in the 19th century, men could transit freely in public spaces, whereas women were often limited to their homes. Servants occupied certain spaces within a bourgeois home that were clearly separated from the spaces used by their masters. Being a servant or a woman meant taking up spaces delineated by their social identity, that is, it meant inhabiting certain cultural territories. In the case of tourism, an example of cultural territory are the all-inclusive resorts, such as the ones found in the Caribbean, Cape Verde or Southern Spain, where lodging, entertainment, food, beverages, sports and leisure can all be found within the same delimited space and are included in the package. Tourists are restricted to a specific area and rarely ever meet local inhabitants, unless the latter work in the resort. In this example, differences between the two identities (tourist/host) are displayed explicitly and marked in space.

The discourse of tourism reclaims the preservation of cultural identities associated with a territory allegedly threatened by globalization, desertification or marginalization, of which some examples are Tana Toraja, Ibiza, Madeira, Nazaré, Ria de Aveiro, Óbidos and the Vicentine Coast. This can involve the appropriation and adaptation of elements from other cultures, in order to create something that is not purely traditional nor exclusively modern, but a culture in a constant state of dynamism. And that is precisely this dynamism that a non-condescending perspective should incorporate, albeit critically, because cultures, as well as their accompanying cultural identities, evolve continuously in any part of the world and should not be expected to remain perfectly stagnant in time.

The tourism industry is aggressive in its ceaseless pursuit of increasingly exotic and remote new attractions and destinations, such as Papua New Guinea, the Amazon or even Antarctica. When tourism is established in a region, its peoples and cultures are marketed, typecast by advertising and sold to an international tourism consuming public. International mass tourism has triggered one of the largest population movements ever, where millions of occasional travellers from industrialized nations seek, on the outskirts of globalization, living vestiges of their imagination, embodied as exotic, erotic or as Rousseau's "noble savage". French Polynesia, for instance, is described in tourist language as a tropical paradise with pristine beaches, a place of purity and charm, where people live blissfully, away from civilization and close to nature, in a culture that is unchanging, harmonious and sustainable. This myth of the primitive man that resists the threats of civilization not only overlooks real living conditions of local inhabitants, but also describes a culture that has actually never existed. The descriptions about many tourist sites away from Western metropoles resonate the Orientalist discourse analysed by Edward Said, as well as the anthropological monologues based on a redemptive ethnography.

Tourism takes place in a border zone that is not natural, which exists in order to be discovered by tourists, as all borders are human constructs. Most tourists, mainly those who travel in organized groups, do not only visit an actual country; they visit selected tourist destinations instead, that are located within a border zone[4]. Tourist border zones are fluid, they may change over time; by definition, no migrants live therein, but a recurring wave of temporary travellers, a population of tourists in constant movement and renewal. The collective identity category and the presence of tourists is permanent, but each single individual comes and goes constantly. The resident population is somewhat permanent, but they must get out of their daily routine to meet tourists, to sell their goods and services or to exhibit themselves and their culture. The tourist border zone is a cultural territory that resembles a stage in anticipation of a spectacle, both for the tourists-audience and for the inhabitants-actors. Thus, inhabitants also have to come and go constantly in this tourist border zone. Notwithstanding, the perceptions of both groups are not the same, as what is a territory of leisure and exoticism for tourists, is a territory of work and profit for inhabitants.

What the tourist discourse announces as being authentic, pure and unknown has been, in fact carefully fabricated, sold and advertised. The inhabitants of the Maldives, Salvador da Bahia, and the French Polynesia, among others, acknowledge this thirst of tourists for the exotic and authentic. Thus, they present themselves and their cultures in a way that

---

[4] We have adapted here the concept of the border zone described by Gloria Anzaldúa (1987), Guillermo Gómez-Peña (1993), Emily Hicks (1991) and Coco Fusco (1989), who developed their theories based on the border between the United States and Mexico, as a place of migration between two countries.

properly reflects preconceived tourist representations. From the outside, tourists visit primitive inhabitants; from the inside – according to the inhabitants' perspective – tourism is a means to achieving economic development and ensure subsistence. However, the richer and more modern local populations become, the less interesting they will become for tourists, therefore, the less money they will get from tourism. If the abovementioned peoples renounce their role as the exotic noble savage, they risk losing their major source of income. What most inhabitants do in this situation is to collaborate with the production of a tourist discourse and representation, staged as a strategic essentialism. However, tourists are not a passive agent in this process: they collaborate with the inhabitants by tacitly accepting the fictional tourist enactment. The tourist border zone is a territory of cultural invention on a wider scale. Tourists wish to experience a fictional past that is untouched by globalization. Hence, the industry invents versions of this utopian past and turns them into tourist consumption assets. Tourists do not travel to experience the post-colonial present nor the territories that emerge from economic development; they travel in order to enjoy an immutable colonial past, lost in time.

That said, tourists travel to a border zone between their 'civilized' culture and 'another' culture that is 'exotic' and 'savage', in order to explore a fantastic territory of the Western imagination. In reality, this 'other' 'savage' is the post-colonial subject, who has long travelled in the opposite direction, as people from Sub-Saharan Africa, India, South America, China and the Maghreb have migrated to Western metropoles many decades ago. Paradoxically, the Western elite seems to be ready to spend thousands of euros travelling thousands of miles in order to encounter those they might easily meet in their hometown, in their day-to-day lives. In Western metropoles, the efforts of privileged classes to avoid acknowledging the presence of other ethnicities in their midst are striking. This takes the form of self-segregation in private condominiums, upscale suburban towns or gated communities. When they are forced to observe 'other' people who surround them, they normally do so by means of a selective representation that emphasizes poverty and marginalization. Westerners enjoy going to ethnic restaurants and folkloric shows, as long as they take place in restricted, controlled and legitimate spaces. The elite avoids seeing the 'other' in first world cities, but on their vacation, they travel to tourist border zones expressly aiming to observe that same 'other'. According to the discourse of hegemony, the 'other' in Western territories is a source of criticism; the 'other' in the territory of their alleged distant origin is a source of pleasure and instagrammable moments collected as trophies. In fact, this is a longstanding phenomenon, existing already for well over a hundred years in the United States, where Native Americans living in their reserves, become exotic and romantic, but when they go to urban metropoles they are generally perceived as undesirable. In a third world space, the 'other' is domesticated, works for tourists, is frozen in time or out of time, fabricating a westernized version of their culture, where they participate as mere actors (Bruner, 2005: 191-5).

While travelling for adventure, experience, status or exploration of the exotic 'other', tourists can bring back a hypothetical, intangible, decontextualized and pristine 'other', who they own and control through the stories they tell and the images they display. Tourists insert the post-colonial subject into a new narrative frame, where tourists become the heroes of the trip and the 'other' is the object of their demand. Thus, it is extremely important to guide the attention of the tourism sector, as well as of the research on the topic, towards host communities, more or so than towards the motivations of the tourist, that is to say, this perspective should become truly intercultural.

4. Opportunities for development through intercultural tourism

Speaking of intercultural tourism is somewhat redundant, as tourism always implies a contact between different customs, uses, traditions and structures of feeling, that is, between different cultures. In order to illustrate this topic, we will use the case of Portugal, a country with approximately 10 million inhabitants that, in 2019, welcomed a total of 27 million tourists, 7.3% more than in 2018, a significant advance in the pace of growth, according to data from the National Statistics Institute (INE)[5].

---

[5] In 2019, tourism revenues increased to 4.28 billion euros in Portugal. In terms of stay, hotels continue to lead the choice, concentrating around 58 million stays, ahead of local accommodation with 10 million stays. Rural tourism counted with 1.0 million overnight stays. When it comes to growth, hostels stood out with overnight stays skyrocketing 23.5% (INE). Most of the tourists kept coming from the United Kingdom, with a total of 9.38 million people, rising 1.5% when compared to 2018, followed by Germany, with 5.88 million guests, and Spain, with 5.22 million. In terms of growth, the highlight goes to the North American (29.2%), Canadian (27.6%) and Irish (26%) markets. With tourism expanding more and more, the national authority "Tourism of Portugal" approved the construction of 105 new hotels. In the specific field of sustainability, Portugal received the 2019 Accessible Tourist Destination Award during the 23rd General Assembly of the UNWTO, held in St. Petersburg. In the World Economic Forum's

The economic and commercial exploitation of culture is increasingly guided by the reinvention of traditions arising out of controversial exogenous and political interests. Regarding the intercultural study of tourism, two fundamental approaches can be addressed. The first approach is interested in economic matters and addresses the problem of change, development and modernization. The second approach relates to the cultural dimensions of tourism, that is not seen as a mere instrument of destruction, but as a potential factor for creativity and reinvention. The combination of these two approaches concludes that the reification of culture through tourism may not always destroy it but, instead, transform culture and boost its growth. However, some major challenges remain: the issue of cultural authenticity, the cultural homogenization of mass tourism, as well as the relationship between economic improvement and cultural impoverishment. Tourism can respond creatively to local cultures and positively influence their path towards development, because barring all changes is as infeasible as sanctioning all modifications. Therefore, an intermediate position becomes a strategy of productivity and sustainable development. We shall call this perspective "intercultural tourism".

Nowadays, the notion of 'traditional' is often associated with an idea of 'authenticity', which is not always correct. Conversely, 'traditional' and 'typical' are two concepts that are often mixed up, as they are not necessarily synonyms. The maintenance of authenticity is a phenomenon directly related to the process of continuity and change; tradition not always corresponds to authenticity, as it can be invented or reinvented; 'typical' is often artificial, imported or transposed, therefore, not authentic. Likewise, after the industrial revolution, Western societies tended to invent traditions, in order to establish a connection with the past and with a lost community identity (Hobsbawn & Ranger, 1988: 9). In Portugal, we can highlight the example of the typical yet invented tradition of the carnival of Ovar, famed for its samba schools and dancers dressed in

---

2019 Tourism Competitiveness Report, an in-depth analysis of tourism in over 130 countries, Portugal achieved unprecedented results when, for the first time, ranked first in the quality of tourist infrastructure and 12th in the global competitiveness ranking (WEF). During the current COVID-19 pandemic, the Portuguese Government has been taking strict public health measures to protect the population. General behaviour guidelines were enacted by the Directorate-General of Health, concerning social distance, the use of face masks, sanitisation measures, and vaccination, with specific recommendations for each sector of the economy. In tourism, the "Clean & Safe" seal, defined by the Tourism of Portugal, was implemented, granting tourists greater security and confidence in accommodation, services and attractions.

tropical Brazilian fashion, who parade under the cold rain and wind, in the height of the winter of Northern Portugal.

The main purpose of intercultural tourism consists in favouring the in-depth knowledge of tangible and intangible assets of local, regional or national cultures. This is how they should be addressed, not as mere attractions for meeting visitors' expectations, which is often the case. A growing interest has been perceived in considering 'intercultural' as a process that manifests itself on occasions where different groups are led to confrontation, so that later they reconcile their points of view and meanings. Tourism, with its multiple border territories, becomes an excellent opportunity for practicing intercultural processes of communication and for inventing new forms of cultural expression.

4.1. The risks of cultural commodification and (over) mediated activities

Greenwood questions the possibility of culture being considered a commodity. Indeed, everything that is marketed is a product stemming from a combination of production factors. However, this is not so evident when tourists are attracted by a local cultural characteristic, such as the Vila Franca de Xira bull run, the appearance of the Virgin Mary in Fatima or the congress of folk medicine in Vilar de Perdizes. Hence, Greenwood claims that culture is a peculiar, altered and often destroyed commodity, when addressed as tourist attraction (1989: 172-3). In fact, culture commodification, either as a natural resource or as service, is potentially destructive and should be reconsidered by all those involved in the tourism industry. A good example would be the landscape and environmental concerns in the Algarve and the Troia Peninsula that were only taken into account in the late 20th century, after decades of ecological and urbanistic neglect.

In the past, relationships between travellers and their hosts were considerably more direct than they normally are in contemporary tourism. Travel conditions were largely determined by hospitality conventions, much more than by travellers' rules and requirements. The advent of mass tourism changed it all, to a point where, in certain situations, the distinction between tourists and hosts became almost irrelevant. Indeed, while opting for cruises, hotel chains, resorts, theme parks, shopping malls and casinos, tourists are frequenting places that are only vaguely foreign. Conversely, local communities are often prevented from engaging in any type of relationship with visitors. In some cases, their work is no longer necessary, as importing labour, catering, entertainment, technology and other goods required by tourists has become easier. As stated above, if the representation of local inhabitants is deemed desirable, it would be limited to the cultural picturesqueness and elements of local colour, according to the expectations that tourists create and bring along with them.

Some popular tourist destinations can now be considered 'tourist cultures', due to the predominance of cultural influences of visitors, such as Ibiza, Dubai, the Cayman Islands or Acapulco, with little or no relationship with the local population amidst which they have been established. These communities are based on recreational lifestyles, located within beach, ski, nightlife and ecotourism resorts, evoking those theme parks which are designed deliberately as fantasylands. But the development of heritage tourism can also generate 'tourist cultures' alienated from reality, as it is frequently associated with the invention of communities erected from idealized images of the past, such as Sortelha, Óbidos, Monsanto and other villages that have been renovated for tourist purposes in the countryside of Northern and Central Portugal. In many cases, these tourist communities have acquired a strong cultural symbology, but were rarely built in a vacuum, as they have arisen from – and sometimes in stark contrast with – preexisting communities, widely ignored in the decision, design and execution of tourism projects.

Tourism is an increasingly mediated activity, depending on the intervention of agents who are neither hosts nor visitors. This is obvious when we consider large-scale tourist enterprises, such as theme parks, resorts and the recuperation of historical centres. The motivations for the tourism mediation activity vary, as well as the ideas and values that these agents aim to convey, in their attempt towards balancing the interests of tourists and those of the communities they visit. However, most agents tend towards invisibility, such is the case of owners of large resorts in the Algarve and Alentejo or the real estate agents of Óbidos, Lisbon and Porto. This trend is stimulated in part by the desire of keeping – at least on the surface – the most traditional host/guest relationship possible. Nevertheless, the agent's invisibility is also motivated by the desire of concealing inequality in the distribution of wealth derived from tourism. This has become almost axiomatic in the tourism industry: those who profit the most with its development are those who suffer the least with its impact and vice-versa.

4.2. Heritage and the development of intercultural tourism

In Portugal, the tourism industry re-emerged in the eighties of the 20th century, in a format far removed from its roots in the 19th century, when predominant cultural values emphasized the preservation of cultural heritage and the picturesque aspects of Portuguese rural life. In the 20th century, tourism was no longer an isolated activity and became an economic and political issue. Therefore, the fascist regime of *Estado Novo* sought to promote the image of a traditional, hospitable and peaceful country, isolated from foreign influences and stagnated in time, especially from the 1940s onwards. Only in the seventies, tourism in Portugal took the form of an industry, when the traditional view of popular culture as folklore was replaced by the values of popular mass culture, based on the promotion of a 'sun and sea' product. Notwithstanding, some elements of the original Portuguese approach to tourism and culture remain at the core of current policies.

The Portuguese cultural heritage, both tangible and intangible, constitutes a strong identity element and a powerful resource to attract national and foreign tourists. Compared to other European countries, Portugal does not have a large number of monuments and museums to offer its visitors. Thus, the attention of travel agents has turned to the preservation and exploitation of the valuable heritage resources available, which include castles, sacred art, gastronomy, wine, architecture, tiles and fado, among other practices of what can be generally called the Portuguese way of life, i.e., the Portuguese culture. We should not forget that Portugal ranks amongst the fifteen countries in the world with the most tangible and intangible cultural heritage listed by UNESCO, as follows:

Tangible Heritage	Intangible Heritage
Historic Centre of Angra do Heroísmo, 1983	Fado, 2011
Jerónimos Monastery and Belém Tower, 1983	Mediterranean cuisine, 2013[6]
Monastery of Batalha, 1983	Cante (singing) from Alentejo, 2014
Convent of Christ of Tomar, 1983	Traditional Portuguese musical shaker art, 2015
Historic Centre of Évora, 1988	Black pottery of Bisalhães, 2016
Alcobaça Monastery, 1989	Portuguese falconry art, 2016
The cultural landscape of Sintra, 1995	Estremoz clay figures, 2017
Historic Centre of Porto, 1996	The Careto tradition in Podence, 2019
Prehistoric Rock-Art Site of the Côa Valley, 1998	
Laurel Forest of Madeira, 1999	
Historic Centre of Guimarães, 2001	
Alto Douro Wine Region, 2001	
The Landscape of the Pico Island Vineyard, 2004	
The Garrison Border Town of Elvas, 2012	
University and the upper city of Coimbra, 2013	
Sanctuary of Bom Jesus do Monte of Braga, 2019	
Royal Buildings of Mafra, Convent, Garden and Hunting Park, 2019	

Portugal was essentially a rural country for many years, not acquainted with industrialization. Agriculture, though obsolete, was the main source of income for a large part of the economically active population until recently. Hence, for structural reasons, Portuguese rurality also turned out to be a symbolic resource to be valued and preserved in the tourism

[6] With Spain, Morocco, Italy, Greece, Cyprus and Croatia.

industry, as it can be seen in the Alentejo, Minho, Azores and Portuguese Beira villages. Intercultural tourism is an appropriate response to the maintenance of local and regional identity, as the imitation of mass tourism models that occurred in the Algarve – following the examples of Costa del Sol, the Greek Islands or the French Riviera – has only led to an uncharacteristic offer, without competitiveness or identity, thus reducing the territory and the profit margin.

Research on tourism as an intercultural phenomenon tends to focus on international aspects and on the impact of the relationship between wealthy Western visitors and developing nations, who crave their wealth. The assumption of this relationship is described as an important aspect of contemporary tourism, whose growth often followed Western imperialist routes, when travelling was one of the many privileges of the colonizer. However, this can be reductive, as it obliterates the increasing dependence of the so-called developed Western countries, where Portugal is included, along with Spain, France or the United Kingdom, in relation to tourism, in a phenomenon that makes the notions of host and visitor even more ambiguous, especially when one bears in mind the intense economic flows of domestic tourism. In Portugal, for instance, international tourism represents 70% of tourist demand, with the domestic market accounting for the remaining 30%. Residents of Portugal spent a total of around two billion euros on domestic tourism in 2018. The Northern region of the country (the *Norte*) was the most visited destination by domestic tourists in 2019, with approximately 2.8 million visitors, with Lisbon and the surrounding region attracting about 2.2 million domestic visitors that same year (INE).

These calls for attention are an opportunity for the productive intervention of Social and Human Sciences in the intercultural tourism industry, both in the case of Portugal and beyond. They are firstly aimed at contributing to improving the offer, enhancing local territories and communities, and privileging residents as dynamic actors interested in the tourist offer. The risks and opportunities involved in the process of transforming monological affirmative actions into dialogical transforming actions through intercultural tourism can be summarized along these ten guidelines:

Intercultural Tourism	
Risks	**Opportunities**
Local culture limited to picturesque.	Implementation of inclusive, dialogue generating projects, by acknowledging integration, diversification and complementarity as critical tools to improve offer.
Predominance of cultural influence of visitors.	Promotion of international tourism through digital media campaigns, trade marketing actions and initiatives of economic diplomacy, with updated and scientifically reviewed information on local history, traditions, customs and ethnographies.
Idealized image of the past.	Historically correct marketing strategies, reinforced by critical collections, carried out in the field, with scientific oversight.
Cultural symbolism detached from reality.	Creation of comprehensive circuits across the region, supported by sustainable equipment and infrastructure, with broad and inclusive themes, easy access and adequate signage.
Deletion of existing communities.	Engage local populations in decision-making processes and in the execution, consolidation and development of tourism projects, privileging local resources, both human and material.
Dependence on international guests.	Focus on the domestic market.
Unequal distribution of tourism generated wealth.	Accountability of mediating agents, promoting actions of social entrepreneurship.
Cultural commodification.	Promote UNESCO tangible and intangible cultural heritage, safeguarded by rigorous environmental and urbanistic measures.
Invented traditions.	Reinvented and creative traditions that offer authentic though innovative experiences.
Prohibit all changes/Accept all modifications.	Creative and sustainable development.
Monological affirmative actions.	**Dialogical transforming actions.**
Intercultural Tourism	

Conclusions

Addressing tourism as an intercultural business is both an opportunity and a challenge. The opportunity to develop routes of cultural tourism while empowering and engaging communities in the protection of cultural heritage; the challenge to enhance sustainable tourism, with an impact on employment, economic growth, poverty reduction, environmental protection and the general preservation of authenticity in culture and heritage. In fact, cultural tourism is one of the newest trends in the industry, supported by a postmodern style of demand, growing levels of cultural capital, rising educational levels, a desire for direct forms of experience, and global mobility. In the present context of international tourism, there is an increased interest for the use of literature, arts, crafts, and traditions, as well as for tangible and intangible cultural products and practices in general, to promote places and destinations, while preserving the expressions, memories and identities of social-cultural territories. This cultural turn in tourism and related business practices is likely to lead to the development of economic strategies where culture and creativity play a relevant role in the branding of competitive cities, regions and countries, using innovation and technology to promote their international image.

According to UNWTO, there is a new trend in the profile of tourists: more and more, they are solo and multigenerational travellers, as a result of aging populations and single households, pursuing a healthy lifestyle, valuing walking, wellness, sports and the environment. The rise of the access economy and of the importance of sustainability has led to travelling with the purpose of either 'changing', in a quest for authenticity and transformation, living like the locals; or 'showing', by collecting experiences, destinations and instagrammable moments. New intercultural perspectives must be offered in tune with the shifting preferences of modern visitors, while creating alternative routes that are not usually offered to mass tourists, thus fostering sustainability and economic growth, with a more effective branding and marketing strategy.

A strategic, integral, and inclusive sense of identity and territory sustains cohesive communities, capable of addressing their own needs and developing their own resources, within the complex framework of global tourism. By recognizing the cultural value of different sections of the community – including groups that face social and economic exclusion – cultural resources and heritage that could otherwise be seen as ordinary become exceptional. And the exceptional is what tourists seek, as opposed to the commonplace routine of everyday life.

Bibliography

ABDALLAH-PRETCEILLE, M. (2006) "Interculturalism as a Paradigm for Thinking about Diversity". *Intercultural Education*, 17:5 (475-83).

ANZALDÚA, G. (1987) *Boderlands/La Frontera, The New Mestiza.* São Francisco: Spinsters/Aunt Lute Foundation.

APOSTOLOPOULOS, Y.; LEIVADI, S; YIANNAKIS, A. (eds) (1996) *The Sociology of Tourism: Theoretical and Empirical Investigations.* London: Routledge.

BARANOWSKI, S. (2001) *Being Elsewhere: Tourism, Consumer Culture, and Identity in Modern Europe and North-America.* Ann Arbor, Michigan: University of Michigan Press.

BELL, C.; LYALL, J. (2001) *The Accelerated Sublime: Landscape, Tourism and Identity.* Westport: Praeger Publishers.

BRUNER, E. (2005) *Culture on Tour: Ethnographies of Travel.* Chicago: The University of Chicago Press.

BURNS, P. (2002) *An Introduction to Tourism and Anthropology.* London and New York: Routledge.

COHEN, E. (1996) "A phenomenology of tourist experiences". In Y. Apostolopoulos, S. Leivadi and A. Yiannakis (eds), *The Sociology of Tourism: Theoretical and Empirical Investigations.* London: Routledge.

COHEN, R.; KENNEDY, P (2000) *Global Sociology.* Basingstoke: Palgrave.

CROUCH, D. (ed.) (2000) *Leisure and Tourism Geographies: Practices and Geographical Knowledge.* London: Routledge.

CROUCH, D.; LUBBREN, N. (eds.) (2003) *Visual Culture and Tourism.* Oxford: Berg Publishers.

DANIEL, A. C.; RAMOS, F. (2002) "Modelling Inbound International Tourism Demand to Portugal", *International Journal of Tourism Research* 4:3 (193-209).

DERVIN, F., GAJARDO, A.; LAVANCHY, A. (eds.). (2011). *Politics of Interculturality.* Newcastle-upon-Tyne: Cambridge Scholars Publishing.

DERVIN, F.; ZEHAVIT, G. (eds.) (2016) *Intercultural Competence: Alternative approaches for different times.* London: Palgrave MacMillan.

DUGAY P. (1997) *Doing Cultural Studies: the Story of the Sony Walkman.* London: Sage/Open University.

DUGAY, P. (2007) *Organizing Identity.* London: Sage Publications.

FUSCO, C. (1989) "The Border Art Workshop/Taller de Arte Fronterizo, Interview with Guillermo Gómez-Peña and Emily Hicks", *Third Text* 7 (53-76).

GÓMES-PEÑA, G. (1993) *The New World Border: Prophecies, Poems, and Loqueras for the End of the Century.* San Francisco: City Lights Books.

GREENWOOD, D. (1989) "Culture by the Pound: An Anthropological Perspective on Tourism as Cultural Comoditization", in Valene Smith (ed.), *Hosts and Guests: The Anthropology of Tourism*. Philadelphia: University of Pennsylvania Press.

HALLAM, Elizabeth; STREET, Brian (eds.) (2000) *Cultural Encounters: Representing Otherness.* London and New York: Routledge.

HARRISON, D. (1995) "Tourism, Capitalism and Development in Less Developed Countries, in L. Sklair (ed.), *Capitalism and Development*. London: Routledge.

HICKS, E. (1991) *Border Writing: The Multidimensional Text.* Minneapolis: University of Minnesota Press.

HOBSBAWN, E.; RANGER, T. (eds) (1988) *The Invention of Tradition.* Cambridge: Cambridge University Press.

HOLLIDAY, A. (2011) *Intercultural Communication and Ideology*. London: Sage.

HOLLIDAY, A. (2013) *Understanding Intercultural Communication*. London: Routledge.

HOWARD, P. (2003) *Heritage: Management, Interpretation, Identity.* London: Continuum.

IBANEZ, B. P.; SAENZ, M. C. L. (eds.). (2006). *Interculturalism: Between Identity and Diversity*. Bern: Peter Lang.

IMBERT, P. (ed.) (2014). *Multicultural Interactions: Canada and the World, Politics and Literature*. Ottawa: University of Ottawa Press.

INE – Instituto Nacional de Estatística (2019), *Estatística do Turismo*, https://www.ine.pt/xportal/xmain?xpgid=ine_tema&xpid=INE&tema_cod=1713 (accessed August 2020).

ROJEK, C.; URRY, J. (eds.) (2002) *Touring Cultures: Transformations of Travel and Theory.* London and New York: Routledge.

SAID, E. (2004 [1978]) *Orientalismo: Representações Ocidentais do Oriente*, trans. Pedro Serras. Lisbon: Livros Cotovia.

SANTOS, Maria da Graça Poças (2010) *Turismo Cultural, Territórios e Identidades.* Porto: Afrontamento.

SARMENTO, C. (2014). "Interculturalism, Multiculturalism and Intercultural Studies: Questioning Definitions, Repositioning Strategies". *Intercultural Pragmatics* 11:4 (603-18).

SARMENTO, C. (2016). "Intercultural Polyphonies against the 'Death of Multiculturalism': an Essay on Concepts, Practices and Dialogues". In Fred Dervin & Zehavit Gross (eds.), *Intercultural Competence:*

Alternative approaches for different times (121-42). London: Palgrave MacMillan.

SARMENTO, C. (ed.). (2010). *From Here to Diversity: Globalization and Intercultural Dialogues*. Newcastle-upon-Tyne: Cambridge Scholars Publishing.

SARMENTO, C.; PASCOAL, S. (eds.) (2020) *Cultural Tourism and Heritage in Northern Portugal*. Newcastle upon Tyne: Cambridge Scholars Publishing.

SMITH, V. (ed.) (1989) *Hosts and Guests. The Anthropology of Tourism.* Philadelphia: University of Pennsylvania Press.

UNWTO – United Nations World Tourism Organization (2020a). *World Tourism Barometer and Statistical Annex*, volume 18, issue 1, January.

UNWTO – United Nations World Tourism Organization (2020b). *World Tourism Barometer and Statistical Annex*, volume 18, issue 2, May.

URRY, J. (2002) *The Tourist Gaze.* London, California and New Delhi: Sage.

WEF – World Economic Forum (2020), *The Travel & Tourism Competitiveness Report 2019*, https://www.weforum.org/reports/the-travel-tourism-competitiveness-report-2019 (accessed August 2020).

WILLIAMS, R. (1961) *The Long Revolution*. London: Chatto and Windus.

WILLIAMS, R. (1976) *Keywords: A Vocabulary of Culture and Society*. London: Fontana.

CHAPTER 6

THE VALUE OF PRODUCTS AND SERVICES IN TOURISM: THE CASE OF VIRAL SOCIETY

PEDRO ANDRADE
UNIVERSITY OF MINHO, COMMUNICATIONS AND SOCIETY RESEARCH CENTRE

Introduction

In contemporary times, tourism constitutes a fundamental part of global economies, societies and cultures (Andrade, 2020a, 2020b). However, Covid-19 virus pandemic turned this situation on its head. Therefore, it is also necessary to put reflection and action conducted by Social Sciences upside down. The present text aims to discuss the different types of value of tourism goods and services, in the context of the current '*viral society*'. This unprecedented emerging paradigm of virulent social formations, can be understood and defined, among other terms, as a social dialectics among confinements and lack of confinements, in what regards social spaces and times.

In sociological terms, such social clash may be translated as relations among three central concepts: 'social mobilities' (John Urry, 2007), signifying that 'everything is on the move': capital, labor, means of production, goods, services, etc. After this pre-pandemic mobile era, under a rising pandemic stage, '*social demobilities*' are associated with a relative lack of freedom, in what regards social and physical movements. Thirdly, '*social remobilities*' is a post-pandemic idea that the sociologist may use, to overcome this demobililities conjuncture, in articulation with the participatory remodeling of social activities and discourses by citizens. In fact, today a '*viral culture*' is also emerging, founded on cultural activities undertaken in a novel '*viral public space*', where new dialectics of demobililities and remobilities occur.

Viral public space means a collective social sphere conditioned by the characteristics of the viral society, which leads, for example, to cultural events developed more frequently and deeply in cyberspace and cybertime, especially within digital social networks (Web 2.0) and inside Web 3.0's socio-semantic networks. In the context of tourism, the model of '*viral tourism'* is designed as an unprecedented way of traveling, which inherits some of the characteristics of viral society, such as the preponderance of virtual travel on the internet, and a greater development of locative tourism driven by mobile phones, even if used in a somewhat virtual way.

Table I: Society regimes and respective central value type

society regime	**predominant (but not exclusive) value type**
pre-capitalist societies (primitive communism / community driven / artisanal / slave dependent / medieval / Asian regimes: Prehistory, Antiquity and Middle Ages, until the middle of the 15th century)	use value
capitalist and modern societies (stages: concurrential-liberal capitalism, since the middle of the 15th century, corresponding to the emergence of the world economy (Immanuel Wallerstein); organized capitalism, in two phases: monopoly capitalism, which started around the economic crises of 1870, and monopoly capitalism of State, since the 1929 crisis)	exchange value
capitalist and modern societies (stage of disorganized capitalism and post-Fordism (Scott Lash, John Urry), since the mid-1970s)	sign-value, informative-textual value
post-capitalist societies (socialist or utopian)	reciprocal-distributive value

1. Historical types of value

As for the reflection on value, this text debates, in particular, '*informative-textual value'*. This is a configuration of the value of products and services, which integrates and combines some of the components of use and exchange value defined by Marx, as well as some features of Baudrillard's sign-value, but also differs from them in some aspects. To this aim, it is necessary, first of all, to guard against the ambiguity of the term, confronting the various interpretations of the concept 'value', within the various social spheres: economic, political, cultural-discursive spheres, etc. Such prior care allows to create the conditions for a wide-ranging debate and not the dominance of a unique thought. However, for now this discussion will be necessarily incomplete. At least, it may shed some light on the scientific and sociological value of the social phenomenon 'value', as a relevant explanatory concept of the Social and Human Sciences (See Table I).

Use and exchange values, sign value

According to Marx (1887), exchange value is defined considering, as a unit of measure, the socially necessary abstract labor time, on average, to produce a given commodity. That is, exchange value, in the beginning of this process, refers to the temporalities, places and social circumstances of the production of a good or service. However, after its production, the commodity will be exchanged for others, the value of which will ultimately be expressed in the use value of an ultimate reference commodity. In capitalism, this fundamental and ultimate good is essentially money, meaning the universal equivalent of value, still as Marx opines. In addition, and as I see it, money may work within capitalism, not just as the measure of all things, but also, in some way, as the measure of all measures.

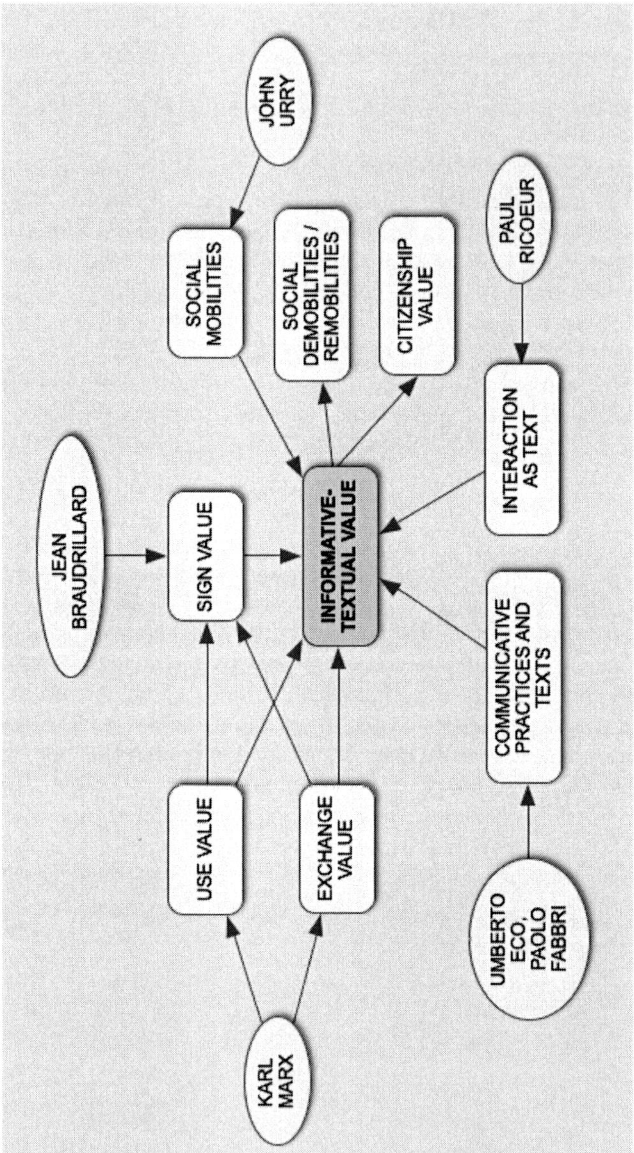

Figure 1 The debate on textual informative value and citizenship value.

Let us see how Jean Baudrillard understands this issue of *value within capitalist production and consumption.*[1] The *consumer society* that guarantees such a new status of the object is also circumscribed by this sociologist.[2] Finally, the 'exchange value / sign', according to Baudrillard, is delimited.[3]

Such sign-value, circumscribed by Jean Baudrillard, originates in the contemporary society regimes of capitalism (2nd phase). However, some critics of Baudrillard, such as Fredric Jameson and Roy Porter, argue that sign-value does not explain everything, or has already been explained, in other ways.[4]

---

[1] "Consumption is not a material practice, nor a phenomenology of 'abundance', it is not defined by the food that is digested (...) nor by the oral and visual substance of images and messages, but by the organization of all this in substance significant; it is the virtual totality of all objects and messages constituted from the present in a more or less coherent discourse. Consumption, as long as it has a meaning, is an activity of systematic manipulation of signs. (...) In order to become an object of consumption, it is necessary that the object becomes a sign, that is to say, external in some way to a relationship that that object does nothing more than signify - therefore arbitrary and not consistent with this relationship. concrete, but taking its coherence, and therefore its meaning, in an abstract and systematic relation to all other sign-objects. It is then that the object is 'personalized', that it enters the series, etc.: the object is consumed - never in its materiality, but in its difference." (Baudrillard, 1968, 233).

[2] "If the consumer society no longer produces myth, it is that it is its own myth. (...) In other words, it is a word from contemporary society about itself, it is the way our society speaks of itself. And, in some way, the only objective reality of consumption, is the idea of consumption, this reflective and discursive configuration, indefinitely taken up by everyday speech and intellectual speech, and which has become a force of common sense." (Baudrillard, 1970, 311-2).

[3] "The sign is the height of the commodity. Fashion and merchandise are one and the same. It is in this form of exchange value / sign that the differentiation of the commodity is suddenly inscribed (and not in the quantitative logic of profit). The fulfilled state of the commodity is one in which it imposes itself as a code, that is, as a geometric place for the circulation of models, and therefore as a total medium of a culture (and not just of an economy)." (Baudrillard, 1972, 259).

[4] "Baudrillard offers an evocative, if impressionistic, picture of contemporary capitalism. What needs to be emphasized from the historical viewpoint is that this characterization of capitalism as a fevered, frenzied epidemic of signs is not applicable solely to *late* capitalism. At least since the seventeenth century, capitalism been inseparable from the incitement of imagination, the creation of blitzes of speculation, fantasy, fiction, hyperstimulation (…) But the historian also requires to take all this with a large pinch of déjà vu. *Mutatis mutandis*, all this could have been

Figure 2 Informative-textual value inside goods' labels: about the origin and characteristics of Portuguese touristic wines.

According to David Harvey, the recent economic regime within the capitalist system, post-Fordism, is based on the process of *flexible accumulation* which, unlike Fordist accumulation, allows for high flexibility in production, distribution, trade and consumption. As for the consumption that underlies this flexibility, the author clarifies such issue. [5]

In turn, John Urry (1990), applying these theses to tourism consumption in postmodernity, provides the most complete definition and differentiation of the two moments. The consumption of the Fordist period receives the following traits: mass production determines mass consumption, which is, therefore, secondary to the productive sphere; poorly differentiated goods; limited product choices reflect the interests of producers. On the contrary,

---

said - and was being said – of the age of Locke. And, after all, Nietzsche died, and *The Interpretation of Dreams* was published, in the nineteenth century. Yesterday's tomorrows suggest that we have been there before." (Porter, 1993, 7,16).

[5] "Flexible accumulation has been accompanied on the consumption side, therefore, by a much greater attention to quick-changing fashions and the mobilization of all artifices of need inducement and cultural transformation that this implies. The relatively stable aesthetic of Fordist modernism has given way to all the ferment, instability, and fleeting qualities of a postmodern aesthetic that celebrates difference, ephemerality, spectacle, fashion, and the commodification of cultural forms." (Harvey, 1990 , 156).

post-Fordist consumption, which began during the 70s of the 20th century, is defined in these terms: the increase in consumer purchasing power causes more expenses and a predominance of consumption dynamics; new forms of credit encourage more spending, but create alarming situations of indebtedness; most aspects of social life are commercialized; the differentiation of purchase models is organized according to market segments; consumer preferences are very varied; the increase in consumer movements testifies to the growing politicization of consumption; we are witnessing the emergence of new products not mass produced, but following consumer demand, such as 'natural products'; importance given to information about the product and its aestheticization.

Figure 3 Informative-textual value within goods: on souvenirs at a Lisbon touristic shop.

In short, nowadays, consumption seems to be somewhere among economics, citizenship and culture, or between socio-symbolic practices and the new forms of value of consumer objects mobilized by these practices. For example, the 'informative-textual value', circumscribed here (Cf. Figures 2-12), consists of written and read information in daily practices, and embedded in products and services enjoyed or subjected to criticism by consumers, and sometimes inscribed in their own body.

Informative-textual value

This is a type of value, still little discussed, but whose reflection seems pertinent. However, not only this mode of value in particular, but also the information in general, or the notion of text itself, are always problematic, requiring, for this reason, an adequate criticism. Such strategy allows, in a second step, the elaboration of a '*theory of informative-textual value*', one of the possible contributions to a larger hermeneutics of value within society.

Paul Ricoeur is explicit on this matter, characterizing action and interaction as an objectified text. [6] Consider also the semiotic-textual theory of communication, proposed by Umberto Eco and Paolo Fabbri, whose main theses are as follows. Firstly, social actors do not exchange simple messages, but share social 'textual sets'. Secondly, such communication does not involve just messages and codes, but several social 'textual practices', based on social grammatical systems of rules. Thirdly, social speakers exchange a multiplicity of messages and texts, both diachronic and synchronic (Eco; Fabbri, 1978: 570).

Bearing these observations in mind, and starting from Marx and Baudrillard, let us see what is happening today in the consumption scene. In particular - and here lies the heart of the matter - it should be stressed that *informative-textual value consists of a particular case of exchange value,* as indeed exchange value / sign also is, as Baudrillard points out.

In effect, exchange value constitutes the main type of value that capitalism circumscribes, according to Marx, to measure the products of human labor, although in different forms under post-Fordism. It should also be noted that Baudrillard makes connections between the economic and cultural spheres. However, it seems to us that, in addition, today, spheres and social dimensions are related in unusual ways, especially in terms of their hybridization. *In the contemporary socio-symbolic scene, we are not only witnessing the circulation of signifiers, but as well, new breeds of social information and texts*, as Paul Ricoeur, Eco and Fabbri emphasize.

---

[6] "Just as the interlocution undergoes a transmutation by writing, the interaction undergoes an analogous transformation in the countless situations where the action allows itself to be treated as a pinned text. (...) This objectification is made possible by means of some internal features of the action, which bring it closer to the structure of the act of language and which transforms doing into a kind of enunciation. In the same way that the fixation by writing is made possible by a dialectic of intentional exteriorization, immanent to the actual act of discourse, a similar dialectic within the transaction process allows the meaning of the action to stand out from the event of the action." (Ricoeur, 1986, 213-4).

Figure 4 Textual informative value as a service: information at a Lisbon touristic café, about its meeting and working space, wifi and portable devices charging, drinks, snacks, timetable.

What is more, texts are not only and mere places of inlay of signifiers, but they themselves become nomadic and are inscribed and described through multiple social actors and authors. This process is intensified inside cyberspace and cybertime, in particular across social networks, blogs and sites. In short, social texts are written, continuously, within other social texts. Therefore, text is no longer just a support, but as well a sort of pen or computer mouse and ultimately, together with other conditionalities, the subject of its own object or service, intended for consumption within the network society.

In sum, *informative-textual value* can be defined as a type of hybrid value, halfway between Marx's 'exchange value' and Baudrillard's 'exchange value / sign'. On the one hand, it is defined as *the socially necessary abstract working time to introduce, in a commodity, components of information and knowledge* about it, in particular its conditions of production, exchange and use, and also about our society in general. In addition, on the other hand, informative-textual value pursues such objective, partially, from a *circulation of signifiers of the contents in play, functioning equally as code or, more properly, as information and textual knowledge* conveyed by an object / product or service. In fact, what informative-textual value measures

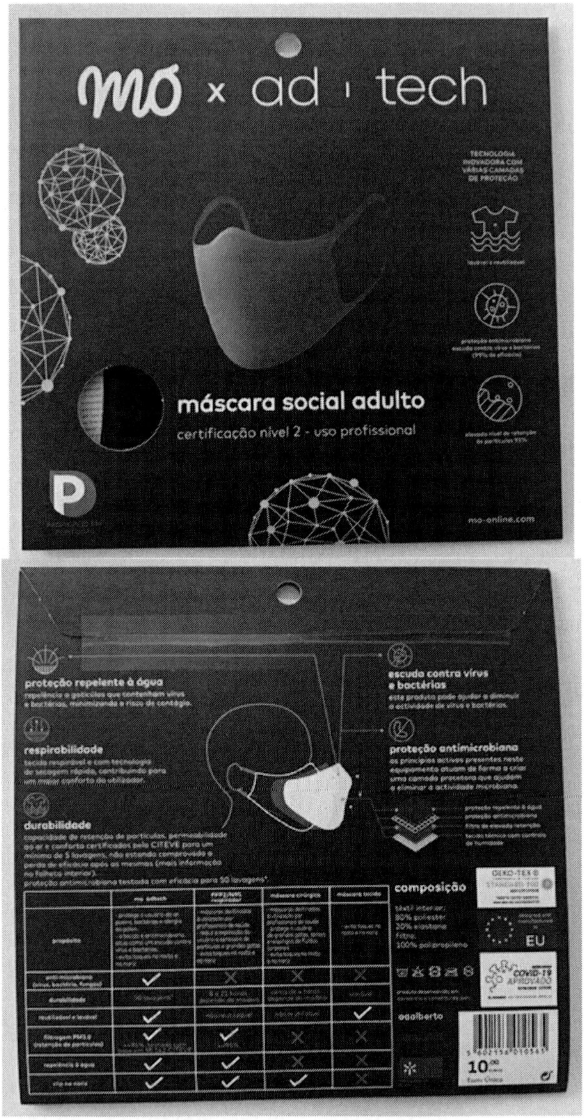

Figure 5 Textual informative value within a product cover: about an innovative mask against Covid-19, made in Portugal.

efficiently, is the capacity to allow access and exchange information and knowledge for all and everyone, deposited in the material and symbolic products and services of our societies. As mentioned above, this phenomenon occurs today in greater scale and depth within cyberspace and cybertime, and in particular inside digital social networks. Concretely, these daily data that each commodity provides, refer to the adequacy, real or virtual, between, on the one hand, the needs and interests of social agents and, on the other hand, the actual consumption made by them. Or, still, such daily data inscribed in a good or service are focused on the space-times where consumption and production of consumers are founded and hybridized.

From a more specific level, concrete information – the one which sociologically and empirically indicates the abstract informative-textual value - is printed and published, on the one hand, in labels and packaging, in the case of physical products (see Figures 2, 3, 5) and services (cf. Figures 4, 6-12) within face-to-face interaction. On the other hand, in the case of virtual products and services, the abstract informative-textual value is shown, concretely, through texts, images and other media circulating across the internet. These elements of any commercial, scientific, technical or cultural product or service, insofar as they relate to other texts, work in a transtextual way, if we also call on Julia Kristeva (1974), who introduced the concept 'intertextuality', as well as Gerard Genette (1979: 187-90; 1987: 2). For example, such textualized information, that is, data embedded in a product label as a touristic wine bottle (Fig. 2), or in the cover of a mask against Corona virus (Fig. 5), resend or are cited via 'paratexts'. According to Genette, 'paratexts' are texts that present other texts. In our case, the commercial adds that advertise the consumer objects on which information labels are located. Furthermore, textualized information is linked to 'metatexts', that is, those texts that 'speak' socially and succinctly, and in the second degree, of the object or service to consume, for example a commodity's brand. Moreover, textualized information connects to 'architexts', which classify product and services types, such as supermarket sections and the names of commercial areas or 'streets' in some shopping centers. Later, these varied text configurations will be read and interpreted by consumers. In short, if, as Baudrillard advances, within the consumer society, the exchange value / sign realizes the exchange value, in some way *exchange value and sign value are as well resolved, of course partly, via the informative-textual value, mainly within post-Fordism.*

2. Information and knowledge about consumption

Other authors warn of this role of information, especially in the sphere of consumption and urban life, which is useful for the present reflection on the consumption of tourism. In fact, such a phenomenon, although much more visible today, has been observable since the beginning of the exchange of goods and services for humanity. [7]

Therefore, if, at first, the exchange of goods generates information about them, this information and, even more deeply, knowledge on them, also provide a framework for deciding on the choice of purchasing these products and services.

On the other hand, Scott Lash and John Urry seek to delimit the current contours of this centrality of information, relating it to the sphere of production, based on the concept of 'reflexive accumulation'. [8]

For his part, Manuel Castells is even more involved in the discussion of the relevance of the information that underlies the capitalist mode of production in its current phase, by identifying, but also by demystifying, the main historical consequence of this association, the network society. [9]

---

[7] "Man needs goods for communicating with others and for making sense of what is going on around him. (...) communication can only be formed in a structured system of meanings. His overriding objective as a consumer, put at its most general, is a concern for information (...) a concern to control it. (...) Being near the center [of the information system] requires a strategy of organizing the exchange of marking services (...)" (Douglas, 1996, 67).

[8] 'Reflexive accumulation' has a number of important characteristics. It emphasizes how knowledge and information are central to contemporary economies. Knowledge though is not just a question of increasing information intensivity as a way of coping with a complex and uncertain economic environment. Knowledge on the basis of reflexivity operates via not just a single but a double hermeneutic, in which the very norms, rules and resources of the production process are constantly put into question. (...) We shall argue that specialized consumption and flexible production entail knowledge-intensive production. (Lash and Urry, 1994, 60-61)."

[9] "The information, global economy is organized around command and control centers able to coordinate, innovate, and manage the inter-twined activities of networks of firms. (…) They all can be reduced to knowledge generation and information flows. (Castells, 1996, 409).

Figure 6 Textual informative value as a service: circulation rules at Lisbon Amoreiras mall, in the context of Covid-19.

In addition to these macrosocial determinants, which certainly influence micro-social consumption practices, the following process, in reverse, is also true: consumption, at least in advanced modernity, does not take place without any information or awareness on the part of the consumer, in the same way that the use value presupposes a certain knowledge of the needs of each one, although associated with the exchange value, mainly in the society regimes articulated with capitalism.

Figure 7 Textual informative value as a service: at shops, on Covid-19 (masks, social distance instructions, bottles with disinfectant liquid, etc.).

3. The Viral Society

How does the informative-textual value works, in the context of the pandemic originated by Covid-19? It should be noted that the impact of this virus may have caused irreversible changes in the social fabric, originating a harbinger of '*Viral Society*'. As mentioned above, this seems to be an emerging social formation, where *viral economies and technologies* flourish, based on: capitalism's global weaknesses and economic crises, caused not only by computer viruses, but also and increasingly, by biological viruses; *viral policies, politics and politicians*, such as the possibility that certain states, institutions, organizations, associations, or other social agents, use various types of viruses as weapons of threat, aggression or surveillance, local or global; *viral cultures and cults*, that is, ways of exercising science and the arts, or other knowledge and leisure, in virulent ways. For example, through *virulent strategies*, that is, according to the idea that the more followers and / or friends (or, in certain cases, the more enemies) are articulated or branched with a given social subject, individual or collective, the more cultural and cultic value that subject accumulates and / or distributes across the social fabric.

Within viral society, *viral tourism* is understood as a way of traveling conditioned by forced confinement: that is, tourists make more virtual trips in cyberspace and cybertime, to the detriment of physical travel. Or they prefer to do a *virtual locative mobile tourism* through cell phones, which can become progressively more frequent than the classic mass tourism. In particular, viral tourism includes activities for the displacement and enjoyment of culture or within leisure spaces that occur largely in situations of social distance. Some consequences are the greater difficulty in physically visiting cultural spaces and institutions, such as archaeological sites, museums and galleries, which are closed or imposing a limitation on the number of visitors. Or the loss of contact in terms of sharing identity with local communities, partly due to the widespread use of masks. Or the compartmentalization and demarcation of restricted or controlled areas, in local social and cultural territories, such as squares and streets.

In sum, viral society causes *social demobilities*, as it metamorphoses mobile *pre-pandemic* social fabric into a partially immobile society. In view of this situation, social agents need to revitalize cultural and tourist citizenship, through a counter process of *post-pandemic 're-mobilization'*. In other words, *social remobility* may be defined as a position of resistance to viral society, aiming at overcoming it and reinventing social mobility actions and activities, to be carried out among citizens, tourists and migrants. This means, among other things, the re-creation of innovative urban mobilities as well as unprecedented re-mobilizations, in the areas of economics, politics, culture, ecology, etc. For example, novel connections between urban cultures and mobile cultures, e.g. tourist cultures hybridized with the cultures inherent to digital social networks and practiced by mobile phone tribes.

One of these initiatives to resist Corona virus is the project *Viral Cultural Tourism via Mobile Devices* (see Andrade, 2020c, and site: Andrade, 2020d).

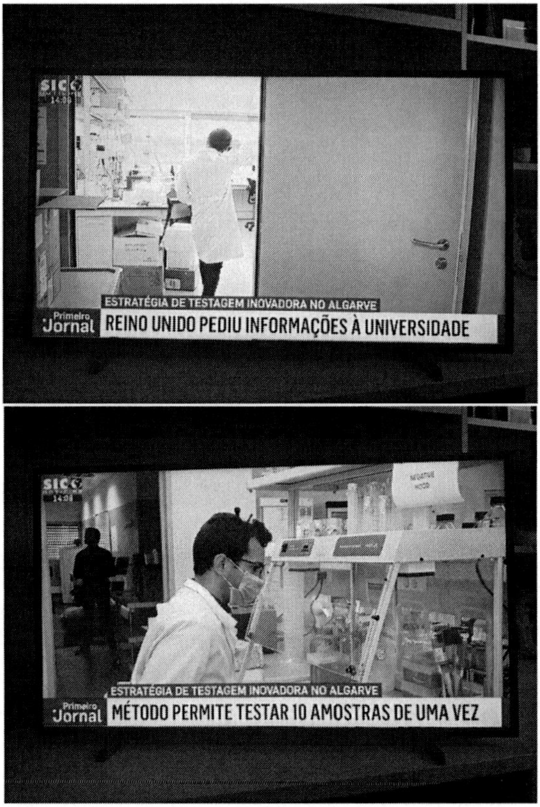

Figure 8 Textual informative value as a research knowledge service: information demand by UK health administration, on a successful method for testing Covid-19, developed by Portuguese Algarve University.

4. Informative-textual value of tourism within the Viral Society

In our contemporaneity contaminated by Covid-19, it is necessary to move to a more refined stage of self-conscience of the tourist interests, in terms of *tourism consumption associated with tourist citizenship,* a process that is still babbling. It was noted above that viral society favors the contacts that took place in cyberspace and cybertime. Therefore, the use of the internet is likely to allow its users to update *tourist citizenship value*, linked to the informative value or to the text value of these goods or services, which are not only of an economic nature, but also, and sometimes predominantly, of a political-symbolic nature. The value of citizenship underlying tourism, is exercised, in part, in three moments that we will develop below: pre-purchase, the acquisition itself and post-contract actions to purchase products or services within activities concerning tourism.

An outline of this ternary dialogue of the *moments of tourist consumption*, may be observed when problematizing the phenomenon of consumption as a journey in search of sociability, prestige or information about goods and merchandises related to tourism activities. This dialogue finds another, the historical process of the main commercial and tourist establishments, which allow daily trips of consumption and information on goods and services, and which, in the History of Western societies, are linked, in turn, to the modes of consumption production, as follows:

Firstly, a diachronic figure of a commercial place, the *small commer*ce, appears associated with societies developed before the dominance of the capitalist and modern 'world system', in part analyzed by Immanuel Wallerstein. The clients of these local establishments are frequently recruited in their neighborhood, and their consumption include "... intermediary practices of solidarity and community and local's exchange of information" (Andrade, 1993: 56).

Secondly, in the 19th century, the large *department store* or the *specialized shop emerges*, more characteristic of contemporary social modes of organized capitalism, in its two stages, the competitive and monopoly stage. The supermarket is one of the last incarnations of such process, although obeying to the same basic logic as the specialized store. In other words, "... consumerism no longer is manifested only via the circulation within the supermarket, where the acquisition is often subordinated to the ostentatious dynamics of the buying agent, representing a lifestyle with a certain power purchase (...) " (Idem, Ibidem); finally, inside the society regimes connected to post-Fordism, the *shopping center* is dominant, "... in which people stroll not only to buy or talk, but essentially to see who will buy and find out about what to be acquired. This is a kind of pre-purchase, a fragmented and dispersed visual and informative conditioning, predecessors of an acquisition that is often not achieved, but that shapes the desire and consumption styles through an involving and uninterrupted way." (Idem, Ibidem).

Figure 9 Textual informative value as a service: on touristic boat tours, at Fuseta, Algarve, South of Portugal.

Nowadays, the *three moments of consumption* in general and tourism in particular, take place in terms of the informative-textual value underlying all goods and services.

In the first instance of consumption, the *pre-acquisition stage*, before the purchase of a tourism product or service (e.g. a travel to a given vacation destination), the tourist is asked several questions, and is assisted by a huge mass of information about the products and services available, namely in three ways:

(a) regarding the socio-economic sphere, in the form of consumption precepts, in this case in relation to travel, for example, via travel agencies travels;

(b) within the political and powers sphere, as duties and rights of consumption and the respective conflicts, for example, through consumer protection associations, such as DECO in Portugal; and by the state apparatus itself via central administration services, such as *Turismo de Portugal (Tourism of Portugal)*;

(c) inside the discursive, cultural or ideological sphere, in terms of arguments about the advantages and disadvantages of a product or service, advanced by advertising in the mass media, on the websites of travel agencies or museums, etc. If we bring together the economic and the discursive spheres, we will notice, in its synthesis, frequent power relations among the actors concerned, for example, in the practice of consuming food: "Consumers are perceived to be removed from appropriate knowledge on what they eat. They need to be properly informed and persuaded to respond accordingly." (Fine, 1993: 22o).

In the second moment of consumption, the *concrete act of acquisition*, the information about the product or service appears embedded in the very 'shopping experience' carried out, on a large scale, inside the contemporary 'consumption temples':

> There is a difference between 'going shopping' and 'doing the shopping'. Going shopping is a vague activity, an extravagance - literally, 'wandering out'. It is open-ended, with no precise plans or destinations: you can spend all day or not, you may just look and not buy. (…) is pleasurable, and possibly transgressive. (…) Doing the shopping, on the other hand, suggests an obligation or a regular routine. 'The' shopping implies something both planned and limited (...) the future itself is envisaged in the image of a great supermarket in which citizen- consumers move about making their more or less informed, more or less random individual choices. (Bowlby, 1997, 102,109).

In short, there is an immense volume of information, available in societies founded on capitalism and advanced modernity. This process, besides conditioning the choice of goods to buy, remains one of the sources of democratic opinion. *Thus, there is an informative-textual value of goods and services, closely associated with exchange value and sign-value.* That is, as mentioned above, the former appears as a more specific manifestation of the latter.

Figure 10 Textual informative value as a service: at a café, on the use of masks (Fuseta), and at the Ria Formosa beach, Algarve, about circulation rules.

Thirdly, in the *post-purchase period*, the consumer (the cultural tourist, etc.) can accept his purchase contract, even if often reduced to a receipt. In that case, the products and services will be subsequently *used, abused or disused*, within the framework of the continuous dialogue between overvaluation and undervaluation of commodities, dictated mainly by the information available on these products or services, often in a textual form, but also through images, sounds, campaigns, periodical events, etc.

In such context, the citizen, the tourist or the migrant, even applying different levels of power, may contest the value of the sale and purchase operation, according to democratic consumer rights, one of which is exactly the right to information, which in Portugal, takes the form of the following regulation norm, among others:

> Article 9, Right to information. 1- The consumer has the right to be fully and loyally informed, with a view to forming his decision to contract, and in any case before the conclusion of the contract, about the essential characteristics of the goods or services that are going to be provided to him, in order to make a conscious and rational choice between competing goods and services, and to use these goods and services with complete safety and in a satisfactory manner. (Santos, 1997. 21-22).

This information must be provided on the labels (paragraph 2), by previous economic agents in the production-consumption cycle, such as the producer, distributor, etc. (point 3). Other recent legal collections relating to consumer rights and duties are: Braga, 1994; Ferreira, 1995.

Figure 11 Textual informative value as a service: information about the beach and bar services, and on Covid-19 safety (Ria Formosa).

5. Conclusion

What about the future of tourism within pandemic and post-pandemic societies, in connection with the value of textual information that underlies it? The economic/social/cultural value of information on products and services, can be articulated with other goods, through social practice and via sociological reflection. Indeed, at least in the society regimes that may rise as utopian, the value of the merchandise will probably integrate new informational utilities and unprecedent wisdoms, in close connection with the need for the exchange of global and local information and knowledge, inherent to our complex societies. In other words, within our risk society but now also viral society, remobilized information and knowledge about viral tourism are simultaneously becoming some of the most central means of production and consumption of commodities and services.

Figure 12 Textual informative value as a service: at the beach, about Covid-19 safety (Ria Formosa).

However, the emerging exchange values and sign-values, underlying the irruption of this recent circulation of information / knowledge, and inherent to the respective social interruption perpetrated by the Corona virus, combined with novel use values, should be guided by the need for a stronger and egalitarian redistribution of information and knowledge. For this reason, the informative-textual value may eventually be transformed into a *reciprocal-distributive value*, a kind of deeper hybridization of the previous types of value. In the present viral age, such a process will probably occur through a more frequent and profound exchange of both information and knowledge with other goods, preferably for the common good. This will allow that commodities and services where this value is printed and expressed, may act, more effectively and affectively, as vehicles for the equal sharing of wealth and social justice among peoples.

Likewise, research knowledge must accompany such deep social metamorphoses, reflecting on them within a critical, emancipatory, political and sociological way, but also inside a cultural imaginative manner, in order to counteract the novel socio-economic inequalities and 'viral wars', such as those between vaccine subscribers and negationists, that are already circulating inside the present *viral social fabric*.

References

Andrade, Pedro. 2020a. "Rua Augusta, an intercultural space: touristic communication via locative media for territorial sustainability". *Livro de Atas do XII Congresso da Geografia Portuguesa: 'Geografias de transição para a sustentabilidade, 13-15 de Novembro de 2019*, edited by Paula Romoaldo et al., 326-331. Guimarães: Universidade do Minho.

Andrade, Pedro. 2020b. "Cultural Tourism and Mobile Digital Devices: An analysis of Tourists in Lisbon through Sociological Comics and Video Paper". *Intercultural Routes across Multicultural Spaces: From Theory to Dialogue,* edited by Clara Sarmento and Manon Quincé, 39-56. Porto: Centro de Estudos Interculturais.

Andrade, Pedro. 2020c. *Viral Cultural Tourism via Mobile Devices: Open Research using Open Methods and Open Media.* Lisbon: Social Web Lab Publishers. [e-book, app]

Andrade, Pedro. 2020d. "Viral & Intercultural Tourism City". Accessed December 20, 2020: www.sites.google.com/view/viral-tourism-city

Andrade, Pedro. 1993. "Sociology of Travel". *Revista Crítica de Ciências Sociais*, No. 37, 51-77.

Baudrillard, Jean. 1968. *Le système des objets: la consommation des signes*. Paris: Denoel Gonthier.

Baudrillard, Jean. 1970. *La société de consommation: ses mythes ses structures*. Paris: Gallimard.

Baudrillard, Jean. 1972. *Pour une critique de l'économie politique du signe*. Paris: Gallimard.

Bowlby, Rachel. 1997. "Supermarket futures". *The Shopping Experience*, edited by In Pais Falk and Colin Campbell, 92-110. London: Sage.

Braga, Armando. 1994. *Legislação de Defesa do Consumidor*. Porto: Porto Editora.

Castells, Manuel. 1996. *The Information Age: Economy, Society and Culture. Vol I: The Rise of the Network Society*. Oxford: Blackwell.

Douglas, Mary and Isherwood, Baron. 1996. *The World of Goods: towards an Anthropology of Consumption*. London: Routledge.

Eco, Umberto and Fabbri, Paolo. 1978. "Proggetto di ricerca sull' utilizazionne dell' informazione ambientale". *Problemi dell' informazione,* No. 4, 555-597.

Ferreira; A. & Liz, J. 1995. *Direitos do Consumidor: colectânea de Legislação*. Lisboa: DECO.

Fine, Ben. & Leopold, Ellen. 1993. *The World of Consumption*. London: Routledge.

Genette, Gerard. 1987. *Seuils*. Paris: Éditions du Seuil.

Harvey, David. 1990. *The Condition of Postmodernity: An Enquiry into the Origins of Cultural Change.* Cambridge, MA: Blackwell.

Lash, Scott. and Urry, John. 1994. *Economies of Signs and Space.* London: Sage.

Kristeva, Julia. 1974. *Révolution du langage poétique*. Paris: Éditions du Seuil.

Marx, Karl. 1887. *Capital; a Critique of Political Economy* (Vol.I). Progress Publishers.

Porter, Roy. 1993. Baudrillard: history, hysteria and consumption. *In Forget Baudrillard?* London: Routledge.

Ricoeur, Paul. 1986. *Du texte à l'action : Essais d'herméneutique II*. Paris: Seuil.

Santos, Beja. 1997. *(Quase) tudo o que o consumidor deve saber*. Venda Nova: Bertrand.

Urry, John. 1990. *The Tourist Gaze*. London: Sage.

Urry, John. 2007. *Mobilities*. Cambridge: Polity Press.

CHAPTER 7

USING CULTURAL HERITAGE TO CREATE BUSINESS OPPORTUNITIES: SUCCESSFUL CASES FROM FRANCE, GERMANY AND SPAIN

MARCO FURTADO, LAURA TALLONE AND SARA CERQUEIRA PASCOAL

CENTRE FOR INTERCULTURAL STUDIES (CEI)
ISCAP – P.PORTO, POLYTECHNIC OF PORTO

Introduction

Today's society is increasingly characterised by the emergence of a powerful "cultural economy", in which cultural tourism and cultural and creative industries play a major role. Tourism has been influenced by what is known as a cultural turn, which, together with the creative turn that followed (Richards, 2011), has paved the way for the development of economic strategies in which culture and creativity play a crucial role. Due to place branding and marketing, cities compete with one another using innovation and technology, in order to foster social and economic development. Cultural tourism is thus one of the most recent trends in the tourism industry, underpinned by a demand for postmodern style, as well as by a growing interest in culture and in cultural knowledge. Stimulated by higher educational levels and increasing mobility, as well as by a crave for authentic, first-hand experiences, contacts between cultures have allowed for the creation of new tourist-related businesses. In addition, this more diversified supply has stimulated cultural tourism even further and advanced the external image of entire regions, with a consequent boost in income levels and job creation.

Against this background, the Master in Intercultural Studies for Business (MISB) offered by the Porto Accounting and Business School (ISCAP) provides training focused on the business world, developing entrepreneurial skills within the context of culture, along with practical, analytical and critical skills for intercultural communication. The German, Spanish and French Culture course units have been promoting a set of interdisciplinary pedagogical strategies, through which students are challenged to participate in and reflect on the transformation of cultural heritage into marketable products, thus developing entrepreneurial skills and creativity.

This chapter analyses some cases of the French, German and Spanish cultural heritage, which have become successful marketable products, proving not only that cultural heritage plays an essential role in the development of cooperation between regions and countries, but that cultural entrepreneurship accounts for a growing percentage of countries' GDPs, labour force and circulation of goods and services (Zaman, 2015).

Cultural heritage commodification and business opportunities

Cultural heritage has recently become a driver for economic growth and employment, namely in Europe, where it is considered a key factor not only to strengthen citizens' sense of identity and belonging, but also to attract tourists, thus contributing both to the revitalization of cities and buildings and to the preservation of arts and traditions (Sarmento & Pascoal, 2020). As the "cultural economy" (Bourdieu), the "cultural industry" (Adorno), and cultural tourism thrive in postmodern societies, there is a growing need to reflect upon the strategies and uses of commodified culture. Although these strategies entail clear socio-economic benefits at a regional level, as they raise awareness of a common cultural heritage and engage local communities in its protection, the business opportunities fostered by the marketing of culture should however be conscientiously and meticulously considered and applied. They should be used to enhance sustainable tourism, while empowering local populations and encouraging employment, economic growth, poverty reduction, environmental protection (Cardia, 2018) and the preservation of authenticity in culture and heritage.

Of course, the commodification of culture is not free from controversy. In *Dialect of Enlightenment*, Adorno and Horkheimer (2002) critically saw the emergence of a "cultural industry" in the merge of cultural goods and commercialization. Standardization and reproducibility lead to the impoverishment of culture and to the production of a mass culture, stripped of "singularity, originality or authenticity" (Southerton, 2011). Adorno argues that the commodification and massification of culture "impedes the development of autonomous, independent individuals who judge and decide consciously for themselves "(Adorno, 1975: 14).

Also approaching the relationship between economy and culture, Bourdieu (2000) explores the social impacts of culture commodification, in order to underline that in late capitalist societies, as culture is increasingly commodified, commodities too are increasingly culturalised. This commodification is not limited to the process of culture creation, subordinate to market interests, but affects the reception and consumption of cultural goods. For both Adorno and Bourdieu, through culture commodification, the exchange value takes precedence over the symbolic value of culture, and autonomy and creativity are hostages to standardisation.

In view of these threats and challenges, it is thus a priority to promote, conserve and manage cultural heritage even within a free market, as it represents a legacy from past generations, which contributes to the preservation of identity and history. Cultural heritage entails a large and complex set of assets comprising tangible culture (buildings, books, monuments, artefacts, landscapes), intangible and digital culture heritage (language and knowledge, folklore, oral history, traditions, customs, aesthetic and spiritual beliefs, etc.), and cultural natural heritage (bio and geo diversity and natural landscapes). The commodification of cultural assets plays a positive role in the preservation of traditions, monuments and sites that otherwise could be lost or neglected, but it also raises concerns about the possible negative impacts of tourism. As Zaman (2015: 5) points out, cultural heritage entrepreneurship has to be linked to

> strategic objectives and policy mix implemented by public authorities and private entities for good conservation, maintenance and affordability for cultural goods consumption by the population, as well as of their integration into the current environmental landscapes in a productive, educational and efficient manner. The population accessibility of CH products and services is a fundamental factor for maintaining communities' identity, legacy and possibilities of national and international contacts, in the context of good practices and sustainable strategic management.

In this paper, three case-studies are presented and analysed of successful commodification of cultural assets, which have become major tourism attractions in three European countries, France, Germany and Spain. These and other examples are approached in the German, Spanish and French

Culture course units of the Master in Intercultural Studies for Business at ISCAP, in order to reflect whether these three examples comply with the OECD Report on The Impact of Culture on Tourism guidelines (2009: 43). By analysing and identifying the factors that stimulate the increasing use of cultural assets to make places more appealing and competitive, this report points out that the main drivers for developing culture and tourism policies are:

- Enhancing and preserving heritage.
- Economic development and employment.
- Physical and economic regeneration.
- Strengthening and/or diversifying tourism.
- Retaining population.
- Developing cultural understanding.

France: An oxymoron country

As the world's leading tourist destination, France attracts both foreign tourists and French holidaymakers. The diversity of its landscapes, the great variety of its sites, the exceptional richness of its historical, artistic and cultural heritage as well as the ease of access, its geographic location and its climate, make France a country offering multiple possibilities in terms of stays and vacations.

However, the economic advantages of art and of cultural heritage were for a long time neglected, crystallizing a set of pejorative perceptions on the part of artists, writers or cultural mediators, who feared the misrepresentation of the mission and identity of art and culture. As already mentioned, Bourdieu argued that "réintroduire le règne du commercial dans des univers qui ont été construits peu à peu, contre lui, c'est mettre en péril les œuvres les plus hautes de l'humanité, l'art, la littérature et même la science" (Bourdieu, 1999: 18). However, this romantic idea of the cultural sector in France has been losing ground, and cultural institutions are increasingly using marketing strategies to respond to two main factors: (1) the need for their own resources and economic growth and (2) to new cultural behaviours rooted in the generalisation of the internet and of digital experiences in cultural trends (Chiapello, 1998).

Supporting this new attitude towards the commodification of culture is the renewed branding and positioning of the country, which has been headed by Phillipe Lentschener since 2013. Former CEO of Publicis and of the Mccann Erikson group in France, Lentschener (2013) calls for a renewed economic attitude by the country, as France must find its true mission and values embedded in the nation's brand[1]. He argues that branding France's image will strengthen the country's reputation, meeting the goals already pinpointed by several researchers. The design of "La Marque France" will help "(1) remould national identities; (2) enhance the nation's competitiveness; (3) embrace political, cultural, business and sport activities"; (4) promote economic and political interests at home and abroad; and finally (5) alter, improve or enhance a nation's image /reputation" (Fan, 2010: 3).

With these purposes in mind, Lentschener (2013) puts forward three major pillars to reshape the national economic narrative. The first pillar is the "love of gestures", based on the famous French "savoir-faire", found in almost every French industry, from retail to luxury and gastronomy. The second pillar is "vision". France gives a meaning to everything that it does. The TGV train, for instance, originally intended as a premium service for business travellers, has become a commitment to democratisation by promoting speed, frequency, reservation policy, affordable rates, and broad accessibility to the service under the slogan "Progress means nothing unless it is shared by all". Finally, Lentschener identifies "the art of surprise" as the third pillar. As a nation, France sees itself as a role model to the rest of the world and a country that does not copy or imitate other countries, focused on creativity and innovation.

These three pillars determine the brand's promise, which is described in Marketing as an extension of a company's positioning. It is a statement of what customers may expect in terms of benefits and/or experience, i.e., the value proposition. According to Lentschener, France does not create value, but multiplies it. Consequently, the famous French social, historic and cultural narrative of "Liberty, Equality and Fraternity" should embrace the economic narrative, which has been concealed and erased by the weight of social aspects. And this, even though an oxymoron, should be the French promise to the world.

---

[1] According to Fan (2006: 12), "[a] nation brand is the total sum of all perceptions of a nation in the mind of international stakeholders which may contain some of the following elements: people, place, culture/language, history, food, fashion, famous faces (celebrities), global brands etc. A nation's 'brand' exists, with or without any conscious efforts in nation branding, as each country has a current image to its international audience, be it strong or weak, clear or vague."

Le Puy du Fou: The French History rebranded

A paradigmatic example of the synergies that can be created by merging the economy and cultural heritage is the commodification of French History, told and retold in live history shows or reenactments.

In France, historical reenactments began to appear in 1960, when a "Son et Lumière" (Sound and Light show) was created at Lude Castle in the banks of the Loire river. It was the first show to use over 350 actors, all from the local town. This magnificent show, which lasted four decades, received the most distinguished tourist and cultural awards. Inspired by this success, aristocrat Philippe de Villiers created a truly unique performance in the ancient ruins of a castle situated in the Vendée region, in Western France. He put on a production called *Cinéscénie* about a local family, the Maupilliers, and their history, set against 700 years of history in the Vendée region. Over the years, the show's success grew enormously, and in 1989, the Puy du Fou's Grand Parc was established[2], offering accommodation and attractions, fun, leisure, history, education, spectacle and emotion – a true living history show.

Voted best park in the world[3], Puy du Fou hosts about 2.2 million visitors every year, being the second most visited park in France, after Eurodisney. *Cinéscénie* is now a show of epic proportions, covering a 23-hectare stage and featuring 2,400 actors, 130 horse riders, 80 technicians, 28,000 costumes, 31 drones and 3,000 projectors[4]. Other shows, experiences and villages have been added through the years to *Cinéscénie*. Each village tells the story of a period in French History, from the Roman Empire to World War I, and provides immersive walk-throughs as well as thematic restaurants and hotels.

Puy du Fou's success is probably explained by its roots in the local community, the local "Puyfolais", and a sense of authenticity that attracted even the attention of some of France's most important historians, like Michel Vovelle, Claude Langlois and Jean Clément Martin. The commodification of history is always controversial, especially in a country like France. Langlois

---

[2] https://www.puydufou.com/fr

[3] https://www.puydufou.com/en/our-awards

[4] Due to Covid-19, *Cinéscénie* has reduced that number to 5,000 spectators (https://www.nouvelobs.com/coronavirus-de-wuhan/20200726.OBS31558/face-a-une-polemique-le-puy-du-fou-limite-sa-cinescenie-a-5-000-spectateurs.html?utm_term=Autofeed&utm_medium=Social&utm_source=Twitter#Echobox=1595753742).

(1987) and Martin (2000) have pointed out the dangers of a misrepresentation of History and its exploitation for political purposes. In the mid 1990's, when the Front National began to appear in the French political scene, Vovelle warned about the dangers of such an emphasis on national identity, especially since the initial show featured a "Grand Parcours" that further promoted a nationalistic view of history (Vovelle, 1994).

Those critiques highlighted some of the main issues involving culture commodification, i.e., the possibility of political manipulation for economic or nationalistic reasons and its oversimplification for marketing and consumption purposes, which may sometimes produce a digested version of culture and cultural heritage. Organisers argue their non-partisan position, promising not to enter into polemics and/or politics[5]. These performances respond to the public's urge to recover "the spaces of nostalgia, that permit a tactile encounter with the past and a recovery of the self at the margins of civilization" (Gerson, 2003: 285).

Nevertheless, Puy du Fou is a prototypic example of how culture and sites can be commodified in response to tourist demands and benefit both entrepreneurs and local communities. In recent years, Puy du Fou has spun into international branches. In 2016, the Vendée park, via its subsidiary Puy du Fou International, has put in place *Kynren*, a live show inspired by *Cinéscénie*, in the settings of the neo-Gothic castle of Auckland, telling the history of England from the Vikings to the World Wars, not forgetting King Arthur. The international Puy du Fou branch, created in 2010, has exported its success and is about to open other parks in Hungary, Holland, Russia and China. In 2019, Puy du Fou Spain opened its doors in Toledo, retracing "the great hours in the history of Spain [...], from the Gothic Kings to the arrival of the Railway", always with the same winning recipe which combine historical reconstructions, life-size battles, special effects and waterfalls.

---

[5] "L'ASSOCIATION DU PUY DU FOU et du GRAND PARC DU PUY DU FOU n'ont jamais prétendu faire un travail d'historien : elles proposent de spectaculaires romances historiques qui permettent un voyage poétique dans le légendaire français à travers ses merveilles, ses drames, ses grandeurs et ses égarements, de l'Antiquité au XXème siècle. Le Puy du Fou emprunte à l'imaginaire collectif des images parfois inspirées de la grande Histoire sans autre prétention que de mettre en scène des poèmes divertissants, mêlant légendes et réalité" (Association Puy du Fou, 2019).

Germany: The Oktoberfest – bringing the world's biggest beer festival to the world

Despite having the largest outbound tourist trade in the world, Germany is not as much visited as France or Spain. This country is, however, among the world's top ten destinations and the eighth most visited country after France, Spain, the US, China, Italy, Turkey and Mexico. According to the UNWTO, almost 40 million international tourist arrivals were recorded in Germany in 2018, accounting for an overall income worth more than 37 billion euro.

Germany is attractive for both national and international travellers. According to the *Statistisches Bundesamt*, the number of overnight stays related to travel accommodation has been steadily rising for more than a decade, ranging from almost 369 million to over 495 million between 2009 and 2019 (Statistisches Bundesamt/Statista, 2020). The accommodation and travel industry has therefore been recording growing levels as regards the contribution to the country's GDP, with more than 300 billion euro per year (WTTC/Statista, 2020).

As the largest and strongest economy in Europe, and the fourth largest at a global scale, Germany is certainly one of the most popular destinations and well known for its promising business opportunities to be found in international conferences, trade fairs and exhibitions in cities like Hanover, Düsseldorf, Berlin, Cologne, Munich, etc. However, the country has become better known and understood by foreigners since the Fall of the Berlin Wall in 1989 and the Reunification a year later, having gained a prestigious status as a tourism destination to be explored for cultural and leisure purposes. With more than forty UNESCO World Heritage sites, 6,000 museums, theatres, orchestras, castles, cathedrals and a number of historical buildings and monuments with outstanding architecture and historical treasures to be discovered, forests and natural landscapes for hiking or cycling tours, "culture and nature are two central elements at the core of the 'Destination Germany Brand' […]. Germany offers a wide range of options for sustainable travel. Its leafy towns and cities boast excellent public transport networks and a good cycling infrastructure. [...] Many amenities also cater for disabled guests through the 'Tourism for all' project" (German Convention Bureau, n.d.). One can visit and explore, for instance, the Romantic Rhine Tour, with its famous section of the river between Koblenz and Bingen and its steep vineyard-covered hills; the Black Forest; the picturesque medieval-looking village Rothenburg ob der Tauber; the outstretching Saxon Switzerland National Park, which extends to the Czech Republic, and is also known on the other side of the border as the

Bohemian Switzerland National Park; the enchanting *Weihnachtsmärkte* (Christmas markets), the most famous of which is found in Nuremberg; Aachen Cathedral, the oldest in northern Europe; the German Reichstag and the Brandenburger Gate in the capital city Berlin.

Furthermore, Germany invites its visitors to experiment regional products within a diversified gastronomic scene, most appealing to anyone who enjoys the flavours of good food and drink. Beer in particular has traditionally played an important role in German history and society.

> [It has been produced] for mass consumption since around the end of the first millennium, the year 1000. The beer-producing monasteries were predominantly located in Southern Germany, and some of them are still around today, such as Kloster Andechs, St. Gallen, Weihenstephan, or Weltenburg. Drinking beer back then was safer than drinking water. Beer was regarded as safe, nutritious and caloric, even good for small children (Germanfoods, n.d.).

Meussdoerfer (2011) points out the role of beer in German culture throughout the past centuries during which it became the most popular beverage. To this author, in fact, it is "unsurprising that Germans and foreigners perceive beer to be important in national identity, but [on the other hand] he also stresses the significance of the federal, rather than the unified, history of Germany and how that has led to a regional diversity on the beers for which Germany and its neighbours are famous" (Schiefenhövel & Macbeth, 2011: 6).

Another relevant aspect as regards the importance of beer in German cultural heritage is the *Reinheitsgebot*, i.e., the German Beer Purity Law, which to a certain extent is still in force. The original Bavarian Beer Law had been established under the Bavarian duke Wilhelm IV in Ingolstadt in April 1516, establishing that only clean water, malt and hops were to be used as ingredients to brew beer. According to van Tongeren (2011),

> the 1516 law later morphed into the German 'Reinheitsgebot' […]. [It] is often seen as one of the oldest known food laws, and German brewers take pride in referring to it as a guarantee of traditional quality. […] the European Court decided in 1987 that the German standard hampered the free movement of goods in the European Community and forced a national repeal of the law. Today, German beer producers are still subject to legal production standards that have their origins in the original Reinheitsgebot, but imported beers need not adhere to strict requirements concerning the ingredients to be used in brewing.

Bekker (2012) claims that Bavaria is the most popular and visited holiday destination for domestic travellers and international tourists. Its capital city Munich has a vast range of cultural attractions and is the home of many breweries, beer halls (being Munich's *Hofbräuhaus* the most popular), beer gardens, and the world's most famous beer festival, the Oktoberfest. According to Touropia, it is ranked sixth among the most popular 25 top tourist attractions in Germany, closely following Neuschwanstein Castle, the most photographed building in Germany, the Brandenburg Gate in Berlin, the romantic city Heidelberg, the Holstentor in Lübeck, and Cologne Cathedral (Touropia, 2020).

The Oktoberfest marks the royal wedding of the Crown Prince Ludwig (later King Ludwig I) to Princess Teresa of Saxony-Hildburghausen on 12th October 1810. The citizens of Munich were invited to attend the celebration in the fields in front of the city gate, which in honour of the princess have been called *Theresienwiese*, also known by locals in the shortened form *Wies'n* (Das offizielle Stadtportal München, n.d. & The Oktoberfest international guide, n.d.). Beer has distinguished the festival from its very first edition. Gaab (2006: 24) states that to celebrate his son's wedding, King Maximilian organised games and horse racing that lasted a week, on the *Wies'n*. At the time, the Munich Chamber of Commerce had put forward to the King the organisation of a 'Maximilian Week', including a children's carnival with rides and games. "In addition to the games and the carnival, the King allowed free beer for the entire week" (*ibidem*). The first beer concessions were permitted in 1815. Fifteen years after the first Oktoberfest over 100,000 visitors attended the festival and consumed 250,000 litres of beer.

Nowadays, the number of visitors to the Oktoberfest averages 7 million per year. According to official data (Die offizielle Website zur Wiesn, 2019), 6.3 million guests from all over the world attended the 2019 edition of the festival, having consumed 7.3 million litres of beer. The city's economy generated more than a 1.2 billion profit thanks to the Oktoberfest (THE LOCAL de, 2019).

The home of Germany's largest *Volksfest* may be in Munich, but visitors can experience its atmosphere inside and outside the country. It has parallel editions, usually at a smaller scale, in other German cities like Stuttgart, Frankfurt, Nuremberg in the South, or even Berlin and Hamburg in northern Germany.

Fig. 1: The 2019 edition of the Oktoberfest at the Spitalerstrasse in Hamburg (Photo credit: Marco Furtado)

The Oktoberfest is also celebrated overseas, for instance, in cities all across the American continent:

> the second-largest reported Oktoberfest outside Munich, with over half a million visitors, takes place in the American city with the biggest German population: Cincinnati, Ohio. There, Fifth Street becomes the stage for 'Oktoberfest Zinzinnati', a quintessential German celebration that remains Midwestern through and through. And all across the US, hundreds of Oktoberfest celebrations, both large and small, testify to the significant contribution made by German migrants over several hundred years. […] South America […] is a long way from Munich. But Blumenau, Brazil, founded by German settlers, plays host to the largest Oktoberfest in South America and one of the largest in the world. More than 500,000 people have reportedly been attending each year (Stolarz & Atkinson, 2012).

Even Portugal has become inspired to host beer festivals in five different cities: Caminha and Porto in the northern part of the country, Sertã in the centre and Lisbon and Faro in the south. The first edition of the "Lisbon Beer Fest" was held in 2015; the festival in Porto took place just one year later.

Several business sectors and industries in Germany have also become inspired by the Oktoberfest for the past few years. Munich, Lufthansa's southern hub in Germany, is an important gateway to the world. Once a year, the German airline company offers an extra taste of the Bavarian atmosphere on board selected long-haul flights from Munich to San Francisco, Montreal, and São Paulo. Cabin crew members become ambassadors for the Bavarian festival, wearing uniforms created by Bavarian designers: men wear traditional Bavarian-style suits, while women are dressed in *Dirndls* in Lufthansa colours[6].

Germany and its cultural heritage have been successfully promoted around the globe as a travel destination for many years. The country has occupied a leading position in the international travel market for its many cultural, historical, and geographical attractions. In addition, Germany, as a leading global trade fair venue, is Europe's top international destination for conferences and conventions. A positive image of the country and the successful marketing and promotion of the Destination Germany Brand around the world have indisputably boosted the economy at home and inspired other countries to commodify Germany's cultural heritage.

Spain: The Tomatina Festival, from Buñol to the world

Spain has been for years the second most visited country in the world after France. With more than 82 million visitors in 2018 (Rubio, 2019), Spain concentrates 23% of all overnight stays in the EU (INE, 2018: 49). About 16% of these 82 million (El Diario, 2018) go to Spain for cultural reasons, following the appeal of long-established attractions like Camino de Santiago, and iconic Spanish cultural manifestations such as flamenco, bullfighting and its Moorish architecture. More importantly, cultural tourism is steadily rising, with a 38% increase in the number of visitors and a 62.5% leap in visitors' spending between 2016 and 2017 (*idem*). Coincidence or not, it must also be pointed out that Spain has forty-one UNESCO Cultural Heritage Sites, the second highest number in the world (after Italy, that totals 49).

The importance of tourism in Spain may be seen in its impressive contribution to the country's economy. According to the World Travel & Tourism Council, in 2017, travel and tourism accounted for almost 15% (totalling approximately 173 billion euro) of the Spanish GDP, and its total contribution to employment (direct, indirect and induced jobs) reached 15.1% (WTTC 2018: 7-8). According to the *Anuario de Estadísticas Culturales 2018* (Ministerio de Cultura y Deporte, 2018: 179-180), cultural tourism has generated more than 20 billion euro each year. As an example,

[6] https://www.youtube.com/watch?v=XUW39gQCL1U

in 2016, Bilbao's Guggenheim Museum received 1.2 million visitors, who collectively spent 32.2 million euro (Uribarri, 2017).

Cultural tourism and the use of Spain's heritage as a marketable commodity to attract visitors is not a completely new phenomenon for the country, and began in the mid-1990s (Vizcaino, 2015: 78), when the traditional tourist model based on seaside resorts became stagnated, though it became a stronger trend in the mid-2000s (Cánoves, 2016: 433). This shift coincided with a new way of perceiving culture, from the descriptive contact with mainly the artistic heritage (intended to be enjoyed by a cultivated minority), to a vehicle to get to know a society's way of life, from which increasingly larger numbers of people may benefit (*ibidem*). In other words, there has been a move from a paradigm in which culture may be "appreciated" or "enjoyed", to a new one in which culture may be "experienced".

The creation of the Spanish "Marca España" in 2003 (though only made official in 2012 by a national law[7]) came to offer, among other things, a cultural product ready to be consumed, on the basis of a notion of guaranteed quality (Vélez, 2018: 108). Therefore, branding implies an interpretation of culture that captures the most recognizable and/or profitable features of the country and turns them into the image intended to be perceived from abroad.

An interesting example of branding and of culture as experience is provided by the Tomatina de Buñol, a festival featuring tomato fights that has become extremely popular in recent years.

Between 1945, when it started spontaneously during a parade, and the mid-1980s, the Tomatina was a strictly local event, shared by the few thousand inhabitants of this small town 40 minutes away from the city of Valencia. In 1983, after it was featured in a TV show by Televisión Española, its popularity began to grow, and in 1987 the City of Buñol took over the organisation and management of the event. In 2002, the Tomatina was declared Fiesta de Interés Turístico Internacional by the Spanish Department of Tourism[8].

---

[7] Royal Decree 998 dated 28 June 2012 establishing the creation of the High Commissariat for Marca España – https://www.boe.es/buscar/act.php?id=BOE-A-2012-8672

[8] https://www.xn--buol-hqa.es/la-tomatina-0

It was only in 2013 when the city changed the management model for the festival, until then fully financed by public money. A specific enclosed area was demarcated, with capacity for 22 thousand participants (more than twice the number of local inhabitants), and an admission fee of €10 was charged to all visitors except locals. That year of 2013, the city invested about €90,000 in the organisation of the Tomatina, which accounted for an income of €193,550 (Cuenca & Giménez, 2017: 26-27). According to city sources (*ibidem*), the profit was reinvested in the branding of the event and its international dissemination, which included a fresh, joyful logo[9] clearly appealing to young people.

Fig. 2: Tomatina's logo. Source: https://ticketstomatina.com/i/home/official-tomatina-tickets

Today, the Tomatina is an event with wide coverage in traditional and social media. It has parallel events, like a mini Tomatina for children and an after party featuring the two most traditional items of Spanish cuisine: paella and sangria. Its website offers a downloadable free app, as well as different packages and merchandise for visitors. Another smart move was to make more than half the tickets available through tour operators (*ibidem*). As a result, almost 65% of visitors to the Tomatina are foreigners, mainly from England, but also coming from as far as Japan, South Korea and India.

The internationalisation of the Tomatina product resulted in the event being increasingly present in social media. A simple Google search shows hundreds of thousands of pages with references. The event has in fact been replicated in other countries, like the United States, Colombia, Costa Rica, China and even Portugal (Tomatina de Almeirim[10]). In 2011, the Tomatina was featured in a Bollywood movie, *Zindagi Na Milegi Dobara*, taking advantage of tax incentives offered by the Spanish government to

[9] https://ticketstomatina.com/i/home/official-tomatina-tickets

[10] https://www.evasoes.pt/noticias/a-tomatina-a-portuguesa-vai-ser-em-almeirim/

international productions[11] (Tax incentives 2017). In that movie, a group of friends enjoy the care-free life of the Spanish summer, while visiting the country's most iconic places and events, including Barcelona, Seville and Pamplona's San Fermín. During Buñol's Tomatina, the protagonists engage in a sensuous dance[12] in the middle of a tomato fighting crowd – thus, the playful, almost mischievous, original tomato fight has gained an erotic undertone, particularly suitable for the youth.

If we agree that the processes of cultural product generation lead to new ways of interpreting authenticity and express the dynamism and imagination of local groups to adapt to the demands of the global market (Santana Talavera, 2003: 35), then it is undeniable that the Tomatina has managed to generate a cultural product that caters for an audience who is ready to validate and consume the widespread, archetypical Spanish image of wild "fiesta" and carefree fun, while sharing in the "true" Spanish spirit.

Conclusions

The synergies between culture, tourism and economy have become evident in recent years. Countries have invested considerable efforts to develop their tangible and intangible cultural assets, in order to increase their attractiveness and competitiveness in a global market. Even if challenges and difficulties need to be acknowledged and tackled – namely questions of authenticity, social value in employment, accessibility, assets knowledge, significance and interpretation, inclusiveness, sustainability, copyright and contribution to local development (Zaman, 2015) – cultural heritage commodification is increasingly being considered as a fundamental development strategy by public or private sectors.

The case-studies presented cannot be taken as exemplary of all culture commodification in these three European countries – Germany, France and Spain. Nevertheless, these examples seem to embody what could be described as the process of branding cultural identity, in which the symbolic value of culture is commodified, more or less standardised, to meet the demand for some degree of authenticity, identity or alterity, with the potential to attract tourists. Local communities seem to be at the heart of

[11] These incentives are part of a long-term policy to attract international film productions, which has led Spain to be a stage for hundreds of films and TV productions since the 1980s, like *Indiana Jones and the Last Crusade* (1989), or *Game of Thrones* season 7 (2017).

[12] https://www.youtube.com/watch?v=6EHpMmSyU5o

these case studies, mixing and embedding stereotypes within identities and combining the static and simple nature of the first with the complex and heterogeneous nature of the second. These tourist products are tailored from a set of "cultural markers", *topos* or stereotypes, which, once purged of all pejorative connotations, become the quintessence of cultural identities. Oktoberfest, Puy du Fou and Tomatina may be considered symbolic icons of German, French and Spanish cultures, although they are merely synecdoches of these cultures, namely of the regions Bavaria, Vendée and Valencia. Nevertheless, since these products appear to encapsulate the archetypical essence of these cultures, they are easily understood by heterogeneous audiences and, thus, internationalised.

Finally, these examples seem to match the guidelines suggested by the OECD (2009), once their success and longevity appear to prove their role in developing the economy and employment, retaining local populations, preserving cultural heritage and contributing to cultural understanding.

References

Adorno, T. (1975). Culture Industry Reconsidered. New German Critique, No. 6, p. 14.

Anholt, S. (2007). Competitive identity: The new brand management for nations, cities and regions, Basingstoke: Palgrave Macmillan.

Anholt, S. (2008). Why nation branding does not exist?, available at http://www.orangecontest.nl/docs/SimonAnholtNationBranding.pdf.

Aronczick, M. (2013). Branding the nation. The Global Business of National Identity, US: Oxford University Press.

Association Puy du Fou (2019). Re: Mazeau, G. (2019, 19 March). Le Puy du Fou: sous le divertissement, un «combat culturel» [right of reply]. The Conversation, available at https://theconversation.com/le-puy-du-fou-sous-le-divertissement-un-combat-culturel-113888.

Bekker, H. (2020). Berlin & Beyond Travel Adventures, New Jersey: Hunter Publishing, Inc.

Bond, R., McCrone, D., and Brown, A. (2003). "National identity and economic development: reiteration, recapture, reinterpretation and reputation". Nations and Nationalism, 9, pp. 371-391.

Bourdieu, P. (1999). Maîtres du monde, savez-vous ce que vous faites?, discours à la réunion annuelle du Conseil international du musée de la Télévision et de la Radio, le 11/10/1999, available at http://www.homme-moderne.org/societe/socio/bourdieu/varia/maitres.html.

Bourgeon-Renault, D., Debenedetti, S., Gombault, A. & Petr, C. (2014). Marketing de L'Art et de la Culture, Paris: Dunod, 2ème édition.

Cánoves, G. et al. (2016). Turismo en España, más allá del sol y la playa. Evolución reciente y cambios en los destinos de litoral hacia un turismo cultural. Boletín de la Asociación de Geógrafos Españoles, Nº 71, pp. 431-454.

Cardia, G. (2018). Routes and Itineraries as a means of contribution to sustainable tourism, in Katsoni, V., Verlander, K. (eds.) Innovative approaches to Tourism and Leisure, Springer Proceedings in Business and Economics, XXIII, pp. 17-33.

Chiapello, E. (1998). Artistes vs Managers. Le management culturel face à la critique artistique, Paris : Ed. Métaillé.

Cuenca, E. & Giménez V. (2017). La fiesta popular de la Tomatina de Buñol: gestión e impacto de una fiesta internacional. Gran Tour: Revista de Investigaciones Turísticas, nº 16 Julio-Diciembre de 2017 p. 23-42.

Das offizielle Stadtportal München (n.d.). The History of the Oktoberfest, available at https://www.muenchen.de/int/en/events/oktoberfest/history.html.

Die offizielle Website zur Wiesn (2019). Facts and figures: The Oktoberfest review 2019, available at https://www.oktoberfest.de/en/magazine/oktoberfest-news/2019/the-official-oktoberfest-review-2019.

El Diario (2018, 7 December). El turismo cultural internacional en España sube un 38 % y gasta más, available at https://www.eldiario.es/cultura/turismo-cultural-internacional-Espana-gasta_0_843765945.html

Fan, Y. (2004). Nation branding: Confusion and paradox. 33rd EMAC Conference, Murcia.

Fan, Y. (2006). Branding the nation: what is being branded?. Journal of Vacation Marketing, 12:1, pp. 5-14.

Fan, Y. (2007). Soft power and nation branding. Brunel Business School Research Papers, available at https://bura.brunel.ac.uk/bitstream/2438/1594/3/FullText.pdf.

Fan, Y. (2010). Branding the nation: Towards a better understanding. Place Branding and Public Diplomacy, 6/2, available at https://bura.brunel.ac.uk/bitstream/2438/3496/1/NB%20Towards%20a%20better%20understanding.pdf.

Gaab, H. (2006). Munich: Hofbräuhaus & History: Beer, Culture & Politics. New York: Peter Lang Publishing, Inc.

Germanfoods (n.d.). A Brief History of German Beer, available at https://germanfoods.org/german-food-facts/brief-history-of-german-beer/.
German Convention Bureau (n.d.). Tourism & Culture in Germany, available at https://www.gcb.de/discover-germany/tourism.html.
Gerson, S. (2003). The Pride of place: local memories and political culture in Nineteenth Century France, New York: Cornell University Press.
Horkheimer, M., & Adorno, T. (2002). Dialectic of enlightenment, Stanford: Stanford University Press.
INE Instituto Nacional de Estadística (2018). España en cifras, available at https://www.ine.es/prodyser/espa_cifras/2018/ .
Langlois, C. (1987). La révolution malade de la Vendée. Vingtième Siècle, revue d'histoire, n°14, avril-juin 1987, pp. 63-78, available at www.persee.fr/doc/xxs_0294-1759_1987_num_14_1_1857.
Lentscehner, P. (2013). La Marque France, Paris: Éditions du Cerf.
MacLeod, D.V. (2006.). Cultural commodification and tourism: a very special relationship. Tourism, Culture and Communication, 6(2), pp. 71-84.
Martin, J. C. (2000). A propos du 'génocide vendéen'. Du recours à la légitimité de l'historien. Sociétés contemporaines, N°39, pp. 23-38, available at www.persee.fr/doc/socco_1150-1944_2000_num_39_1_1799.
Meussdoerfer, F. (2011). Beer and Beer Culture in Germany, in Schiefenhövel, W., Macbeth, H. (eds.). Liquid Bread: Beer and Brewing in Cross-Cultural Perspective, New York: Bergbahn Books, pp. 63-70.
Ministerio de Cultura y Deporte (2018). Anuario de Estadísticas Culturales 2018, available at http://www.culturaydeporte.gob.es/dam/jcr:eb5b8140-e039-42ab-8e24-500fddc5b2a4/anuario-de-estadisticas-culturales-2018.pdf.
Richards, G. (2011). Creativity and tourism: the state of the art. Annals of Tourism Research, 38(4), pp. 1225-1253.
Rubio, R. (2019). España bate récord en 2018: 82,6 millones de turistas extranjeros y un 3,1% más de gasto, available at https://www.europapress.es/turismo/nacional/noticia-espana-bate-record-2018-826-millones-turistas-extranjeros-09-31-mas-gasto-20190116130415.html.
Santana Talavera, A. (2003).Turismo cultural, culturas turísticas. Horizontes antropológicos, 9(20), pp.31-57.
Sarmento, C. & Pascoal, S. (2020). Cultural Tourism and Heritage in Northern Portugal, Cambridge Scholars Publishing.
Schiefenhövel, W. & Macbeth, H. (2011). Introduction: Assembling perspectives on Beer, in Schiefenhövel, W., Macbeth, H. (eds.). Liquid

Bread: Beer and Brewing in Cross-Cultural Perspective. New York: Bergbahn Books, pp. 1-12.

Statistisches Bundesamt/Statista (2020). Number of overnight stays at travel accommodation in Germany from 1992 to 2019, available at https://www.statista.com/statistics/560792/overnight-stays-german-accommodation/.

Stolarz, S. & Atkinson, C. (2012). Oktoberfest overseas. Deutsche Welle, available at https://www.dw.com/en/oktoberfest-overseas/a-16241753.

THE LOCAL de (2019). Oktoberfest in numbers: An inside look at Germany's multi-billion Business, available at https://www.thelocal.de/20190923/oktoberfest-in-numbers-an-inside-look-at-germanys-multi-billion-business.

The Oktoberfest international guide (n.d.). History of the Oktoberfest, available at https://www.oktoberfest.net/history-oktoberfest/.

Tongeren, F. van (2011). Standards and International Trade Integration: A Historical Review of the German 'Reinheitsgebot', in Swinnen, J. (ed.). The Economics of Beer, New York: Oxford University Press.

Touropia (2020). 25 Top Tourist Attractions in German, available at https://www.touropia.com/tourist-attractions-in-germany/.

UNWTO (2019). International Tourism Highlights - 2019 Edition, available at https://www.e-unwto.org/doi/pdf/10.18111/9789284421152.

Uribarri, R. (2017). Los museos del fútbol desplazan a las obras de arte. Revista Contexto Nº 134, available at https://ctxt.es/es/20170913/Deportes/14942/museos-futbol-arte-estadios-afluencia.htm.

Vélez, V. L. (2018). La marca-país. Reflexiones sobre la obsesión por rentabilizar la cultura. Indi@logs, Vol.5, pp. 107-115.

Vizcaino Ponferrada, M. L. (2015). Evolución del turismo en España: el turismo cultural. International Journal of Scientific Management and Tourism, Vol.4, pp 75-95.

Vovelle, M. (1994). Un historien au Puy du Fou. Spectaculaire revision de la Revolution Française. Le Monde Diplomatique, pp. 16-17, available at https://www.monde-diplomatique.fr/1994/08/VOVELLE/7410.

WTTC (2018). Travel & Tourism. Economic Impact 2018. Spain, available at https://www.wttc.org/-/media/files/reports/economic-impact-research/countries-2018/spain2018.pdf.

WTTC/Statista (2020). Total contribution of travel and tourism to GDP in Germany from 2012 to 2028, available at https://www.statista.com/statistics/644714/travel-tourism-total-gdp-contribution-germany/.

Zaman, G. (2015). Cultural Heritage Entrepreneurship (CHE) – Challenges and Difficulties. Procedia - Social and Behavioral Sciences, vol. 188, available at https://www.researchgate.net/journal/1877-0428_Procedia-Social_and_Behavioral_Sciences.

CHAPTER 8

TRANSLATING THE CULTURE OF THE RIBEIRA SACRA'S VITICULTURAL BUSINESS: AN INTERCULTURAL DIALOGUE

REBECA CRISTINA LÓPEZ-GONZÁLEZ
UNIVERSITY OF VIGO

1. Introduction: Wine and Culture

The origin of viticulture can be located in the Eastern areas of the Mediterranean Sea. Some of the first written references to vineyards and wine can be read in the Holy Bible dating back three thousand years. The Aryan people were responsible for the introduction of these crops in this area of Europe. Proof of such labour has survived centuries in the form of paintings and relieves, which reveal vines and grapes in Assyria, Armenia, Mesopotamia, Eastern shores and Egypt (Zamora, 2000).

It was precisely in Egypt where references regarding the production of wine were recorded over 4,000 years ago. This activity was also reported through artistic representations reproducing each of the 5 stages of wine making: harvesting, crushing and pressing, fermentation, clarification, aging and bottling.

These stages, which may experience deviations and variations in the process, were broadly celebrated by the Greek and Romans, who humanised their gods by representing them surrounded by vine leaves and grape cluster crowns. The Greeks named their god Dionysius, who is frequently represented in the company of satyrs, maenads and bacchants. This visual recreation of wine festivals did endure through centuries and was a theme for 15th Century artists. Romans honoured Bacchus during grape-growing and wine-making stages as well.

This connection between agriculture, art, and worship had its impact on the development of religion, from polytheistic to monotheistic. Originally, wine was associated with royalty and power, and progressively priests became another influential social class. In the Holy Bible the process of winemaking is quoted at least 150 times according to Manglano (2003), and the vineyard is part and parcel of a settled society due to its multiannual nature as a crop. All throughout European Christian history, paintings and relief artwork of vineyards and wine have been used as symbols for praise in religious rituals. Jews celebrate the Sabbath with bread and wine, the Eucharist in the Catholic Church uses wine to represent the Blood of Christ, and although Islam, the Abrahamic religion, forbids the consumption of alcohol, grapes and vine leaves are frequently used in Muslim gastronomy.

Also, priests of the Catholic Church used vines metaphorically to propagate this religion. As part of their duties, cereals and vines were planted wherever they would go. From a Eurocentric perspective vine crops and winemaking was exported to the New World as of the 16th Century. Countries such as Argentina, Chile, Mexico, The USA, Australia, New Zealand and South Africa have become excellent winemakers, all claiming top positions in the rankings of Enotourism or what is also known as Wine tourism (Manglano, 2003, p. 75).

From a linguistic perspective one can observe the evolution of producing wine as human nourishment by analysing the idioms that have arisen throughout centuries and in differing cultures. Among the several expressions which may be used in English, one can hear idioms such as "good wine needs no bush" meaning that good quality does not require advertisement; "new wine in old bottles" and "new wine in old wineskins" share a similar idea linked to the innovations applied or added to an establishment or longstanding organisation, system or method; "there is truth in wine" is the translation of the first part of the Latin phrase "in vino veritas" and refers to how overdrinking might lead a speaker to be more honest. This same Latin phrase "in vino veritas, in aqua sanitas" was translated into Spanish "en el vino está la verdad, en el agua la salud" and into Portuguese "no vinho, a verdade" (Martin, 2020, n. p.).

As aforementioned, wine and vines have been part not only of mankind's nourishment, but have also been constituent elements of religions, an artistic metaphor of beliefs represented in paintings, relief artwork, codices, sacred literature… As soon as winemaking and vine growing processes were part of texts, individuals using their own language related wine and vines to everyday situations by creating idioms, proverbs and expressions, still in use today.

This use of language is a clear example of how we live in a shrinking world (Spitzberg, 1997, p. 379) where the production and trade of wine has crossed frontiers and become a global business accessible to eager customers. Yet, this process has required the interaction of people; a dialogue, in other words, which demands the know-how of translators and interpreters. These professionals are mediators capable of "gaug[ing] the distance between the worldviews of Insider (or original recipients of tourism texts) and Outsiders (recipients of translations)" (Agorni, 2018, p. 255).

This chapter is aimed at precisely discussing how "new wine in old bottles" is being introduced with a catalogue, originally written in Spanish and translated into English, to promote the wine-making region of Ribeira Sacra (Galicia, Spain) as an attractive, intercultural touristic destination. To this end, there are some points, such as the definition of Enotourism and Intercultural Communication, which are to be stated for a better understanding of how viticulture is being conveyed.

2. Enotourism: Cultural Tourism

According to Núnez (2015, pp. 27-28, my translation) Enotourism is "that which is offered so as to enjoy, make known, learn and value every single thing behind the making of a glass of wine: the vineyards, the production, the facilities, the tradition, the people involved, all adding to another more familiar heritage".

Tourists have much to gain from Enotourism. In fact, this whole industry teaches a lesson to those who want to know more about wine and the historical process surrounding it. It is the awareness of the heritage and the people who have made possible the existence of this beverage through tradition and experience. Winemaking is then an added value to cultural tourism because tourists have an opportunity to learn about the history and traditions of the location where cellars began their activity. One can discover the landscapes, regions and wine-making countries.

Furthermore, entrepreneurs may boost the economy of a geographical area by allowing visitors' access to their facilities, which frequently are part of the architectural heritage of the site. This touristic business plays a strategic role in the development of regions by providing direct and indirect employment. As an example, workers are not only needed in the wine-making stages in cellars but also staff who guide visitors and sell their wine bottles; and logistics may also be part of the process since customers might be offered a home delivery service for their purchases on the premises as well.

The expansion of this mode of tourism has been the concern of institutions such as the Secretaría de Estado de Turismo (Secretary of State for Tourism) in the Spanish scenario, who has been a key agent in the touristic promotion of Spain in international markets. Regarding Enotourism, this institution's main activity is centred on structuring and consolidating a high-quality touristic offer while promoting Spain's wine industry abroad.

Blanco (2015, p. 4) also mentions ACEVIN, the Spanish Association of Wine Cities, as a touristic engine aimed at the consolidation of the quality of Enotourism in the country through the Product Club "Wine Routes", born in 2001.

Turespaña also works towards the positioning of the online brand of Enotourism in Spain by implementing a specific website within the official tourism website, www.Spain.info. This site includes information on different offers related to viticultural trips, the main wine-making regions, and the Product Club mentioned above. In 2013, a site was attached to this website to promote touristic experiences related to Enotourism, targeting tourists who search for unique and original experiences.

Some institutions of the Autonomous Community of Galicia, where the Ribeira Sacra is located, work towards the promotion of this type of cultural tourism. Turgalicia has published several materials online, such as the digital leaflet *Galicia, paseando entre viñedos* (Galicia, strolling among Vineyards) and YouTube videos showing the wonders of Galician architectural heritage, landscapes and vineyards, in other words, Enotourism.

The Xunta de Galicia (the Galician Regional Government) and the Consellería do medio rural (this is the Regional Ministry for the Rural Environment) have also promoted wine tourism through the website, http://rutasdovino.xunta.gal/en/, purposely compiling six unfamiliar wine routes including the "Rota dos vinhos verdes", vinho verde, being a fruity wine which is produced in North-Western Portugal. The marketing of this wine and its producers is the result of the cross-border cooperation between Spain and Portugal. Among the wine routes of the Euro-Region Galicia-Northern Portugal described in this website, the following five routes are proud bearers of the Designation of Origin qualification: Ruta do viño

Monterrei, Ruta do viño Rías Baixas, Ruta do viño do Ribeiro, Ruta do viño Ribeira Sacra and Ruta do viño Valdeorras.

This chapter will focus on one of these, namely, the Ribeira Sacra wine route, since the catalogue to be analysed below belongs to this wine-making Galician territory.

3. The Ribeira Sacra Wine Route and the Denomination of Origin

The land bathed by the Sil and Miño Rivers just where both rivers meet in the inland area of Galicia is known as the Ribeira Sacra (The Sacred Riverbank). This region covers the area between the provinces of Lugo and Ourense, where the Sil flows into the Miño River. After centuries this abrupt landscape has turned into a deep and impressive canyon up to 500 m deep in some spots and was a settlement for monks and hermits in search of an ascetic life at the beginning of the Christian era. Written evidence since the 12th century registers the rise and fall of the monasteries built in the region, which were the cradle of the artistic and cultural development of the region and the rest of Galicia (Ocupación histórica del territorio, 2020, n. p.).

The Ribeira Sacra comprises a rich 1,500-year legacy including castles, churches, *pazos* (manor houses), in which cultural events and traditional festivals are held, as well as bridges. Archaelogical remains from the Bronze and Iron Ages and the Roman Empire's mark reveal the historical wealth of this site.

In addition to its landscape and archaeological history, the Ribeira Sacra's waters become navigable along a 40-km stretch due to the construction of several reservoirs. This circumstance has promoted touristic catamaran cruises, which allow the discovery of inaccessible spots hidden by the terrain. Several natural scenic spots overlooking the rivers invite the tourist to take in the unspoilt landscape.

Indeed, the Ribeira Sacras' landscape is another of its wonders. Oak, chestnut, birch and alder trees along with broom, gorse and heath bushes change season after season modifying the colour palette of the canyon. Cypress trees can be seen along with the vines cultivated on descending terraces, harvesting the grapes, which are the main crop of this region. In 2015 wine was made in about 95 cellars in this region entailing 20 municipalities. Abadía da Cova, Amedo, Finca Millara, Regina Viarum,

Ribada, Rousel do Sil, Val da Lenda, Vella and Via Romana can be mentioned to name just a few of Ribeira Sacra's cellars.

These cellars are represented by the Ribeira Sacra Regulatory Council (Rutas do viño, Galicia e norte de Portugal, 2020, n. p.), who oversees the management of this Denomination of Origin. A Denomination of Origin helps identify a product that is created, developed or transformed in a specific geographical area. It is a guarantee and recognition of product quality. Within the wine industry, a Denomination of Origin represents the cellars and the wine producers who agree on which is the best way to take care of the crops and produce wine in accordance with the characteristics of the geographical site and the know-how gathered with the passing of time (Denominación de origen Ribeira Sacra, 2020, n. p). The Ribeira Sacra comprises the wineries located in the following Subregions along the Miño and Sil Rivers: Subregion of Amandi, Subregion of Chantada, Subregion of Quiroga-Bibei, Subregion of Ribeiras do Miño and Subregion of Ribeiras do Sil.

4. Intercultural Communication, Translation and the Wine Business

Mansouri (2017, p. 13) has used the term "conceptual conundrum" to describe 'interculturalism'. As stated by this author, this is an ambiguous definition. Yet, over time academics have favoured "focus on relations between citizens and groups in civil society" (*ibid.*) as an acceptable definition. The literature regarding policy, on the other hand, has addressed this matter as "a state-oriented endeavour centred on the global war against terrorism" (*ibid.*). These are just a few of the multiple interpretations of this term.

Interculturalism is a label which has been coined to discuss social and cultural diversity derived from globalisation, population mobility and the development of information technology. Other terms such as 'multiculturalism' and 'assimilation' have fulfilled similar functions but not without controversy among expert academics from transversal fields.

Sarmento (2020, p. 400), for example, has employed 'interculturalism' as a synonym for "movement, communication, and encounter between cultures". When cultures meet there is a need for dialogue; an intercultural dialogue, that is, "a process that comprises an open and respectful exchange of views between individuals and groups with different ethnic, cultural, religious and linguistic backgrounds and heritage on the basis of mutual understanding and respect" (Council of Europe, 2008, p. 17).

Precisely, this process entailing exchange is grounded on language which should communicate and even share culture and heritage. Intercultural dialogue, therefore, implies the need for communication quite often covered by cultural mediators such as translators. The term 'intercultural communication' was coined by Hall in 1959, in *The Silent Language*, and refers to "the combination of diverse forms of relationship, interaction and communication between individuals and groups belonging to different cultures" (Soter, 2016, p. 89).

Communication is also a key factor in the tourism and hospitality industry. Travellers need to search for information about their destinations, make plans related to every day's journey, book hotel rooms and read restaurant menus. These are but a few of a tourists' communication needs which can be fulfilled by translators. These intercultural communicators will help tourists access the foreign culture by cutting down the distance from a lingua-cultural point of view, gauging the distance between Insiders and Outsiders (Agorni, 2018, p. 255).

Therefore, translators must develop at least two intercultural communication competences (Spitzberg, 1997, pp. 379-380) to engage tourists in their cultural and heritage discovery; 1. Appropriateness, as a non-violation of the rules, norms, and expectancies of the relationship; and 2. Effectiveness, as an accomplishment of valued goals or rewards regarding costs and alternatives. Hence, an actor's goals are accomplished in an appropriate way regarding context and relationship.

Apart from describing these two skills, Spitzberg (1997, p. 380) has also addressed intercultural communication's Interactional Quality which can be measured by considering three standards applicable to the practice of translation: 1. Communication may be minimising, that is, inappropriate and inefficient, and as a result poor, low quality; 2. Communication may be sufficing. It is appropriate but ineffective; 3. Communication may be maximising, inappropriate but effective. This category includes messages which are ethically problematic, as seen in certain advertising campaigns. The optimal interpersonal communicator must be appropriate and effective when rendering the message.

In the context of tourism, the success of the business very much relies on the know-how of translators and their use of language, even when "language issues do not seem to have place in tourism research. Translation as language mediation is hardly ever mentioned" (Agorni, 2018, p. 257). And still, the amount of new information to be offered, for example, in translated brochures is a dilemma among translation scholars, such as Kelly (1997, p. 35) who worries about communication breakdowns. The language of tourism is essential as Dann (1996, p. 249) has affirmed: "without it, tourism would surely cease to exist. […] the world's largest industry would simply grind to a halt, and we would remain at home –deaf, dumb, and blind to the beauties of creation and the voice of the Other."

In fact, the Ribeira Sacra is one of the beauties to be discovered and enjoyed. However, in numerical pre-Covid terms, it only represented 3% of the total Galician figure of booked hotel rooms in 2016. Moreover, according to the Galician Statistics Institute (IGE, in Galician), in that same year, 65.4% of the Ribeira Sacra's tourists were foreigners as opposed to the 34.6% of Galician travellers to this destination (La Voz de Galicia, 2016). These percentages reveal two findings which determine the future intercultural business to be developed in the region along with its sustainability.

First, the region of the Ribeira Sacra and Enotourism as cultural tourism have not yet fallen victim to human exploitation and environmental damage, nor to the imposition of one culture over another, nor even to the evasion of laws and regulations of one's country of origin (Sarmento, 2020, p. 403). There is a chance of bringing wealth to the region and reviving local heritage while preserving the long-lasting wine making tradition. Galician autonomous and central government authorities seem to have noticed the opportunity and the positive economic effects drawn by promoting tourism in the area. Therefore, €2 million have been allocated in October 2020 to support sustainable tourism in the Ribeira Sacra (La Voz de Galicia, 2020).

Second, and because of the needs of the industry to promote the region, the off/online publication of leaflets, brochures, and tourist guides which require the use of the language of tourism aimed at national and international enotourists will demand the mediation of intercultural professionals as translators. They are the ones who can keep an open, culturally aware and informative dialogue with potential travellers. This chapter is a clear example of how these social and cultural demands are being currently covered in this context.

5. Objective

The first part of this chapter has dealt with how the production of wine is related to culture such as religion, language and the appearance of social statuses associated with occupations and the organization of social hierarchies. Also, attention has been paid to the definition of Enotourism as a new form of tourism in Galicia, the Northwest autonomous region of Spain. The involvement of national, regional and local institutions in the promotion of Enotourism has been a key element in order to disseminate online the touristic offer of the region. A description of the Ribeira Sacra Denomination of Origin contextualises the commissioner of the translation to be discussed in the following pages. Precisely, this is the objective of this chapter: to discuss how this viticultural business is being advertised as a cultural touristic destination in a 288-page bilingual brochure and in four of its fourteen chapters. Is the translated text into English capable of attracting international tourists by communicating an appropriate and effective message? Will the intercultural communicator, i.e., the translator, render a functional text in English?

6. The Source Text: A Bilingual Brochure

This brochure was published in 2016 by the Ribeira Sacra Regulatory Council with headquarters in Monforte de Lemos (Lugo) with the mind set in a bilingual document Spanish>English. It can be retrieved from the website: https://ribeirasacra.org/media/documentos/guia_Rs_2016_web.pdf.

The director of this touristic text was Simón Vázquez. Ramón Bazarra and Álvaro Liste were the producers of this document together with Teresa Candal, who worked on the design and layout. The texts in Spanish were written by Victoriano Nodar and were translated into English by Claire Teed. Antía Cundíns and Dolores Villar Sánchez worked on the translated files.

This brochure is a 288-page online document with colourful visuals of the sites, most important monuments, landscapes and wineries photographed by Simón Vázquez.

Titled *Ribeira Sacra el sabor de un paisaje (The Taste of a Land). Guía de bodegas y vinos de la denominación de origen Ribeira Sacra (Guide to the Wineries and Wines of the Denomination of Origin Ribeira Sacra Regulatory Council)*, this brochure has been structured according to the following sections to fulfil an advertising purpose:

A brief historical approach about the land where the grapes are grown titled "El vino de los heroes" ("The Wine of the Heroes") pages 11-16. Data about the Subregions is offered from page 17-22 under the heading "La denominación de origen" ("Denomination of Origin"). The Regulatory Council is described in pages 23-24 under the title "El consejo regulador" ("The Regulatory Council").

Pages 25-30: "La fortuna de la Rovoyra Sacrata" ("The Fortune of Rovoyra Sacrata") deals with the name, Rovoyra Sacrata (El topónimo, 2020, n.p.), which has been a Constitutional privilege of the Monastery of Santa María de Montederramo, granted by Queen Doña Teresa of Portugal. Rovoyra Sacrata was the original name of the Ribeira Sacra, popularised in modern history. This section also includes the history of the hermits, Benedictine and Cistercian, and the monks' heritage in the region.

"El terroir" ("The Terroir") (pages 31-34) describes the special orography of the zone, followed by two chapters which are essential in this brochure, "Las uvas" ("The Grapes") (pages 35-42) and "Los vinos" ("The Wines") (pages 43-46).

Of special interest for this chapter, the section "El carácter internacional" ("International Scope") (pages 47-52) explains the impact of the Ribeira Sacra's wines in the international scenario. The longest section of this brochure consists of a thorough introduction for the reader to each of the cellars that produce and trade wine within the Denomination of Origin and analysed in this chapter: "Bodegas y vinos de la Ribeira Sacra" ("Ribeira Sacra Wineries and Wines") (pages 53-265). Pages 265-272 discuss Enotourism under the Spanish title "El turismo del vino". This same chapter's title in English is "International Scope", differing from the ST. From page 273 to page 276 there is a chapter about gastronomy, where the best wines to eat are being recommended "Vinos para comer" ("Food and wine pairing"). The next section (pages 277-278) deals with the relation between the wine industry and relaxing moments of leisure as suggested by its title "Sin prisas" ("Taking it easy"). Two more chapters complete the brochure with the following titles: "Para reflexionar" ("A moment of reflection"), pages 279-280, and "Para recordar" ("Things to remember"), pages 281-288.

As the table of contents of this document reveals, this brochure is divided into three main parts: Part 1 is about the history of the wine industry in the region, the crops and the land, the grape varieties and the Ribeira Sacra Denomination of Origin and its international marketing approach. Part 2 deals with the introduction to the reader about the cellars that are involved in the production of this beverage. Part 3 discusses how the production of wine and the surrounding enjoyable, relaxing experiences obtained create a touristic offer. In other words, the feelings and emotions felt by enotourists are described.

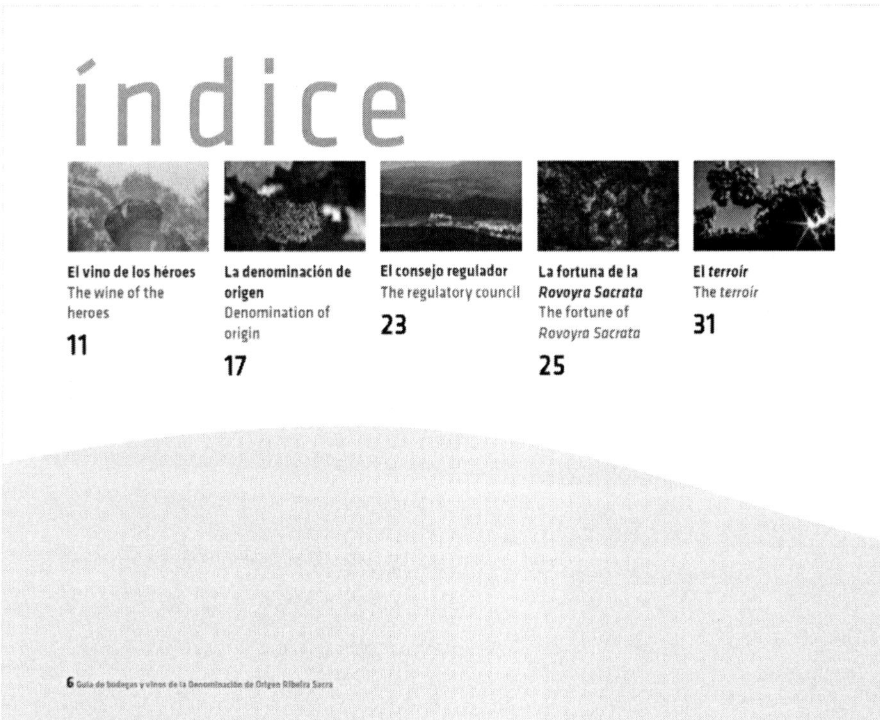
índice

6 Guía de bodegas y vinos de la Denominación de Origen Ribeira Sacra

Image 1: Example of one of the pages of the table of contents included in the brochure.

Regarding the ST, mention must be made of which is the main objective of this text: this brochure, available online to a broad audience, is also a printed document gifted to touristic and gastronomic fair visitors as an informative and appellative document, aimed at attracting their interest in the region, its wine products and culture. The following section will detail how this has been done by analysing the translation from Spanish into English of four of its fourteen chapters from a cultural point of view.

7. The Target Text: Analysing how culture is being internationally advertised

The *Ribeira Sacra, the taste of a land. Guide to the Wineries and Wines of the Denomination of Origin Ribeira Sacra Regulatory Council* brochure's most important sections were described in the previous section. This content was considered by the Ribeira Sacra Regulatory Council to be essential information in order to promote its activity and trade. Out of the fourteen sections included in this 288-page-long brochure, attention will be paid to four sections which are centred on the enotourist experience and thought to be the least technical sections of this brochure. Therefore, these sections should be the most appealing to foreign visitors, eager to add new leisure experiences and emotions to their personal memories. Creating an emotional attraction through these texts will probably facilitate selling the enotouristic product, while visitors are introduced to a new culture.

7.1. El Carácter Internacional > The International Scope

This part of the brochure is aimed at describing the procedures followed by these Galician cellars in order to promote their wines. The text in Spanish demonstrates the prestige of the Ribeira Sacra's wine industry in three foreign and cultural scenarios. The interesting point is that by mentioning foreign elements in the Spanish text the author enriches this national production. The foreign culture ratifies the importance of local culture in the source text (ST).

The first foreign element consists in naming two wine experts in the USA:

ST (source text): Concretamente es en Estados Unidos donde gozan de un gran prestigio gracias a la difusión que Robert Parker y Gerry Dawes, dos de los profesionales con mayor renombre y credibilidad en el mundo del vino a nivel mundial.

TT (target text): In fact, the United States is a place where these wines are held in high esteem thanks to articles by the likes of Robert Parker and Gerry Dawes, two of the most renowned and respected wine experts in the world.

Moderna sala de barricas en una bodega de la subzona de Ribeiras do Miño.
Modern barrel room, in a winery in Ribeiras do Miño

gracias a la difusión que Robert Parker y Gerry Dawes, dos de los profesionales con mayor renombre y credibilidad en el mundo del vino a nivel mundial. Ahora, el gran reto de los productores de la Denominación de Origen Ribeira Sacra son los nuevos mercados de China y Japón ●

teem thanks to articles by the likes of Robert Parker and Gerry Dawes, two of the most renowned and respected wine experts in the world. The new challenges facing the winegrowers of the Ribeira Sacra Denomination of Origin are the markets of China and Japan ●

Guide to the Wineries and Wines of the Denomination of Origin Ribeira Sacra Regulatory Council 49

Image 2: Extract where the prestige of Ribeira Sacra is ratified through foreign opinions in the brochure.

The second foreign element has to do with the use of an international wine contest held in Italy:

ST: Las denominaciones de origen asociadas al CERVIM se reúnen en el Certamen Internacional de Vinos de Montaña que se celebra en Aosta (Italia) donde los vinos de la Ribeira Sacra son frecuentemente premiados por su elevada calidad.

TT: The denominations of origin associated with the CERVIM come together at the International Mountain Wines Competition held in Aosta (Italy) where Ribeira Sacra wines often receive awards for their quality.

By including this international competition, the source culture is placing value on the local product, which is exactly what happens in the third extract:

ST: "La pasión y la devoción de sus productores es parte de lo que hace de la Ribeira Sacra tan distintiva" Eric Asimov, crítico de vinos del periódico New York Times de Nueva York.

TT: "The passion and devotion of the wine producers are part of what makes Ribeira Sacra so distinctive." Eric Asimov, New York Times wine critic.

Image 3: Foreign critics grant prestige to the Galician wine sector in the source culture's brochure.

This third cultural insert in the text is a quote by an expert on his opinion about these wines. This is another example of how international opinion, i.e., a foreign culture, on the quality of these products is being used to advertise the product among Spanish consumers in the SC (source culture). The translator has chosen to keep the reference in the translated document. Also, there are various punctuation mark errors. In the Spanish text the quotation marks are incorrectly used, and there is no period at the end of each sentence in both languages. Furthermore, italics have not been chosen to refer to the title of the newspaper. As interpreted, the translator has imitated the ST's layout.

In this first section, literal translation was the strategy chosen by C. Teed in order to transfer the cultural elements into English.

7.2. El Turismo del Vino > The Tourism of Wine

The translation of this section's title into English is a free translation of the source text's meaning ("el turismo del vino" could be literally translated as "the tourism of wine"). This might have been a mistake in the processing of this section's title since it is the same text as the previous translation provided for the section discussed in this chapter's Section 7.1.

Despite this different approach in content, the rest of the translated section is extremely faithful with regard to the ST. Literal translation, not word for word, but nearly, reflects the ST's information.

Regarding the advertised cultural features, there is a deep interest in describing what the translator has named as 'artistic patrimony'. These are the monuments which recall the history of the region and the history of how wine has been made there. Sightseeing the Romanesque churches and monasteries dating from the Middle Ages, visiting mountainous areas such as Cabeza de Manzaneda and O Faro and enjoying the architectural and ethnographic heritage are some of the activities offered in both the Spanish and English texts.

Image 4: Sightseeing the mountainous Ribeira Sacra as part of wine tourism. Detail from the analysed brochure.

The following extract of the text demands some further attention:

ST: La Ruta del Vino de la Ribeira Sacra es principalmente vino: las riberas, las bodegas, la vendimia, los viticultores, los depósitos, los trasiegos, las cubas. Pero a partir del vino hay todo un mundo esperando ser descubierto. Siguiendo esta ruta del vino se pueden conocer pequeñas bodegas llenas de encanto y bodegas, más grandes, con la última tecnología en vinificación. En ellas se pueden catar vinos auténticos elaborados con toda la atención del bodeguero y vinos experimentales que suponen un reto para el elaborador. El alojamiento no es un problema ya que algunas bodegas disponen de servicio de hotel y de restaurante y, sino, existe una importante oferta de casas de turismo rural y hoteles con encanto en los que descansar.

TT: Ribeira Sacra's Wine Circuit is all about wine –riverbanks, wineries, the harvest, winegrowers, tanks, decantation, vats. But there's a whole world waiting to be discovered revolving around wine. On this wine tour, visitors will be introduced to charming little wine cellars as well as the larger, state-of-the-art wineries. All of them offer the opportunity to sip the native wines, served by attentive cellarmen, and to taste the experimental wines which are a challenge to the winemakers. Lodging is not a problem since some of these wineries have hotel and restaurant service. There are also many bed and breakfast establishments and boutique hotels where guests can spend the night.

To begin with, the ST twice mentions "la ruta del vino" translated into English as two different items "Ribeira Sacra's Wine Circuit" and "wine tour". The first is treated as a site or location and uses capital letters, whereas the second just refers to a general tour. Even the capital letters have been dropped in the TT. The translator has used the words 'circuit' and 'tour' to refer to the same concept in Spanish.

C. Teed, the translator, also chose the adjective "state-of-the-art" to advert the wineries that can be visited as opposed to the Spanish ST which speaks about the latest technology applied to wine production. "State-of-the-art" brings the idea of a novelty or modern winery to the English reader when the nuance in Spanish is selling technological advances instead.

The enotourist is advertised a slightly different experience concerning wine tasting in both languages. The Spanish document explains how wine tasting is part of the activities to be enjoyed along the circuit but does not specify who serves the wine. The English version literally states that "attentive cellarmen" will serve the wine to every visitor. This difference might promise a more exciting experience to the English speaking enotourist than to the Spanish one, whose expectations about meeting the cellarmen and cellarwomen might be lower.

This extract of the text also offers lodging services to visitors which according to the Spanish text spend their enotouristic experience in "casas de turismo rural y hoteles". Translating the term "casa de turismo rural" can be a challenge due to the specific services offered by these hotels. Translations into English may be "a country holiday house", "country house hotel", "a rural tourism lodge/accommodation" or "village inn hotel". To bridge the cultural gap between this type of hotel in Spain and a similar type of hotel to be found in the target culture C. Teed probably carried out some research before deciding to use the term "bed and breakfast establishments". Although the term 'bed and breakfast' has been defined as "a room to sleep in for the night and a morning meal or private house or small hotel offering this" (Cambridge Dictionary, 2020, n. p.), further research reveals that experts in tourism do use the term 'bed and breakfast' in rural tourism (Chen *et al.*, 2013, pp. 278-286; Giray *et al.*, 2019, pp. 1-15; Lanfranchi *et al.*, 2008, pp. 1-7; George *et al.*, 2012, pp. 36-54; Quantao, 2019, pp. 44-48). This translating solution does comply with the expectations of an English-speaking expert in tourism and non-expert prospective foreign tourist, both will know exactly what the services that these 'casas de turismo rural' will offer in the Ribeira Sacra.

In a similar manner, the text in Spanish offers other services as hotels, ("hoteles") which were translated as "boutique hotels". These hotels according to the Cambridge Dictionary (Cambridge Dictionary, 2020, n. p.) are "a small stylish and fashionable hotel that is not part of a chain". An expert definition of Jones, Day and Quadri-Felitti (2013, p. 726 and p. 729) states that a boutique hotel offers an aspirational experience, a total experience and a focus on the property experience. These hotels offer a very personalised service and hopefully some charm and/or other unique characteristics. These academics mention a small or historical hotel as an example, but as a more developed definition, Jones, Day and Quadri-Felitti (2013, p. 729) compile the opinion of researchers in the field and provide this final definition for 'boutique hotel': "[…] small hotels that offer high levels of service. Boutique hotels tend to be stylish, trendy and cool and provide an intimate hotel experience. Boutique hotels often provide authentic cultural and historical experiences and interesting services to guests. Boutique hotels are unique".

What this definition demonstrates is the fact that the translator of this extract, C. Teed, decided to use a specialised term to translate the Spanish "hotel con encanto" (literal back translation: charming hotel), which is a more general term in the source culture. This decision may come from the need to attract the English-speaking tourist with a lodging offer that is trendy and provides a cultural and historic value differing from other locations. Here C. Teed has gone from a literal translation strategy to adapting a minimal amount of content in order to fulfil the target text's function, attract visitors and sell the lodging offer.

Image 5: A boutique hotel with panoramic views of the vineyards. Image from the brochure.

7.3. Vinos para Comer > Food and Wine Pairing

Translating gastronomic cultural references is a challenge and has been well-documented for decades in papers such as Chiaro and Rossato (2015); De la Cruz Trainor (2004a and 2004b) and Fallada (2000). The challenges have much to do with cultural constraints and the complete fulfilment of the TT readers' expectations and culinary fancies. The topic has even become part of specialised translation courses aimed at differentiating translator's skills and competences.

This section's gastronomic translation is not far from the strategies implemented by previous professionals who chose to literally translate the content or adapt it so that the client will know what is going to be tasted and enjoyed. The dish "Cocido" is explained as a "hearty boiled dinner" which does not even mention the ingredients of this typical Galician winter dish.

"Caza" making reference to meat obtained from hunting is described as "wild game meat", which does suit the definition provided by the Britannica Encyclopedia Online. "Truchas y/o anguilas" were also literally translated "trout and/or eels", but the term "empanadas" was kept in the TT and explained in brackets ("fish and meat pies"). Other gastronomic cultural references were simplified. "El caldo de huesos de Taboada" (back translation: Bone broth from Taboada) was translated "Taboada's famous broth", omitting the main ingredient of the broth to possibly avoid upsetting the visitor. Sober's famous dessert ("Rosca de Sober") was also described rather than translated: "Sober's pastry ring".

Image 6: Pairing wine and food as a cultural experience; a key point in this brochure.

7.4. Sin prisas > Taking it easy

This chapter is an example of how the terminology of Tourism can be included in a brochure to confer a more technical view to the promotion of a location. Specifically, this text mentions the need to avoid mass tourism in favour of a slower experience, which means a deeper cultural exposure and a profound discovery of the visited location. This type of touristic immersion is mentioned in the ST but incorrectly spelt (slow turism*), a common feature of tourist texts written in Spanish according to Durán (2012, pp. 103-113). This author claims that these badly drafted texts may be confusing and demand double work on the part of the translator, who will need to correct and avoid the mistakes in the TT. C. Teed proceeded in this way and corrected the mistake in the TT: there are innovative proposals that are gradually garnering the attention of fans, like the so-called concept of slow tourism.

In addition, most probably the ST made use of this term in English to add prestige to the wine industry of this rural region by showing it is up to date with recent theories related to sustainable tourism and yet economic development (Hall, 2012; Petrini, 2001).

This section is also an example of how translation can render an exotic or foreign effect on the TT (Venuti, 1995) by avoiding the translation of place names. This has been the strategy followed by C. Teed, who has kept Galician place names throughout the 288 pages. This excellent decision makes it possible for the tourist to ask locals for directions, find these locations in maps and use GPS applications on cell phones and tablets.

En la cascada de Cachón el silencio se rompe con el sonido del agua.
The silence is disrupt by the sound of water, in the cascade of Cachón.

En medio de la vorágine del actual turismo de masas surgen propuestas innovadoras que cada vez captan a más adeptos como el denominado slow turism. Es un tipo de turismo protagonizado por un consumidor más concienciado y responsable y por una máxima de total respeto por la naturaleza y el entorno. Este turismo de descanso y de tranquilidad tiene en la Ribeira Sacra uno de sus paisajes privilegiados en el que tierra y agua se funden en un abrazo eterno. Los cursos fluviales de los ríos Miño y Sil son navegables en catamarán por lo que desde hace años los itinerarios turísticos en barco tienen su recorrido por el corazón mismo del paisaje. El cañón del Miño es de pendientes más suaves, pero obliga al río a doblarse en magistrales recovecos que provocan un espectacular cambio de dirección. En el lugar de A Cova (O Saviñao) a veces denominado como Cabo do Mundo es un lugar donde el tiempo no existe. Es esta la mejor forma de percibir la extraordinaria fuerza de esta tierra y la dificultad del cultivo de la vid y poder así entender la exclusividad y la calidad de los vinos surgidos en estas riberas ●

In the midst of today's maelstrom of mass tourism, there are innovative proposals that are gradually garnering the attention of fans, like the so-called concept of slow tourism. This type of tourism is popular with a more responsible, conscientious consumer, who is highly respectful of nature and the environment. These travellers seeking peace and quiet can find a breathtaking landscape in Ribeira Sacra, where land and water merge in an eternal embrace. The waterways of the Miño and Sil rivers are navigable by catamaran. Boat cruises have long been popular with tourists who delight in sailing through the heart of this landscape. The Miño canyon has gentler slopes but the canyon forces the river to meander around the majestic twists and turns that give rise to spectacular changes of direction. The village of A Cova (O Saviñao), sometimes called Cabo do Mundo, is a place where time stands still. This is the best way to experience the extraordinary strength of this land and the arduous labour of vinegrowing- a way to understand the exclusive nature and quality of the wines that are the product of these riverbanks ●

278 Guía de bodegas y vinos de la Denominación de Origen Ribeira Sacra

Image 7: Galician places names have been kept in the TT to render an exotic and attractive appeal to the destination.

This practical strategy also provides the tourist with cultural information by providing an opportunity to learn the Galician language, its phonetics and hidden meanings place names keep. Here is an example of how the place names were maintained in this brochure:

ST: El cañón del Miño es de pendientes más suaves, pero obliga al río a doblarse en magistrales recovecos que provocan un espectacular cambio de dirección. En el lugar de A Cova (O Saviñao) a veces denominado como Cabo do Mundo es un lugar donde el tiempo no existe.

TT: The Miño canyon has gentler slopes but the canyon forces the river to meander around the majestic twists and turns that give rise to spectacular changes of direction. The village of A Cova (O Saviñao), sometimes called Cabo do Mundo, is a place where time stands still.

8. Conclusions

The descriptive analysis of these four chapters extracted from the *Ribeira Sacra, the taste of a land. Guide to the Wineries and Wines of the Denomination of Origin Ribeira Sacra Regulatory Council* brochure has shown how culture and therefore the wine industry in the region has been translated and advertised into English.

To sell this wine experience to English speaking enotourists, the brochure relies mainly on the fulfilment of expectations by first citing foreign approval naming non-Galician wine experts and its foreign prestige to guarantee the quality of the Ribeira Sacra's wines and Enotourism services. Second, the use of lodging terminology which is easily recognisable in the target culture helps to promote the services offered to English-speaking hotel guests. The third cultural element translated into English and related to wineries and wines puts together the food and beverages binomially. Gastronomy is one of the most relevant attractions of Enotourism. Wine tasting is more pleasing when accompanied by the food of the region, and this brochure includes the Ribeira Sacra's typical dishes. Lastly, the non-translation of place names has also attached an exotic value to the TT, which preserves its practicality in terms of geographical mobility. Foreigners will find each spot in the Wine Circuit due to this strategy. The cultural value of untranslated place names is unquestionable and enriches both the source and target text.

All these elements demand an expert view capable of balancing the range between domestication and foreignization strategies as the translator, C. Teed, has done. It is not a matter of only describing the dishes or not translating the names of each dish (Empanada, for example), but finding solutions which combine and allow the recognition and selection of the dish at the restaurant. The question posed in the objective section above about the TT's ability to promote the Ribeira Sacra's wonders through a successful translation is obviously affirmative.

The translator is the professional who has been able to transfer and transmit the voice of the Other and narrate the ancient history of the Ribeira Sacra while advertising its wine industry. Intercultural communication has been achieved since the translator's training involves acquiring the necessary competences to be appropriate and effective and thus promote the region successfully.

Maximising communication (inappropiate but effective) was exemplified where cost and alternatives were considered in some of the translation extracts discussed above. Yet, maximizing should not be interpreted in this case as the lack of an ethical message or inappropriateness, but as a deep awareness of the needs of the target English reader, who will be eager to visit the region. Enotourism is surely a fledgling post-Covid business in the Ribeira Sacra region due to its fairly isolated geography and rural environment. Perhaps these characteristics will become an asset along with the required intercultural communication in the form of proper translation to ensure a fluid dialogue. Of course, government authorities are key and in charge of the sustainable management of the region to guarantee prosperity and a valuable exchange between insiders and outsiders.

References

Agorni, Mirella (2018). Cultural Representation through Translation: An Insider-Outsider Perspective on the Translation of Tourism Promotional Discourse. *Altre Modernità 20, 11*, 253-275.

Albo, Francisco (October 1, 2020). La Ribeira Sacra recibirá dos millones para fomentar el turismo sostenible. *La voz de Galicia*. https://www.lavozdegalicia.es/noticia/lemos/2020/10/02/ribeira-sacra-recibira-dos-millones-fomentar-turismo-sostenible/0003_202010M2C3991.htm.

Blanco Quesada, Marta (2015). Enoturismo, una propuesta de valor en la estrategia de promoción internacional de Turespaña. *Terruños 25*, 4-9. https://culturadelvino.org/fcv/wpcontent/uploads/pdf/publicaciones/terrunos25.pdf: 8.

Britannica (n.d.). game meat. In *Britannica*. Accessed October 25, 2020, https://www.britannica.com/topic/game-meat.

Cambridge Dictionary (n.d.). bed and breakfast. In *Cambridge Dictionary*. Accessed October 16, 2020, https://dictionary.cambridge.org/dictionary/english/bed-and-breakfast.

Cambridge Dictionary (n.d.). boutique hotel. In *Cambridge Dictionary*. Accessed October 20, 2020, https://dictionary.cambridge.org/dictionary/english/boutique-hotel.

Chen, Li-Chan, Lin Shang-Ping and Kuo Chun-Min (2013). Rural Tourism: Marketing Strategies for the Bed and Breakfast Industry in Taiwan. *International Journal of Hospitality Management 32*, 278-286. DOI: 10.1016/j.ijhm.2012.07.005.

Chiaro, Delia and Linda Rossato (2015). Food and Translation, Translation and Food. *The translator 21:3*, 237-243. DOI:

10.1080/13556509.2015.1110934: 237-243.

Cortés, Carlos (March 6, 2016). Lo que pesa el turismo en la Ribeira Sacra. *La voz de Galicia*. https://www.lavozdegalicia.es/noticia/lemos/2016/03/06/pesa-turismo-ribeira-sacra/0003_201603M6C3991.htm.

Council of Europe (2008). Intercultural dialogue: living together as equals in dignity. *White paper*. Committee of Ministers, Council of Europe. https://www.coe.int/t/dg4/intercultural/source/white%20paper_final_revised_en.pdf.

Cultura de Galicia (n.d.). El topónimo. In *Cultura de Galicia*. Accessed September 22, 2020, https://www.cultura.gal/es/toponimo.

Cultura de Galicia (n.d.). Ocupación histórica del territorio. In *Cultura de Galicia*. Accessed September 22, 2020, https://www.cultura.gal/es/ocupacion-historica-territorio.

Dann, Graham (1996). *The Language of Tourism: A Sociolinguistic Perspective*. CAB International.

De la Cruz Trainor, María M. (2004a). Traducción inversa: una realidad. *Trans 8*, 53-60. DOI: 10.24310/TRANS.2004.v0i8.2963: 53-60

—. (2004b). Traducción al inglés de términos culturales en textos turísticos. In José Antonio Gallegos Rosillo and Hannelore Benz Busch (Eds.), *Traducción y Cultura. El papel de la cultura en la comprensión del texto original* (pp. 83-114). Libros Encasa Ediciones y Publicaciones.

Durán Muñoz, Isabel (2012). Caracterización de la traducción turística: problemas, dificultades y posibles soluciones. *Revista de lingüística y lenguas aplicadas 7*, 103-113. DOI: 10.4995/rlyla.2012.1127: 26-30.

Fallada Pouget, Carmina (2000). Are menu translations getting worse? Restaurant menus in English in the Tarragona Area. *Target 12:2*, 323-332. DOI: 10.1075/target.12.2.08fal: 323-332.

Galicia en vinos (n.d.). Denominación de origen Ribeira Sacra. In *Galicia en vinos*. Accessed October 8, 2020, https://www.galiciaenvinos.es/denominaciones-origen-galicia/ribeira-sacra/.

George, Babu P., Haghiri, Morteza and Okech, Roselyne (2012). Rural Tourism as a Sustainable Development Alternative: An Analysis with Special Reference to Luanda, Kenya. *Cultur Ano 6, 3*, 36-54.

Giray, Fatma Handan *et al.* (2019). Rural Tourism Marketing: Lavender Tourism in Turkey. *Ciência Rural, Santa María 49, 2*, 1-15. DOI: 10.1590/0103-8478cr20180651.

Hall, C. Michael (2012). Degrowing Tourism: Décroissance, Sustainable Consumption and Steady-State Tourism. *Anatolia 20:1*, 46-61. DOI: 10.1080/13032917.2009.10518894

Hall, Edward T. (1959). *The Silent Language*. Doubleday & Company.

Jones, David L., Day, Jonathon and Quadri-Felitti, Donna (2013). Emerging Definitions of Boutique and Lifestyle Hotels: A Delphi Study. *Journal of Travel & Tourism Marketing 30:7*, 715-731. DOI: 10.1080/10548408.2013.827549: 726 and 729.

Kelly, Dorothy (1997). The translation of texts from the tourist sector: textual conventions, cultural distance, and other constraints. *Trans 2*, 33-42.

Lanfranchi, Maurizio *et al.* (2009). *Widespread Hotel: An Example of Sustainable Tourism Development in Rural Areas*, Proceedings of the 2009 International Conference on Tourism April 22-25 Messina, Italy, ISBN: 9788896116203.

Manglano Alonso, Mª Luz (2003). *El vino de los faraones.* Fundación Dinastía Vivanco.

Mansouri, Fethi (2017). Introduction: The Conceptual Conundrum around intercultural dialogue. In Fethi Mansouri (ed.), *Interculturalism at the Crossroads. Comparative perspectives on concepts, policies and practices* (pp. 13-23). UNESCO.

Martin, L. M. (2020). 'In vino veritas': Quotes about wine from around the world. Accessed September 27, 2020, https://delishably.com/beverages/in-vino-veritas-famous-quotes-about-wine.

Núnez Pinto, Lola (2015). El vino es patrimonio. *Terruños 25,* 26-30. Accessed September 17, 2020: https://culturadelvino.org/fcv/wp-content/uploads/pdf/publicaciones/terrunos25.pdf.

Petrini, Carlo (2001). *Slow Food. Le ragioni del gusto*. Economica Laterza.

Quantao, Yu (2019). *Research on the Construction of Rural Tourism B&B in Guanzhong Area of Shaanxi Province*. 2019 International Conference on Social Science, Management and Education (ICSSME 2019), Tokyo, Japan. https://www.clausiuspress.com/conferences/AETP/ICSSME%202019/ICSSME009.pdf.

Sarmento, Clara (2020). Tourism as Intercultural Business: Locating Concepts and Questioning Identities. *European Journal of Sustainable Development 9, 3*, 400-415. DOI: 10.14207/ejsd.2020.v9n3p400.

Soter, Mariia (2016). Theoretical Modelling of Intercultural Communication Process. *Journal of Advocacy, Research and Education 6, 2*, 87-92.

Spitzberg, Brian H. (1997). A Model of Intercultural Communication Competence. In Larry A. Samovar and Richard E. Porter (Eds.), *Intercultural Communication* (pp. 379-391). Wadsworth Publishing Company.

Venuti, Lawrence (2008). *The Translator's Invisibility: A History of Translation*. Routledge.

Xunta de Galicia (n.d.). Rutas do viño, Galicia e Norte de Portugal. In *Xunta de Galicia. Consellería do Medio Rural*. Accessed September 22, 2020, http://rutasdovino.xunta.gal/es/.

Zamora López, José Ángel (2000). *La vid y el vino en Ugarit*. CSIC.

CHAPTER 9

UNDERWATER CULTURAL HERITAGE AS A BLUE TOURISM DRIVER: A PILOT PROJECT FROM LITTORAL ALENTEJO, PORTUGAL

ALEXANDRE MONTEIRO
HTC/IAP, FCSH-UNL

I

The economic sectors related to the ocean and based on the sustainability of the sea constitute the so called blue economy. One major goal of the European Union is "Blue Growth", defined as a long-term strategy to support sustainable growth and job creation in the marine and maritime sectors, using the seas and the oceans as driving forces of the European economy.

With the sea and the coastlines being economic driving forces, coastal and maritime tourism, also called Blue Tourism, is part of the EU's blue growth strategy and constitutes one of the most important sectors of the blue economy. Blue Tourism is also the largest sector in terms of employment and accounts for one third of the economy linked to the sea (EC, 2019). Of the 4 million jobs that the blue economy generated in 2017, 54% were created in the tourism sector. Of the total number of workers of this sector, 45% fall in the 16 to 35-year-old range, a factor that means that growth in this sector is especially important for European youth (FOSSE *et al*, 2019). Research conducted on cultural tourism in coastal regions shows that its growing importance is a powerful engine for sustainable development, being responsible for a third of the total profits generated by the blue economy (DGMA, 2019).

This decade has been nominated the United Nations Decade of Ocean Science for Sustainable Development (2021–2030), therefore, we intend to rise to the challenge and present a pilot project being developed in Portugal as a prototype on how to use Underwater Cultural Heritage as a driver for Blue Tourism, Sea Sustainability and Public Awareness (ARGYROPOULOS & STRATIGEA, 2019).

II

European trade and sea power became inextricably linked by the end of the 15th century, creating new geopolitical tensions, alliances and antagonisms. The newly reunited Spain was then a vast multicultural and multinational empire troubled by domestic uprisings, international conflicts, and cultural revolutions. The costs of maintaining such an empire were immeasurable in economic and human terms. Eager to increase their income, the Catholic rulers, Isabella and Ferdinand, were looking for a way to reach the East Indies and its spices. A tall order, since the eastern route was dominated by the Venetians in the Mediterranean and the Muslims in the Near East, and the Portuguese were exploring a probable route circling Africa.

When Christopher Columbus proposed to get to the Indies through an unknown route to the West, the Catholic monarchs were ready to accept the deal. Although Columbus was mistaken, his journey opened the silver gates of the Americas to Spain. To the Spanish people, the New World was a synonym of wealth, a way of running away from poverty and social constraints. To the natives, who saw their way of life changed forever, three hundred years of intensive colonization obliterated their languages, religions and social organizations. On 14th February, 1503, the Spanish bureaucrats incorporated the trade with the new colonies into the Crown revenue system by creating the *Casa de Contratación* in Seville. Through this institution, the King wanted to encourage and facilitate, but mainly control, the maritime traffic with the Western Indies.

The first step towards the control of the new route was to standardize the oceanic routes and ports of call for the fleets. It was determined that the journey from the Spanish mainland would include a call on the Canary Islands, from where they would use the southern winds to travel to Santo Domingo, in the island of La Española, today´s Dominican Republic and Haiti. From there, the fleet would navigate to La Habana, in Cuba, where they either would wait for the ships arriving from *Tierra Firme* (current Panama and Colombia) or *Nueva España* (current Mexico, California and a few southern states of the U.S.A.) or would start a new journey towards the continent. Commerce between Spain and the New Continent continued uninterrupted until the mid-16th century, when French privateers started raiding the fleets arriving from the West Indies.

In 1580, the union of the kingdoms of Spain and Portugal under King Phillip II brought the hostility of England and France, who challenged the Iberian nautical command of the seas. This challenge was most notably felt in the Azores. Sitting in mid journey from the Old and New continents, amidst the North Atlantic winds, a crucial strategic waypoint in the maritime trade networks of both West and East Indies, these islands were a key port of call in King Philip's overseas ambitions. Eager to take the Azores, where the defiant Dom Antonio, the Portuguese claimant to the throne, was holding positions, the Spanish monarch tried to conquer the Azores between 1581 and 1582. In 1583, Terceira Island was conquered and Don Antonio fled to England. But this did not stop the attacks by the English ships.

In 1587, Philip II was organizing an ambitious plan to invade England and was unable and unwilling to spend the necessary troops and vessels to defend the fleet and the ports in the Americas against Francis Drake's raids. However, the silver and gold lifelines needed to continue to flow from the New to the Old World. In 1588, the Spanish fleet led by Admiral Martín Olazabal departed from Santander on May 15. It called on Cadiz on July 14 and suffered a series of mishaps that postponed its arrival to Veracruz, where it called on September 30. Forced to winter in the Americas, the Spanish fleet needed protection. King Philip sent twelve *zabras*, which had some firepower, but were not as powerful as the twelve galleons that were originally intended. This fleet, led by general Alvaro Flores Quiñones, travelled to Cartagena de Indias, where it gathered the ships loaded with the Crown's gold and silver. From there, it navigated to La Habana, where it met with the fleet of Nueva España, led by the aforementioned admiral Martín de Olazabal. Following the King's instructions, on 12 September 1589, the combined fleet of 90 ships departed from Cuba to Spain.

In the Azores, the privateer ships of Lord Cumberland were waiting for the Spanish fleet. Hidden between the islands of Corvo and Terceira, the Englishmen managed to capture seven vessels. Unable to gather again in convoy, the Spanish fleet left the Azores in disarray, the ships being picked up by the English or sunk by bad weather. Several days after the English attack, the flagship, the *Santissima Trinidad,* and another vessel reached the port of Angra, at Terceira Island. A Dutch merchant, Jan Huygen van Linschoten, left a written account of their arrival, vividly describing the pitiful condition on which the vessels arrived, with the men pumping water, fearing for their lives, and how the ships were unloaded of ingots of silver and gold, of chests full of pieces of eight and unregistered precious stones.

Spanish accounts tell us how, after repairs were made, the treasure was reloaded on the *Santissima Trinidad*, an unnamed ship, and a vessel named the *Nuestra Señora del Rosario*. Although all three ships departed together from Angra on November 26, soon the *Santíssima Trinidad* and the *Nuestra Señora del Rosario* lost track of the other vessel – it either sunk or returned to the Azores, the documentation is amiss on its fate. As the *Santíssima Trinidad* was insufficiently repaired, the flagship began to slowly sink into the ocean in between the Azores and the coast of the Iberian Peninsula. On November 29, its crew and treasure were transshipped into the *Nuestra Señora del Rosario.* Now carrying the cargoes of two ships, archival accounts tally the official treasure aboard the *Rosario* (i.e. minus the expected contraband) in the weight of 397.684 pesos of *tipuzque* (28.7 gr each) and 49.097 *marcos* (230 gr each) - that is, around 22.7 tons of silver and gold bullion.

Now alone in the Atlantic, the *Rosario* caught sight of land on December 6. The four pilots and the "people from Cadiz" onboard determined that the coast in front of them was Larache, in Morocco, so they decided to keep sailing north during that day and the following night. However, alas, the four pilots present were not skilled enough to plot an accurate course to Cadiz. On December 7, they "dawned" dwarfed by the Arrábida mountain coastline, two leagues from Setúbal, Portugal, very close to the shore, with winds blowing from leeward.

The crew fought all morning to maintain the ship at a safe distance from the shore, and even tried to enter the channel that would lead them all to safety, inside Setubal harbor, but to no avail. After having all their masts cut and all anchor lines cast away, they held a meeting in order to decide their fate. Since the seas and winds were increasing their violence, they decided to cut their moorings, in order to have the ship run aground while there was still daylight – to have such an event to occur during the night would seal the fate of all passengers and crewmembers alike. Therefore, at one o'clock, they let go of the mooring lines. Two minutes later, the ship touched ground on the inlet of Tróia and promptly broke into pieces under the heavy surf, the ensuing tragedy ending with over 120 people drowned, of the 230 that were onboard.

Immediately after the sinking of the *Rosario*, local inhabitants recovered 5.554 gold and 133 silver coins. For over a period of 6 months, local fishermen pulled in their nets several dispersed objects from the *Rosario*, such as nautical charts and astrolabes. Several attempts to recover the treasure were made but the Spaniards never found the remains of the ship or of its precious cargo, although the survivors and the soldiers stationed at the nearby castle of Outão described to the scribes that were writing the official accounts how and where the vessel had been lost (MONTEIRO & PINHEIRO, 2012).

III

The *Nuestra Señora del Rosario* is just one of the more than 120 treasure-carrying ships to have sunk in the maritime triangle defined between Portugal, Madeira and Azores islands. It is also one of the 6000 ships estimated to have been lost since 1500 in what are today Portuguese territorial waters. Sunk in storms or in naval battles, shipwrecked by accident or by faulty navigational methods, lost by collision or by stranding, all these shipwrecks are nowadays potential underwater cultural heritage (UCH) sites.

And it is no wonder that so many ships were lost in this area. The strategically located west coast of the Iberian Peninsula has always been a nexus between two worlds: those of the Mediterranean and those of the Northern European cultures. Phoenicians, Carthaginians, Romans, Goths, and Arabs, all left their marks in Iberia's architecture, language, agriculture, religious beliefs, and in many other cultural and technological traits, shipbuilding traditions included.

While wrecks that happened prior to the 16th century in Portuguese waters are seldom documented and have never been found in the archaeological records, the data gathered from the archival records is tantalizing. Indeed, preliminary evidence for the number and type of ships lost since the early modern period gives us a hint to what may lie beneath the waters; but, disappointingly, scarce material remains, when one looks on how that potential translates into actual sites (MARTINS, 2014).

Rough seas, coastal erosion, contemporary and late salvage activities from the 1960´s, as well as coastline human activities such as construction and dredging, may all have contributed to a disappearing heritage. But it is most probable that the lack of archaeological evidence for Portuguese UCH is due more to a lack of geophysical surveys and a general unwillingness to engage fishermen, amateur divers and other sea stakeholders than to any other factors combined (DUNCAN & GIBBS, 2015). This is even more evident by looking at the way *Endovelico* – the National Database of Cultural Heritage, maintained by the Ministry of Culture – treats the Database of Historical Shipwrecks (DHS) contained within it.

The DHS was informally created by Francisco Alves for the National Archaeological Museum and its creation roughly coincided with the brief period (1992-1996) in which the Portuguese government caved in to treasure hunters pressure and put into law the concession of stretches of territorial waters for the commercial looting of UCH (ALVES, 2007). It was at that very moment that the government realized that it had no clue about the whereabouts of the shipwrecks being sought by the treasure hunters and had thus to rely on the historical information provided by them. Thanks to frantic efforts put voluntarily by a handful of archival researchers (BLOT & BLOT, 1992), the DHS gained momentum and was eventually enriched with the database of historical shipwrecks of the Azores (MONTEIRO, 2000), Madeira (MONTEIRO *et al*, 2012), and a score of documented losses of Portuguese Indiamen in the South Atlantic and Indian Oceans.

In 1997, the Portuguese government overturned the treasure hunting legislation and introduced a new one that declared all shipwrecks to be protected UCH. In 2006, Portugal deposited its instrument of ratification of the UNESCO Convention on the Protection of the Underwater Cultural Heritage (CPUCH). According to this Convention and other regulations in force, Portugal was tasked with several legal duties and obligations, which included, but were not limited to, the protection of the UCH lying in its national territory, in the contiguous zone, on the continental shelf, and in its exclusive economic zone; the monitoring of environmental impacts to UCH; the promotion of scientific research, education and public awareness of UCH; the collaboration in international projects that dealt with submerged heritage of Portuguese origin, and the preservation of an effective and up-to-date inventory of UCH.

Regarding this last obligation, the DHS – which is one of the oldest institutional databases on shipwrecks in the world – can hardly be defined as a proper inventory of UCH (MONTEIRO, 2018). First, because it is basically a mere list of historically documented shipwrecks – and not a list of actual UCH sites. Therefore, nowadays, its main purpose is to serve as a quantitative and qualitative tool in order to assess the magnitude and importance of the potential shipwreck sites of a certain area, undergoing environmental studies prior to construction works or dredging. Secondly, the DHS is very incomplete. In a case study recently developed by us for the coast of the municipality of Sines, Portugal, it was found that of the 71 shipwrecks we managed to document for those waters, only 17 were recorded in the DHS, i.e., in general, the DHS only inventories 3 out of 10 shipwrecks that have actually occurred. Also, there are hundreds of phantom or incorrect entries in the DHS. In the above-mentioned case study of Sines, there are 3 records in triplicate for the same ship; there are two duplicate records of a steamer that actually sank in Sagres, 130 km south of Sines; and there are also two data entries for which no record was found in the references indicated. Finally, due to its haphazardly original design, it has scarce scientific value, as shipwreck entries are almost never supported by archival references. This means that the official information provided by the government regarding potential UCH lying in Portuguese waters cannot be peer reviewed by historians without them actually discarding the existing DHS and starting a new one from scratch.

IV

As seen above, there are two main problems regarding the data contained within the DHS: its lack of reliability and its fragmentary nature. To these, we can add a third issue: how limited is the use of the present DHS regarding the new diplomatic, environmental and social concerns tied to UCH, all raised within the last two decades.

In Ireland, shipwreck information is used by maritime-tourist operators, fostering the Blue Economy (KELLEHER, 2007); in Spain (NOTARIO ZUBICOA & TUDELA SÁNCHEZ), and the Netherlands (PARTHESIUS, 2014), shipwrecks serve as cultural diplomatic resources, and their existence in foreign waters is a root cause for the establishment of scientific cooperation agreements between former colonies and colonizers; in the United States and in other European Union countries, UCH inventories are used to inventory dive sites (FABI, 2020) or as predictive models for the location of certain shipwrecks which still contain vast quantities of pollutants and/or explosives inside, and pose even today serious environmental threats (LANDQUIST *et al,* 2013; ALCARO *et al,* 2007).

In order to solve, or at least to mitigate, all those issues, a mixed team of scientists and non-researcher citizen scientists delineated a pilot project that started tentatively in 2011, was promoted in 2018, and funded with €300.000 from the Portuguese National Budget in 2021. The area chosen by the team is the so called Alentejo Littoral, an area that encompasses the Sado river on its 50 km long westward channel, then the Atlantic Troia Peninsula and the 93 km long stretch of coast that runs from Troia to Sardao cape, passing Melides and Sines.

Facing the sea, Grandola – a county 120 km south of Lisbon, with an area of 814 km^2 and 15.000 inhabitants – possesses the world's seventh longest continuous beach: a 66 km long stretch of dunes and small deserted inlets that, on its northernmost end, protects a deep estuarine area that serves as a very sheltered harbour. Within the Peninsula, the port of Setubal has been an important maritime landmark since immemorial times, while the Sado river flows from Alcacer do Sal, a small town that boasts both dwellings from the Iron Age and an important Roman city dating from the 2nd century AD.

The estuarine river environment is well represented by the palaphytic harbour of Carrasqueira, as well as by the rice fields of Comporta, where several Mesolithic shell middens, dated between 7500 and 5000 BP, have been located. More than 100 human burials were reported in them, a tell-tale sign of a hunter-gatherer behavior that can be linked to later habitat sites dated between the 4th and 3rd millennia BP. From that period on, human occupation of that area has been continuous – sites and artifacts from all ages and periods have been found here and there, with the most notable ones coming from upriver. The most important site on this stretch of the Sado river is Abul, a Phoenician enclave that disseminated oriental goods to the *hinterland*, with some artifacts as exotic as Greek attic pottery or Egyptian scarabs from the 6th century BC being found in graves at Alcacer do Sal.

During the Roman period, Strabo praised the importance of this region as a port. Sign of that importance to the Roman world are the fisheries at the mouth of the Sado River, at Troia, where two large fish processing factories have been uncovered. These factories were dated from mid-first century AD, the reign of Claudius, and have remained in operation until the middle of the fifth century AD. Further south, one finds the small village of Melides, nowadays a disappearing lagoon, once part of a vast expanse of water. This huge aqueous body is formed by the ensemble of the Pera, Sancha and Santo Andre lagoons, that used to connect the Roman city of Mirobriga – a town inhabited from at least the Iron Age until the 4th century AD and that now sits 12 kms inland – with the sea. Later on, this area became the site of the largest Islamic naval base of the Peninsula in the early Medieval times. It also provided the Christian Military Order of Santiago with a perfect harbor from which to export salt into Northern Europe. Salt trade, mainly with the Hanseatic League, flourished until the late 19th century.

Bearing all this in mind, the aims of this pilot project are to use underwater cultural heritage as a common, shared heritage, working with local communities on topics such as identity, community feelings and the sense of meaning and continuity. The project intends to develop cooperation with international partners, under Rule 8 of CPUCH, in order to build capacity for intervention in nautical archaeology; train young maritime archaeologists in a multi-disciplinary perspective; disseminate and publish all the information available, mainly via community outreach programs; share the project's results with the public at large, as per Rule 7 of CPUCH; further document written and oral sources that could help our understanding of the maritime history of the littoral Alentejo; and produce a workable, scientifically sound DHS that can serve as a primer for the remaining Portuguese coastline.

As with any harbour and estuarine river that have been under constant use for the past millennia, it is expected that several ships have been lost in the area under research. These could range anywhere, from Phoenician ships to salt trade schooners and late 19th century steamers. But, in spite of all this potential, not a single wreck has been found up until 2011, when this project started out, on a very experimental and small scale. As a matter of fact, it was the public announcement of the project's starting that led to the very first wreck site reporting, by fishermen and local divers. One such example is the site of the Troia 1, and the other is the suspected wreck site of Comporta, from where gold coins and cannons have been reported.

V

The research team's first goal is to survey and locate shipwreck sites, in order to enrich Portugal's Underwater Cultural Heritage database. This is being done with a mix of archival research, tapping into site information held by fishermen and other sea users, and with remote sensing surveys, using Autonomous Underwater Vehicles (AUVs) carrying side scan sonar and magnetometer.

Archival research was conducted between 2014 and 2019 in Portuguese national archives, such as Torre do Tombo and Arquivo Historico Ultramarino; in international archives, such as those of Simancas, Marseille, and the General Archive of the Indies in Seville; in libraries, such as Ajuda, Nacional and Evora; online file repositories, such as *Lloyds Register of Shipping*, and Government Journals and online newspaper archives. Interviews with sea users and other maritime cultural, economic and social stakeholders are still taking place. The information provided by them regarding UCH is then correlated with an open access geographical information system and targeted for remote sensing surveys (GREGORY, & MANDERS, 2015).

If wreck sites are indeed located, it will be necessary to conduct preliminary test probes, in order to assess their condition (POPTA *et al*, 2018). The purposes of the probes are to determine the presence and the extent of preservation of the ship's remains; to identify the site through the location of chronologically and culturally significant diagnostic artifacts, i.e., to correlate the date, nationality, and cargo and/or artifacts present on the located shipwreck site with the known historic record; and to produce visually impacting imagery for documentation, public dissemination and future fund-raising efforts.

VI

Although the 2021-2030 United Nations Agenda for Sustainable Development states, in broad terms, that it aims to conserve and use the oceans, seas and maritime resources for sustainable development, it fails to consider maritime cultural heritage as an important aspect in achieving coastal and ocean sustainability (TRAKADAS *et al*, 2019).

Henderson rightly argues that the maritime archaeological community has not so far directly addressed the 2030 Agenda and is, instead, solely focused on the preservation and protection of the UCH resource rather than musing on what it can offer in terms of economic, social and cultural benefits. The probable outcome of this shortcoming will be that maritime archaeology will continue to be a resource-poor discipline, seen by many governments and institutions as a further financial burden they are not willing to afford (HENDERSON, 2019) – a case perfectly revealed by recent research on Blue Tourism in Portugal (DIAS *et al*, 2019).

We argue that, even in a context of limited financial and organizational capacity, if good practices, tools and methods are used, proper research and promotion of UCH can deliver valuable educational and tourist resources. By using UCH assets for the benefit of the local and global communities, historical and archaeological research can help tourism and heritage practitioners create new products (KARRO *et al,* 2019). These tourism products, drawn from human and cultural maritime landscapes and their gastronomy, legends, festivities, resources and traditions, will generate not only tangible revenue, but also a local drive to preserve and strengthen the memories and the identities of local maritime communities.

Taking into account that coastal and maritime tourism are Europe's most important tourism subsector, archaeologists and other maritime cultural managers simply cannot afford not using UCH as a tourism promoter (UNESCO, 2015). As UCH tourism must be considered a respectful sector in tourism – always safeguarding the integrity of the archaeological sites and establishing synergies with other sectors of the blue economy – it must involve the local communities in its protection and sustainable exploration, in coherence with the natural and social environment in which the UCH is located (MANDERS, 2012). Hence, the importance of governance and of the implementation of a Citizen Science matrix.

Let's look again at the *Nuestra Señora del Rosario* potential wreck site. Though still undiscovered, it is for now an historical episode that stimulates the imagination, provides a sense of mystery, adventure and exploration. In other words, it generates emotions. It is transnational, connecting the past and the present of the two Iberian countries, as well as of Mexico, Cuba and the United Kingdom, and is capable of attracting audiences looking for experiences with high added value in active tourism (PÉREZ-REVERTE MAÑAS, 2020). If the wreck site is found; if substantial, diagnostic, portions of the ship's hull are preserved, if its cargo can be recovered, then the ship's stories will be able to materialize into an exhibition.

The first ever treasure-carrying ship to be archaeologically excavated and presented will certainly provide – with the wealth of information now available from the archives – a myriad of personal and intimate stories. These stories will compose a bigger, larger narrative – a story about emigrants that went to another, far away new world, and got rich with extractive colonialism, only to die on a Portuguese beach, their pockets weighted down by the then useless silver coins.

References

ALCARO, Luigi; AMATO, Ezio; CABIOCH, Fanc'h; FARCHI, Cristina; GOURIOU, Vincent & WRUBL, Carlo (2007) *DEEPP PROJECT, Development of European guidelines for Potentially Polluting shipwrecks - Database for Potentially Polluting Wrecks within the Mediterranean Cetacean Sanctuary*. Istituto Centrale per la Ricerca scientifica e tecnologica Applicata al Mare / Centre de documentation de recherché et d'expérimentations sur les pollutions accidentelles des eaux.

ALVES, Francisco (2007) "Underwater Cultural Heritage Management and Ship Archaeology – the Portuguese Experience" *in* SATCHELL, Julie & PALMA, Paola (eds.) *Managing the Marine Cultural Heritage:*

Defining, Acessing and Managing the Resource. York: English Heritage/Council for British Archaeology, pp. 41-47.

ARGYROPOULOS, Vassilike & STRATIGEA, Anastasia. (2019). "Sustainable Management of Underwater Cultural Heritage: The Route from Discovery to Engagement-Open Issues in the Mediterranean". *Heritage*. 2. 10.3390/heritage2020098.

BLOT, Jean-Yves & BLOT, Maria Luísa (1992) "De la glaciation de Würm aux derniers temps de la marine à voile: Éléments pour une carte archéologique du patrimoine immergé au Portugal", pp. 425-454; *idem*, "Problématique d'une recherche entreprise pour le compte du Museu Nacional de Arqueologia (M.N.A.) de Lisbonne dans le cadre du programme de recensement du patrimoine culturel immergé" in *O Arqueólogo Português*, IV-8/10, pp.469-485.

EC (2019) *Blue Growth: opportunities for marine and maritime sustainable growth.* European Commission, 2012. COM (2012) 494 final.

GMA (2019) *The EU blue economy report 2019*. Directorate-General for Maritime Affairs and Fisheries for the European Commission.

DIAS, Álvaro; PATULEIA, Mafalda & DE BRITO, Mónica. (2019). *Managing, Marketing, and Maintaining Maritime and Coastal Tourism*. IGI Global. 10.4018/978-1-7998-1522-8.

DUNCAN, Brad & GIBBS, Martin (2015) *Please God Send Me a Wreck: Responses to Shipwreck in a 19th Century Australian Community*. Springer.

FABI, Gianna (2020). "The ADRIREEF database: a comprehensive collection of natural/artificial reefs and wrecks in the Adriatic Sea". *Earth System Science Data*, 10.5194/essd-2020-384.

FOSSE, Jeremie; GONZÁLEZ, Alejandro & TONAZZINI, Debora (2019). *BLUE TOURISM - The Transition Towards Sustainable Coastal and Maritime Tourism in World Marine Regions*. 10.13140/RG.2.2.31175.62885.

GREGORY, D. & MANDERS, Martijn eds. (2015) B*est practices for locating, surveying, assessing, monitoring and preserving underwater archaeological sites*. SASMAP Guideline Manual 2. Amersfoot.

HENDERSON, Jon (2019). "Oceans without History? Marine Cultural Heritage and the Sustainable Development Agenda". *Sustainability*. 11. 5080. 10.3390/su11185080.

KARRO, Krista; ROIO, Maili; TEVALI, Riikka; LEHTIMÄKI Marianne & TIKKANEN, Sallamaria (2019) *Status report on socio-economic aspects when linking maritime and underwater cultural heritage to Blue Economy sectors*. BalticRIM - Baltic Sea Region Integrated Maritime Cultural Heritage Management.

KELLEHER, Connie (2007) "Quantification of the Underwater Archaeological Resource in Ireland as a Means to its Management and Protection" in SATCHELL, Julie & PALMA, Paola eds. *Managing the Marine Cultural Heritage: Defining, Acessing and Managing the Resource*. York: English Heritage/Council for British Archaeology, pp. 5-16.

LANDQUIST, H; HASSELLÖV, I-M.; ROSEN, L.; LINDGREN, J. F. & DAHLLÖF, I. (2013) "Evaluating the needs of risk assessment methods of potentially polluting shipwrecks", in *Journal of Environmental Management*, vol. 119, pp. 85-92, https://doi.org/10.1016/j.jenvman.2012.12.036.

MANDERS, Martijn (2012) "Underwater Archaeological Resources" in *Training Manual for the UNESCO Foundation Course on the Protection and Management of Underwater Cultural Heritage in Asia and the Pacific*. Bangkok: UNESCO Office Bangkok and Regional Bureau for Education in Asia and the Pacific, Unit 4 pp. 3-19.

MARTINS, Adolfo Silveira; CARVALHO, António & FERNANDES, Maria Amélia (2014) *O Tempo Resgatado ao Mar*. Lisboa: Museu Nacional de Arqueologia/ Imprensa Nacional Casa da Moeda / Direcção Geral do Património Cultural.

MONTEIRO, Alexandre (2000) "Carta Arqueológica Subaquática dos Açores: metodologia, utilização e resultados na gestão do património cultural subaquático" in *Actas do 3º Congresso de Arqueologia Peninsular*, vol. VIII. Porto: ADECAP/ Universidade de Trás-os-Montes e Alto Douro, pp. 497-523.

MONTEIRO, Alexandre & PINHEIRO, Sérgio (2012), " O naufrágio da nau da prata *Nuestra Señora del Rosario* (Tróia, 1589)", in *Almadan*, II série, nº 17, 2012. Centro de Arqueologia de Almada, pp. 147-159.

MONTEIRO, Alexandre; PINHEIRO, Sérgio; MARTINS, Adolfo; FIGUEIREDO, João & CASIMIRO, Tânia (2012) "The Underwater Cultural Heritage Database: regional contributions from the Madeira archipelago and the Sado/Grândola estuarine complex", in *Actas das Segundas Jornadas de Engenharia Hidrográfica*, Lisboa: Instituto Hidrográfico, pp. 337-340.

MONTEIRO, Alexandre (2018) "Quando o X não marca o lugar: o Caça-Minas 'Roberto Ivens' e a Base de Dados Endovélico" *in* COSTA, Paulo & VALENTIM, Carlos (eds.) *A Marinha Portuguesa na Grande Guerra (1916- 1918): o Afundamento do Caça-Minas 'Roberto Ivens'*. Lisboa: Comissão Cultural de Marinha, pp. 205-210.

NOTARIO ZUBICOA, Carolina & TUDELA SÁNCHEZ, Marta coords. (2009) *Libro Verde. Plan Nacional de Protección del Patrimonio Cultural Subacuático Español*. Cartagena: Ministerio de Cultura.

PARTHESIUS, Robert (2014) *Inventory and analyses of archival sources in the Dutch East India Company (VOC) archives in the Netherlands in order to contribute to possible locations and identification of VOC shipwrecks off the Western Australian Coast*. Centre for International Heritage Activities, Western Australian Museum Report No. 310.

PÉREZ-REVERTE MAÑAS, Carlota (2020) *Tourism Toolkit for European Maritime and Underwater Cultural Heritage*. TIDE Atlantic Network for Developing Historical Maritime Tourism project, Interreg Atlantic Area Programme. Cádiz: Universidad de Cádiz.

POPTA, Yftinus & VAN HOLK, A. (2018) "Where are the Shipwrecks of the Zuiderzee? A new version of the Shipwreck Database Flevoland (3.0), based on spatial and archaeohistorical research into wreck sites in the province of Flevoland" in *Palaeohistoria* 58/60 (2107/2018), University of Groningen, pp. 191-228. DOI:10.21827/5beab08b4d742.

TRAKADAS, Athena; FIRTH, Antony; GREGORY, David; ELKIN, Dolores; GUERIN, Ulrike; HENDERSON, Jon; KIMURA, Jun; SCOTT-IRETON, Della; SHASHOUA, Yvonne; UNDERWOOD, Chris & VIDUKA, Andrew (2019) "The Ocean Decade Heritage Network: Integrating Cultural Heritage Within the UN Decade of Ocean Science 2021–2030". *Journal of Maritime Arch*aeology, 14, 153–165 (2019). https://doi.org/10.1007/s11457-019-09241-0.

UNESCO (2015) *UNESCO's Work on Culture and Sustainable Development: Evaluation of a Policy Theme*. 2015, IOS/EVS/PI/145 REV.2

CHAPTER 10

BRIDGING THE GAP: THE IMPORTANCE OF INTERCULTURALITY IN BUSINESS RELATIONS

ISABEL TORRES
ISCAP – P.PORTO, POLYTECHNIC OF PORTO

The world is a small village - the last generations have been hearing this since middle school. Due to globalisation and the technological advances that progress nonstop, geographical frontiers are less and less imponent when it comes to culture. But how does that impact us? It is not all about sharing and experiencing new things, there are also obstacles that arise when dealing with people from different backgrounds, with different cultures, ideals, and ways of seeing the world. Symmetrically, when it comes to business, it is not simple to communicate interculturally, as this is not a given capacity but rather a soft skill that needs to be worked on. There are several factors that need to be considered in order to communicate effectively or one might end up being misinterpreted, which can cost millions to companies. Therefore, the notion of interculturality and the respective study are a factor of extreme – albeit currently still underestimated – importance for the business sphere.

Before developing this question, it is vital that we define the concept of culture, which very often is opposed to nature, and considered, according to Raymond Williams, one of the most complex words of the English language. While nature is what produces culture, culture is what, simultaneously, changes and shapes nature (Williams, 1958). Trying to deconstruct this opposition is an endless pursue. In the present time, regardless of all the meanings ascribed to culture throughout History, culture is a much wider concept that vouches for a refusal both of complete autonomy of spirit, and of the existence of an organic determinism. Culture is, essentially, what happens in the middle, somewhere between those two concepts (Eagleton, 2013). In the words of Raymond Williams:

> Culture is ordinary: that is the first fact. Every human society has its own shape, its own purposes, its own meanings. Every human society expresses these, in institutions, and in arts and learning. The making of a society is the finding of common meanings and directions, and its growth is an active debate and amendment under the pressures of experience, contact, and discovery, writing themselves into the land. The growing society is there, yet it is also made and remade in every individual mind. The making of a mind is, first, the slow learning of shapes, purposes, and meanings, so that work, observation, and communication are possible. Then, second, but equal in importance, is the testing of these in experience, the making of new observations, comparisons, and meanings. A culture has two aspects: the known meanings and directions, which its members are trained to; the new observations and meanings, which are offered and tested. These are the ordinary processes of human societies and human minds, and we see through them the nature of a culture: that it is always both traditional and creative; that it is both the most ordinary common meanings and the finest individual meanings. We use the word culture in these two senses: to mean a whole way of life - the common meanings; to mean the arts and learning - the special processes of discovery and creative effort. (Williams, 1958, in McGuigan, 2014, pp. 2-3)

Culture is, in conclusion, the universal within the individual. But what about corporate culture? Is there also a "universal within the individual" when referring to business? Stanley Davis argues that corporate culture is a shared pattern of beliefs and values that gives meaning to the members of a given company or institution and that equally and indirectly dictates the rules of behaviour in the organisation (Davis, 1984). Similarly, according to Investopedia (2020), corporate culture "refers to the beliefs and behaviours that determine how a company's employees and management interact and handle outside business transactions". The shared values end up shaping the sense of a group, be it a nation or any other kind of community, and so, of course, the sense of a corporation too. Essentially, the same principle is applied, only the context has shifted.

Consequently, what happens when two or more different cultures collide is called interculturality. According to Dietz (2018), the term has got more complex than that, since it now also encompasses the relations between majorities and minorities and these relations are not simply dictated by culture, but also by language, religion, and other factors (Dietz, 2018). Whether they are different nationalities or different corporations, interculturality is always a sort of third space, that is born in the middle

(Bhabha, 1994). Under Homi Bhabha's theory of hybridity, cultural dimensions can no longer be understood as being homogeneous or self-contained. This implies that the third space represents – quite literally but also abstractly – a place in the middle, a materialisation of the "meet me halfway" expression. In the words of Michaela Wolf:

> There is a Third Space, which can neither be reduced to the self nor the other, neither to the First nor to the Third World, neither to the master nor to the slave. Meaning is produced beyond cultural borders and is principally located in the Third Space, a sort of "in-between space" located between existing referential systems and antagonisms. (Wolf, 2000)

According to Sarmento (2014), interculturality is oriented towards interaction and societal cohesion, without the reductionist attitude of generalising and putting everyone within the same culture into the same box. However, what the author is keen to emphasise is the role of communication as the most important vehicle by which "an intercultural approach aims to facilitate dialogue, exchange and reciprocal understanding between people of different backgrounds" (Wood et al. 2006, as cited in Sarmento, 2014). Therefore, the first step towards interculturality is the existence of a *lingua franca*, which we all know, nowadays, is English. But how and why did English come to be the language of all?

The strong presence of the English language in the global context can be explained, in a first moment, through the story of the expansion of the British Empire. One of the arguments used to validate this expansion was based on the sense of responsibility, on the belief that colonial subjects required leadership, and that otherwise they would fall into anarchy and chaos. This, alongside with several other factors such as economic, political, and military power, asserted the authority of the English native speakers and, gradually, spread their language and implemented it as the go-to form of communication between groups that did not share the same first language. With the rise of the concept of globalization as the coexistence of different cultures, the idea of a language that actively supported Bhabha's third space theory was even more needed and, therefore, explored. The English language became even more popular since it allowed international cooperation, better prospects of employment, access to Western knowledge by non-Western cultures, and the chance to achieve and enforce influence in the business world (Crystal, 2009).

In turn, when discussing corporate interculturality, it is critical to address the weight of power relations, which are equally very much influenced by language itself. This omnipresence of the English language around the world creates an advantage for anyone who speaks it, either native speakers or anyone who learns it by choice or cultural influence. At a first glance, it is easy to understand that the existence of a *lingua franca* democratises access to business and art. The belief that speaking English provides better opportunities in life has shaped the way many parents bring up their children over the last decades. However, a closer analysis will show us the simultaneous and underlying weight of power relations, caused by factors such as social status, level of education, colour of skin, or gender, even when one is fluent in the business language.

According to Sarmento (2015), the way societies or any other groups see the world and see each other influences their interrelationships. It is easy to understand this when looking at discrimination. A community with a more rigid mental structure about racial, social, religious and gender differences, among others, will be much more prone to discrimination, while a community with an open-minded attitude will be much more accepting and tolerant. In short, the way people look at interculturality will define how different cultures are represented and how the majority culture exerts power over minority cultures (Sarmento, 2015).

Bearing that in mind, intercultural studies were born to teach us how to bridge these gaps, not only according to one's level of English, but also according to every other factor that encompasses cultures and the differences that exist among them. This is done not to diminish differences, because they enrich us, but to take advantage of the richness of sharing, always ensuring an effective communication, no matter how different we might be. This is an aspect that has been gaining more and more importance, especially nowadays, in view of the current health situation, whose social effects are incalculable. In the words of Mansouri and Elias:

> In the context of persisting challenges and crises ranging from socio-cultural discrimination and economic inequalities to environmental degradation, and in the face of new acute health crises linked to global pandemics, the global community urgently needs meaningful dialogue, engagement, and collaboration to overcome these problems in inclusive and sustainable ways. These complex challenges require new approaches that transcend cultural differences to harness the benefits of diversity that individuals and communities can bring to the collective task of achieving global peace and sustainable development. (Mansouri and Elias, 2021, pp. 1-2)

Proportionally, when addressing interculturality in business relations, the dialogue must culminate in profit. To do so, in a space that makes room for exchange, communication must serve as a tool to promote both integration and innovation. As several authors have stated, recognizing cultural differences, as well as possessing intercultural communication skills, will not only help companies overcome the communication gap when participating in international trade negotiations, but will also help managers handle cultural differences more effectively inside the company (Washington et al, 2012). Nowadays, companies must consider internationalisation as one of the most important factors in their development, due to the extreme globalisation that all sectors have experienced in recent years. Because of this, interculturality gains a role of enormous value in the world of business, as geographical limitations no longer exist. Internationalisation and interculturality are gaining an immeasurable importance, as thy have become essential for the success of start-ups and growing companies, and for their contribution to sustainable development. There are even emerging companies that have already been created and forged by these concepts (Cerqueira et al, 2021). Another factor that benefits the increase in internationalisation and the consequent importance of interculturality is that younger generations have a greater interest in international work experiences, which will require a greater ability to adapt by the host companies (Neeley, 2017).

A company open to hiring employees regardless of their background, race, religion, culture, and sexual orientation, is the epitome of inclusivity and should be a goal for any business. However, this is not something easy to achieve. Even if "an inclusive team gifts the company with different backgrounds, life experiences and points of view that can be the company's strong suit, a way to attract new talent and enrichment for the team members themselves" (Font, 2020), managing an intercultural team is always a great challenge. The cost of poor management is not simply the absence of reward; it can also have other dangerous consequences for the business. However, I believe that staying on the fringes of interculturality and inclusion can be even more harmful for a company in the 21st century. Different perspectives will result in different approaches when trying to solve a problem, which means that an intercultural team will be able to work on the solution while considering more perspectives and possibilities than a non-intercultural team. It is often said that two heads think better than one, but what if there are several heads and they all think differently? Wouldn't we have many more possibilities of covering a larger area of ground? Yet, to do so effectively, one must face several obstacles, such as lack of financing, cultural issues, and unfair use of unpaid work (Aksenkina, 2018). According to the author, a company must follow certain steps in order to ensure the success of its intercultural team component. The author suggests those steps to be:

- Having a native person on the team.
- Being an active member of the start-up ecosystem, in order to attend events and be able to ask for help or advice from more experienced people.
- Work on your own skills of cross-cultural communication and global thinking.
- Prepare all the paperwork in advance and be aware and ready for possible bureaucracy bottlenecks (e.g. bringing someone in from another country).
- Use a lean start-up methodology.
- Keep an open mind and remember that one's background is not the most important (Aksenkina, 2018).

Simultaneously, and according to Bourbon (2020), a company going international must consider the different economic, social, and cultural realities that coexist in the new markets in which it will operate. In accordance with Washington et al (2012), Bourbon (2020) states that these companies, as well as those that receive employees from abroad, must consider the same factors in the management of their human resources. Considering the dynamic scenario of economic globalisation, now brutally disrupted by the crisis of the COVID-19 pandemic, interculturality becomes fundamental for insuring coexistence, effective communication, and interaction (Cerqueira et al, 2021). In the words of the authors:

> In business, where money rules but not reigns, that is: although, seen as the aim, goal, main objective, in reality, and marked by this fluent world, where anyone can be anywhere in any given time, to be hybrid, to be international and to speak *interculturality* fluently, is to create power: power to reign. Meaning that the power of knowledge is the fundamental approach to reach money; having money and knowledge is the epiphany of the globalised world. (Cerqueira et al, 2021, p. 8)

Indeed, knowledge is important, but intercultural knowledge is just as important. As the authors confirm, an effective and lasting business relationship is built over trust, flexibility, accessibility, and communication, based on secure channels of contact. People need to be prepared to cross the globe in a matter of minutes and approach different interlocutors, who have different backgrounds and mindsets. This goes to say that organisations must carefully consider their foreign and domestic presence and, for this reason, interculturality becomes a necessity (Cerqueira et al, 2021).

The COVID-19 pandemic has only further accentuated the need for an intercultural approach in business relations. According to UNESCO (2020), the pandemic has increased injustice, inequality, and insecurity, while highlighting humanity's interconnectedness and interdependence. This has placed an unprecedented pressure on societies' capacities for intercultural understanding, at a time when unity and collaboration are needed more than ever. The same applies to business, and this is the reason why communication and corporate culture are now hopelessly interdependent. Nowadays, a company cannot exist without a digital presence, and it is imperative that companies have a strong cultural awareness when installing and working on that presence. Stereotypes, common sense, and ethnocentric perspectives very quickly lead to failure and the only way to avoid that mistake is by creating a positive communication channel through clarity and accessibility, that recognises and manages diversity. Change management and adaptability to the diversity of markets are keys to succeed in the hybrid world in which we live (Cerqueira et al, 2021).

Bearing that in mind, Corporate Social Responsibility (CSR) should be mandatory when creating or developing a business, since it encompasses the adaptability to diversity that the authors mention. In fact, according to Amir et al. (2013), a good CSR strategy might be the one thing saving a company during times of change. In the words of the authors, "When these [socially responsible] companies implement change, stakeholders that might be affected by the organizational change and activities have the climate of trust, so they accept the change as they know that the company would not adopt any immoral approaches" (Amir *et al*, 2013, p. 53). This climate of trust will also be of value when dealing with the previously mentioned intercultural teams and the possible problems that can arise from it. One of CSR's focal points regards employees' wellbeing at all levels, one of the objectives of this point being to help foreigners understand the organisational culture they are becoming a part of. Again, in Amir *et al*,'s words:

> Change management would be effective in those companies which have effective CSR policies because CSR improves employees' perceptions of the company, and they will be motivated to adopt those policies. When a company has CSR initiatives, employees are prouder of and committed to the organization. CSR does make a unique contribution to organizational commitment. (Amir *et al.*, 2013, p. 55)

Although there are no strict laws about the implementation of CSR, only a series of guidelines, organizations recognize that their tangible economic and financial success is necessarily linked to their environmental and social performance and are now focusing on the integration of sustainable practices as a competitive advantage. This attitude aims to promote a special attention to the three dimensions of sustainability – environmental, social, and economic – within the business sphere. The theory argues that corporations are members of the moral community and therefore hold economic, legal, ethical, and philanthropic responsibilities, which, amongst others, includes ensuring the well-being of their consumers and employees (Zee, 2020).

Considering all arguments, CSR can be defined as "a management concept whereby companies integrate social and environmental concerns in their business operations and interactions with their stakeholders" and/or as "the way through which a company achieves a balance of economic, environmental and social imperatives" (UNIDO, 2021). The ultimate goal of CSR is to create shared value while understanding that corporate success and social welfare are interdependent. In other words, everything affects everything, in the ordinary world, as well as in the business world (Zee, 2020). This theory seems to have been supported *avant-la-lettre* by the poet Fernando Pessoa, in his 1926 essay on economics and trade. In his words:

> A merchant, whoever he may be, is but a servant of the public, or of a public; and he receives a payment, which he calls his "profit", for the rendering of this service. Now everyone who serves must, it seems to us, seek to please those he serves. To do this, it is necessary to study those who are served - but to study them without prejudice or anticipation; starting, not from the principle that others think like us, or should think like us - because in general, they do not think like us -, but from the principle that, if we want to serve others (to profit from it or not), it is we who must think like them: what we have to see is how they actually think, and not how it would be pleasant or convenient for us if they thought. (...) The study of the public, that is, of the markets, is of three orders - economic, psychological, and social. That is, to enter a market, whether domestic or foreign, it is necessary: 1) to know the conditions of economic acceptance of the article, and those under which the competition works, and in which it offers; 2) to know the character of the buyers, in order, apart from questions of price, to know how best to present, distribute and claim the article; 3) to find out what special circumstances, if any, of a deep social or political nature, or of a superficial fashion or of the moment, require certain corrections in the result of the two previous studies. (Pessoa, 1926)

The author argues that a merchant – to read "businessman" – that does not consider economic, social, and psychological studies, lives only in the present and has a commercial house with no future. They are hurting their own business because they ignore that showing intelligence and studying the conveniences and needs of others is a demonstration of the brand's position and will ensure customer loyalty (Pessoa, 1926). Nowadays, this means that an entrepreneur and businessperson that does not consider interculturality as an essential part of their business from the day one of its creation, is condemned to failure. If they must serve the public, they must first understand it and their needs, and it is no longer enough to simply speak the *lingua franca*. One needs to pair this skill with intercultural skills, so that an effective communication and understanding can take place.

Inherently, as human beings, we need to feel that we add value to the people and the world around us, and that we do not simply work or buy in order to give response to a financial need for subsistence (Sinek, 2011). Building a good relationship with all the stakeholders of one's project or business is a fundamental element for a strong organizational culture and will certainly be a product differentiator that attracts both the targeted consumers and the best workers in the field for the company's team. CSR guidelines are divided into six points[1], two of which refer to consumers and employees, stating that their needs should be equally heard. By listening to those people's needs, their culture must be also considered, therefore intercultural skills must be taken into account. In a world where a company has no chance but to go global, it is crucial that businesspeople have the tools to do it successfully and intercultural skills are capacities that one cannot, definitely, ignore. Communication is indeed key, but it does not serve its purpose unless it is accompanied by true and deep cultural understanding.

That being said, we must stop looking at cultural differences as an obstacle and start seeing them as a competitive advantage. While older generations had to face the challenge of technologies in order to adapt to the hybrid world they were living and doing business in, contemporary business agents must take the challenge of intercultural communication. Failing or succeeding to do so will dictate the future of one's project or business.

Sources

Aksenkina, E. (2018). How Multicultural Startups Manage and Succeed in Finland [Doctoral dissertation]. https://www.theseus.fi/bitstream/handle/10024/149725/Aksenkina_Evgeniya.pdf?sequence=1&isAllowed=y

Amir A., Javaid S., Mahmood Z., & Zafar F. (2013). Effectiveness of Corporate Social Responsibility in Organizational Change Management. *Asian Journal of Managerial Science*, 2(2), 50-55.

[1] Consumers, employees, shareholders/investors, community, environment, and suppliers (Zee, 2020).

https://www.trp.org.in/wp-content/uploads/2016/11/AJMS-Vol.2-No.2-Jul-Dec-2013pp.50-55.pdf

Cerqueira, C., Lamas, M., & Baranovskiy, S. (2021). O papel da Interculturalidade na internacionalização das startups: O caso do programa de aceleração virtual do Eligent Club. *E-Journal of Intercultural Studies*, (8).

Crystal, D. (2009). *English as a global language.* https://doi.org/10.1017/cbo9781139196970

Dietz, G. (2018). Interculturality. *The International Encyclopedia of Anthropology*, 1-19. https://doi.org/10.1002/9781118924396.wbiea1629

Eagleton, T. (2013). *The idea of culture.* John Wiley & Sons.

Font, A. (2020, June 17). The 360° benefits of building an inclusive startup team from day one. EU-Startups. https://www.eu-startups.com/2020/06/the-360-benefits-of-building-an-inclusive-startup-team-from-day-one/

Investopedia. (2020). How to tell if your corporate culture is healthy. https://www.investopedia.com/terms/c/corporate-culture.asp

Mansouri, F., & Elias, A. (2021). The intercultural dialogue index (ICDI): An index for assessing intercultural relations. *Social Indicators Research*. https://doi.org/10.1007/s11205-021-02616-8

McGuigan, J. (2014). *Raymond Williams on culture & society: Essential writings.* https://doi.org/10.4135/9781473914766

Neeley, T. (2017). How to successful work across countries, languages, and cultures and. *Harvard Business Review*. August, 1-5.

Pessoa, F. (1926). A essência do comércio. Arquivo Pessoa: Obra Edita – https://arquivopessoa.net/

Sarmento, C. (2015). *Estudos Interculturais Aplicados: Textos, turismos e tipologias*. Vida Económica.

Sarmento, C. (2014). Interculturalism, multiculturalism, and intercultural studies: Questioning definitions and repositioning strategies. *Intercultural Pragmatics*, 11(4). https://doi.org/10.1515/ip-2014-0026

Sinek, S. (2011). *Start with why: How great leaders inspire everyone to take action.* Penguin UK.

UKEssays. (2017, April 24). Definitions by scholars on corporate culture. UKEssays.com. https://www.ukessays.com/essays/business/definitions-by-scholars-on-corporate-culture-business-essay.php?vref=1

UNESCO. (2020, November 4). Intercultural dialogue during the pandemic: Impact and response. UNESCO.

https://en.unesco.org/news/intercultural-dialogue-during-pandemic-impact-and-response

UNIDO. (2021). What is CSR? UNIDO | United Nations Industrial Development Organization. https://www.unido.org/our-focus/advancing-economic-competitiveness/competitive-trade-capacities-and-corporate-responsibility/corporate-social-responsibility-market-integration/what-csr

Washington, M. C., Okoro, E. A., & Thomas, O. (2012). Intercultural communication in global business: An analysis of benefits and challenges. *International Business & Economics Research Journal*, 11(2), 217. https://doi.org/10.19030/iber.v11i2.6776

Wolf, M. (2000) Chapter 7. *The Third Space in Postcolonial Representation In: Changing the Terms: Translating in the Postcolonial Era.* Ottawa: University of Ottawa Press. http://books.openedition.org/uop/2003

Zee, E. (2020). Lesson 2: Corporate Social Responsibility [Personal Communication].

CHAPTER 11

INTERCULTURAL DIALOGUE IN BUSINESS: MUTUAL BENEFITS AND HUMAN RIGHTS

GEISA OLIVEIRA DARÉ
UNIVERSIDADE ESTADUAL PAULISTA (UNESP)
AND CHARIZE DE OLIVEIRA HORTMANN
UNIVERSITY OF MINHO

1. Introduction

It is well-known and widely discussed that globalization has permanently affected human relations, especially in the business world. With the reduction of the time spent to travel distances, the interconnection of the marketplaces, and the relativization of geographical limits, "companies must now adapt to the new global marketplace to maintain a successful business" (Lawlor 2008, p. 21).

Regarding strategies to survive and add value to the company in the new world scenario, managers must pay attention not only to the demand for technology and information but also to the interculturality that exists at all levels of a company's relations and to the respect for human rights. Interculturality has a wide concept and "is often viewed as a field of study or management tactic" where different cultures interact (Lavanchy, Gajardo, and Dervin 2011, p. 1). This aspect can be observed particularly in the customers, the workers, or the management of the new leadership model of a global society.

The challenges of intercultural dialogue and the fulfillment of human rights are not always easy to solve because cultures have their own codes of conduct, sometimes influenced by religion and/or politics. Nevertheless, the current advantages for business can be compensated by the difficulties encountered along the way and make it worthwhile.

In addition, although following the law is an explicit responsibility of companies, another basic (but not always so evident) responsibility is to respect human rights. John Ruggie (2008, p. 199) stated that:

> Failure to meet this responsibility can subject companies to the courts of public opinion—comprising employees, communities, consumers, civil society, as well as investors—and occasionally to charges in actual courts. Whereas governments define the scope of legal compliance, the broader scope of the responsibility to respect is defined by social expectations—as part of what is sometimes called a company's social license to operate.

Hence, the horizontal effectiveness of human rights becomes a concern not only of the states but also of the enterprises that are willing to follow a corporate culture that considers human rights as an essential part of their business (Ruggie 2008, p. 195).

In this perspective, this chapter aims to analyze the issue of intercultural dialogue in business on the basis of mutual benefits and humanitarian aspects. Also, the advantages and disadvantages of this exchange and some related reflections will be pointed out.

2. Controversial aspects about interculturality and respect of human rights for companies

The countless obstacles and disadvantages that arise with interculturality and the fulfillment of certain human rights in business are undeniable. First, there is the financial slant that does not notice the advantage of investing in human and material resources when adapting the company's internal policy to human rights. The violation of consumer rights such as placing defective or harmful products on the market, with different features from those specified or with the use of misleading advertisement, the use of slave labor, the lack of transparency in management, and tax evasion, among other ploys, are notorious ways to obtain unfair profit.

The financial issue (profit) is an extremely important factor in the business world, especially because the world is fundamentally capitalist, an Anglo-Saxon tradition that assigns a precise function to a company that consists of producing profit (Albert 1992, p. 24). Thus, even today, the profit (that is, roughly speaking, the accumulation of capital) has a significant weight and reflects on the corporate decision-making process.

Second, various situations demand a certain degree of flexibility from a corporation to deal with what is different. Regarding management, for example, some values would need to be rethought, such as correcting an eventual exacerbated nationalism. Because the main concern of a company should be the humanitarian values that focus on social welfare, regardless of the country in which it is installed. In a not-so-distant past, it would have been unthinkable to conceive a company's policy at the cosmopolitan level. Concerning the treatment of consumers, understanding and satisfying the peculiarities of a minority, especially in situations where they are not that expressive, could discourage investment or management.

Nonetheless, multicultural globalization opens the path to a cosmopolitanism scenario, where nationalism is losing its strength. Thus, companies (not only multinationals or transnationals) must invest in the recognition of the other, although the difficulties of dialogue may hinder the relationship.

The companies must also observe human rights not only because of moral necessity but also because they have been a requirement of modern society, as will be explained throughout this chapter.

3. Advantages in respecting human rights: mutual benefits

Although the preamble of the Universal Declaration of Human Rights (UM, 1948) advocates that "every individual and every organ of society" has to promote and respect human rights and that the signatory countries of the pacts pertinent to fundamental rights (UN, 1966) are obliged to comply with and supervise the respect of such rights by entities of the private initiative, the rule is that companies are not automatically submitted to the agreements contained in such diplomas. However, this does not mean that respecting human rights is not generally beneficial, necessary, and interesting for companies.

Feeney (2009) revealed that human rights in the business sphere have become part of the international agenda because of the increased responsibilities of non-state actors in the face of the growing demand for economic and social rights. In this sense, the UN Council (2011) approved the document "Guiding Principles on Business and Human Rights", which, although it is an instrument of soft law, has been widely used as a guideline for non-state organizations to be in coherence with the protection that intends to deliberate fundamental rights.

These guiding principles are aimed at improving standards and actions concerning companies and human rights, in order to achieve satisfactory results, both for individuals and their communities targeting the implementation of sustainable globalization (Conectas, 2012). Furthermore, the so-called Agenda 21 (UN, 2015), to which 179 countries are signatories, foresees among its objectives certain goals, such as goal 09 (industry, innovation, and infrastructure) and goal 08 (decent work and economic growth), whose fulfillment essentially depends on non-state actors. Another important instrument, but nonbinding in the same way, is the International Organization for Standardization (ISO 26000) (Carrieri and Bittencourt, 2005), published in 2010, which institutes international guidelines on corporate social responsibility.

Hence, even if there is no formal document obliging corporations to fulfill human rights rules, such obligation is implicitly brought out by other diplomas besides regional legislation. Presently, companies must promote self-regulated environments to operate in the marketplace because, besides the laws, there is the pressure from modern society, which is becoming more conscious about the human rights issues; thus, enterprises take full responsibility for any external consequence of their practices (Vasconcelos *et al.*, 2012). For example, it can be mentioned that at the beginning of global relations, in the 90s, some companies transferred their operations (Ford, 2016, p. 55), distributing their activities to countries where labor and environment rules would be milder, aiming to maximize profits without considering the social and environmental long-term impacts. However, nowadays, companies that adopt practices capable of violating human rights are no longer tolerated by consumers, or by other companies that have made a commitment with sustainability. When news of companies that subject their employees to degrading situations or cause environmental damage comes to the public, the corporations' market value falls right away, and the companies are forced to pay fines and lose credit in financial institutions. In the same way, other companies that are truly committed to the ideals of sustainability stop acquiring their products, as does the final consumer, for ethical reasons. Conversely, if companies leave their unfavorable reputation and start to adopt sustainable manners, respecting the specific cultural and social elements in which the company intends to operate, the benefits obtained can be seen on a larger scale.

Sustainable development and respect for human rights, based on the environmental, economic, and social pillars, bring a chain of benefits that end up maximizing profits and minimizing eventual losses with mitigation that may occur.

The protection of a balanced environment, the healthiness of the economic system, and social harmony must be understood as interdependent and consequential principles, meaning that one cannot fully exist without the others. In this matter, any sort of damage to one will instantly affect the others; also, any improvement to one will contribute to the others. Enterprises that value these pillars will undoubtedly have long-term advantages, given that a community with greater purchasing power and with no serious social problems will certainly be a better environment for a company to exist.

Specifically, numerous advantages can be highlighted. One advantage is regarding the consumers. Presently, it is known that because of social evolution and the increasing spread of conscious consumption, the identification of corporations with socioenvironmental responsibility certification labels has become a niche market that attracts a larger public (FIEP, 2019) and strengthens brands without the need for major marketing actions (Vogel, 2006).

Moreover, regarding the speed at which information is disseminated, consumers can organize boycotts of companies in an easy way, including through social media, making socially responsible corporations preferred over those that are not committed to the pillars of sustainable development. Similarly, more and more, large corporations are known to have been playing a political role and investing in social projects, besides strengthening their development. This brings a positive return both in terms of improving the image of the corporation among the public and indirectly increasing the living conditions of vulnerable populations, in situations where the state is flawed. Regarding that matter, Elizabeth Melo Rico (1998, p. 155) advocates the following:

> [...] The new corporate social action is looking for something in return, to collaborate with the development of the country, demonstrating that the private initiative must be conscious, have a social responsibility relating to the problems that concern society as a whole. The citizen company is the one that, in addition to fulfilling its economic function, works to improve the quality of life of the entire society. [...]

Another important aspect of companies' compliance with sustainability standards refers to the savings of the possible costs of sanctions. Although sustainable practices are defined by the possibility of preventing, mitigating, and remedying (UN, 2015), research (Bartik, 1988) shows that the study of possible damages and the corresponding preventive measures are better alternatives, in economic terms. Similarly, repairing an existing damage, in general, is recognized to be a more expensive method and potentially incapable of completely restoring the degradation (Andrade, 2008).

Besides all these favorable points directly linked to benefits achieved by enterprises through responsible actions, there is a beneficial counterpart related to workers, which will be explained in more detail in section 3.1.

3.1 Workers and sustainable environment

In terms of sustainability, the first idea that usually comes to mind is the respect for the natural environment through the preservation of resources and the conservation of biosystems. However, there is also a need for sustainability of the artificial environment, and in this spectrum, the conditions offered by enterprises to their employees are included.

The protection of workers' health and safety is regulated by International Labour Organization Convention 155 (ILO, 1981); signatory countries are responsible for supervising the implementation of these measures in companies. Such a tool can be complemented by the guidelines contained in the 17 SDG, especially by objective 8, which concerns decent work. Nonetheless, these guidelines are not always fully implemented by the signatory countries.

As mentioned in the previous section, until recently, some companies chose to migrate their factories and branches to countries where labor rules were more elastic, in order to save on labor costs in developed countries, in which they normally maintain their main headquarters. It turns out that such attitude, besides being currently frowned upon by consumers and investors, is extremely damaging to workers, who can suffer extensive harm because of the insalubrity of the infrastructure and long working hours. This type of global action brings direct losses, giving the company the duty to bear compensation measurements caused by environmental damage and civil liability (Piponnier, 2017) and indirectly by the worsening quality of life of the social environment in which it is inserted. Regarding this, it is worth mentioning that the explanation offered by the governments of the countries for making labor rules more flexible, not offering decent employment conditions, and consequent disregarding of international guidelines, would be the need to increase the economy and to promote an improvement for the generations to come. However, it is clear today that such an argument cannot be sustained, given that the social damage triggered by these practices causes immeasurable harm. Moreover, there remain reflex damages such as public health expenses for workers who operate in unsanitary conditions.

Presently, the marketplace is moving in the opposite direction, toward not repeating the same mistakes of the past and investing more and more in the concept of sustainable work (Bolis, 2014), associating the environmental and social aspects of occupations. In this matter, besides good health and safety conditions for workers, it is possible to include affirmative employment policies through a multidimensional approach, aiming at equal opportunities between genders, people with disabilities, and diverse sexual orientation, with the ultimate scope of benefiting a more egalitarian and fair society instead of exclusively economic interests.

With the increase in globalization and offshore organizations, whether through joint ventures or simply via installing branches (Ferrari, 2012), there is a need to study these new receiving poles and their habits, customs, and culture. In this context, companies must seek to adapt to their values and standards, ensuring a management model that provides the results expected by the headquarters and that also correspond to the demands of the local community, privileging respect for interculturality. Furthermore, global migratory movements that can modify the socioeconomic fabric require companies to seek appropriate training, so that they can obtain the best experience facing new intercultural synthesis. When a company is open to interculturality, it can adapt to new markets and thus get its profits optimized. From a social viewpoint, it also makes minority groups feel included.

3.2 A new leadership model

Because of the current business scenario, based more and more on sustainable and socially responsible practices, the need for a new leadership model emerges, which is the so-called sustainable leader (Rodrigues and Froehlich 2017, p. 129). This concept is based on the premise that the engagement of corporate leaders is essential to leverage issues related to sustainability. The concept of sustainable leadership is under construction since sustainable practices and management efficiency models are instances that are based on dynamism and bear constant improvement.

With that being said, undeniably, a sustainable leader must be open to change and attentive to the social, cultural, and environmental demands of the place in which her7his corporation is located. Ulrich and Smallwood

(2014) define sustainable leadership as attitudes that aim to shape the culture and practices of organizations, strengthening their image before the community and focusing on natural resources. Similarly, Estivalete *et al.* (2016) advocate that sustainable leadership has a focus on social, environmental, and economic factors. The social environment seeks to honor the equality of the community and human capital; the environment intends to preserve the natural capital and the concern with environmental impacts, and the economy relies on the financial viability of the ventures.

Sustainable leadership must seek alignment with compliance practices to improve corporate governance, manage environmental risks, bring transparent management to stakeholders, and seek a good management reputation. In order to standardize and create international standards for this management model, the so-called due diligence in human rights was established.

The human rights due diligence process is not a legal requirement but a set of recommendations and guidelines for managing possible issues and impacts associated with any type of industrial or commercial operation. The procedure is recognized by the UN Guiding Principles on Business and Human Rights. The due diligence process is based on practical guidelines to evaluate risks and impacts in each phase of the project cycle (Mattos and Mattos 2020). The reason for a due diligence process is the necessity to consider human rights impacts associated with business activities, scoping its prevention or mitigation. Otherwise, today's corporate leaders must be aware and seek to adapt to the necessary precepts for sustainable and responsible management. According to Mattos and Mattos (2020, p. 134), making the economic progress of companies compatible with environmental and social protection is a highly complex process, that demands flexibility and adaptation capacity mainly from its leaders.

Finally, besides the socioenvironmental concern in a broad way, the globalized world and corporate offshores raise the issue of the integration of teams with diverse cultures and ideas, as a business challenge. This scenario requires that eventual conflicts shall be treated with sensitivity, responsibility, and respect. Fischer *et al.* (2009, p. 5) stated that it is by recognizing the other that we can know our own self. Furthermore, leaders must be aware that it is essential to know the culture of a particular place when this is a potential targeting market. Consequently, it can be said that respect for diversity and interculturality within an organization is a two-way street because it relates both to the need for empathy and the appreciation of human capital and to the respect for the peculiarities of the local consumer marketplace.

4. Conclusions

Because of the effects of globalization, enterprises had to adapt to the new interconnected reality of the world to survive and add value to their products and services. At this point, the demand for technology and information is evident, but interculturality and respect for human rights are also extremely important. The interculturality discussed here is brought up as a broad concept, regarding the interaction of different cultures. In business, it manifests itself mainly concerning the consumers, the workers, or the management of the new leadership model of a global society.

Nevertheless, some disadvantages for companies in dealing with interculturality and respecting certain human rights still exist. Among them, the financial matter—in a superficial analysis of profit that has existed since the Anglo-Saxon tradition—contrasts the advantages of investing in human and material resources while carrying out this mission. Unfair or illicit competitive practices are profitable and thus are often used by several entrepreneurs. Choosing safety (or standardization) over flexibility is still an existing reason since dealing with humanitarian and intercultural issues requires some effort from the companies.

According to the 1948 Universal Declaration of Human Rights, private initiative is not expressly obliged to promote and respect human rights, but such compliance is healthy and necessary for companies in general. The inclusion of human rights in the framework of business as part of the international agenda is due to the increased economic and social responsibilities of non-state actors. The UN, in 2011 and 2015, as well as the ISO 26000, used soft law instruments to emphasize corporate social responsibility.

The outdated corporate model that pursues profit at any price is no longer viable in a globalized world, where information and humanitarian values have a strong impact on public opinion (consumers, investors, employees, and civil society). Businesses can be benefited on a wide spectrum by taking responsibility for sustainable development from an economic, social, and environmental point of view. Besides strong public pressure, which can promote boycotts of enterprises that fail to fulfill such responsibilities, the enterprises earn long-term benefits, because a more organized community, with better purchasing power, provides an advantageous business environment.

The image of a company that invests in social and environmental projects, and that respects interculturality and human rights, is also positively affected, especially because large corporations have been playing a political role.

Until recently, some companies sought to migrate their factories and branches to countries with more flexible labor rules, causing direct and indirect impacts to workers. Presently, this practice is frowned upon by consumers and investors, and the argument of the recipient countries of such companies that relaxing labor regulations would promote economic improvement has fallen apart. Sustainable work is now a requirement of the relationship between the company and workers, whose implementation requires affirmative policies of employment, equality, and respect for interculturality. This initiative impacts the conquest of new marketplaces and thus the maximization of profits. Socially, it makes cultural minority groups feel included.

With the new leadership model, the figure of the sustainable leader emerges, whose social, environmental, and economic dynamism in the use of sustainable practices can contribute to changing the concept itself. Similarly, the human rights due diligence process for evaluating the risk and impact of each phase of a project's cycle gains strength. Corporate leaders must be very flexible and thoughtful when dealing with the business challenges of integrating teams with different cultures and ideas. Respect for interculturality in business is a two-way street since it relates both to the need for empathy and the appreciation of human capital and to the respect for the peculiarities of the local consumer marketplace.

Hence, the horizontal effectiveness of human rights is currently a real concern for companies, they must follow a corporate culture that respects human rights and interculturality, considering that it is imperative for them to remain in the global marketplace. The entire economic issue that previously existed has made way for the establishment of universal values in terms of the effects of globalization.

References

Albert, Michel. 1992. *Capitalismo versus capitalism*. v. 3. São Paulo: Edições Loyola.

Andrade, Daniel. 2008. "Economia e meio ambiente: aspectos teóricos e metodológicos nas visões neoclássica e da economia ecológica". *Leituras de Economia Política*, No. 14: 1-31. Accessed July 12, 2020. https://www.researchgate.net/profile/Daniel_Andrade/publication/228455195_Economia_e_meio_ambiente_aspectos_teoricos_e_metodologicos_nas_visoes_neoclassica_e_da_economia_ecologica/links/00463522f5827cfae1000000/Economia-e-meio-ambiente-aspectos-teoricos-e-metodologicos-nas-visoes-neoclassica-e-da-economia-ecologica.pdf.

Bartik, Timothy. 1988. "Evaluating the benefits of non-marginal reductions in pollution using information on defensive expenditures." *Journal of Environmental Economics and Management*, V.15: 111-127. Accessed July 12, 2020. https://www.sciencedirect.com/science/article/abs/pii/0095069688900320.

Bolis, Ivan. 2014. "O trabalho para a sustentabilidade: alinhando a estratégia com a operação através de tarefas sustentáveis". Diss., Universidade de São Paulo. Accessed July 13, 2020. https://www.teses.usp.br/teses/disponiveis/3/3136/tde-31122015-103641/publico/Tese_Bolis_Ivan.pdf.

Carrieri, Alexandre, and Bittencourt, Epaminondas. 2005. "Responsabilidade social: ideologia, poder e discurso na lógica empresarial". *RAE-Revista de Administração de Empresas*, V. 45: 10-22. https://rae.fgv.br/rae/vol45-num0-2005/responsabilidade-social-ideologia-poder-discurso-na-logica-empresarial.

Conectas, Direitos Humanos. 2012. "Empresas e Direitos Humanos". São Paulo: *Conectas Direitos Humanos Publishing*, March, 2012. Accessed July 11, 2020. https://www.socioambiental.org/sites/blog.socioambiental.org/files/nsa/arquivos/conectas_principiosorientadoresruggie_mar20121.pdf.

Estivalete, Vânia de Fátima Barros, Andrade, Taís, Costa, Vivian Flores, and Faller, Lisiane Pellini. 2016. "Preocupações com a Sustentabilidade Imbricadas na Missão Social das Organizações: A percepção de empreendedores sociais do Brasil e de Portugal". *Revista de Administração da Universidade Federal de Santa Maria*, V. 9, No. 2: 8-24. Accessed July 18, 2020. http://www.redalyc.org/pdf/2734/273446628002.pdf.

Feeney, Patrícia. 2009. "A luta por responsabilidade das empresas no âmbito das Nações Unidas e o futuro da agenda de advocacy". *Revista Internacional de Direitos Humanos*, V. 6, No. 11: 175-191. Accessed July 3, 2020. https://www.scielo.br/scielo.php?pid=S1806-644520090 00200009&script=sci_arttext&tlng=pt.

Ferrari, Maria Aparecida. 2012. "Gestão da comunicação intercultural nas organizações brasileiras em tempos de globalização". *Comunicologia-Revista de Comunicação da Universidade Católica de Brasília*, V. 5, No. 1: 178-204. Accessed July 13, 2020. https://portalrevistas.ucb.br/index.php/RCEUCB/article/view/3735.

FIEP, Agência Sistema FIEP. 2019. "87% dos consumidores brasileiros preferem comprar de empresas sustentáveis". Accessed July 11, 2020. https://agenciafiep.com.br/2019/02/28/consumidores-preferem-empresas-sustentaveis/.

Fischer, Tânia Maria Diederichs *et al.* 2009. "Competências na Gestão Intercultural: Desafios para a Aprendizagem e Qualificação". *XXXIII Encontro da ANPAD*. Accessed July 18, 2020. http://www.anpad.org.br/admin/pdf/EOR2210.pdf.

Ford, Martin. 2016. *Robôs: A ameaça de um futuro sem emprego*. Translated by José Valle Roberto. Lisboa: Bertrand.

ILO, International Labour Organization. 1981. "Convention 155". International Labour Office, June 3, 1981. https://www.ilo.org/dyn/normlex/en/f?p=NORMLEXPUB:12100:0::N O::P12100_INSTRUMENT_ID:312300.

Lavanchy, Anne, Garjado, Anahy and Dervin, Fred. 2011. "Interculturality at Stake". In *Politics of Interculturality*, edited by Fred Dervin, Anahy Garjado and Anne Lavanchy, 01-25. Newcastle upon Tyne: Cambridge Scholars Publishing.

Lawlor, Benjamin. 2008. "The age of globalization: Impact of information technology on global business strategies". Honors Projects in Computer Information Systems Graduate, Bryant University.

Mattos, Marília Soares de, and Mattos, Nathália Soares de. 2020. "'DUE DILIGENCE' AS AN INSTRUMENT FOR PREVENTION OF POSSIBLE ENVIRONMENTAL DAMAGE IN BUSINESS". In *Natureza, Povos e Sociedade de risco*, edited by Amanda Ferraz da Silveira *et al.*, 133-152.

Piponnier, Florent. 2017. "The 'Rana Plaza' law in France". Responsabilitas Publishing, March. 1, 2017. http://www.responsabilitas.com/blog/rana-plaza-law-in-france/.

Rico, Elizabeth Melo *et al.* 1998. *Avaliação de políticas públicas*: uma questão em debate. São Paulo: Cortez Publishing and IEE/PUC/SP.

Rodrigues, Retiele da Cunha, and Froehlich, Cristiane. 2017. "Liderança sustentável sob a perspectiva de docentes e discentes de um curso de Gestão de Recursos Humanos". *Revista de Gestão do Unilasalle*, *6* (2): 127-141. Accessed July 18, 2020. http://dx.doi.org/10.18316/desenv.v6i2.3507.

Ruggie, John. 2008. "Protect, respect and remedy: A framework for business and human rights". *Innovations: Technology, Governance, Globalization*, v. 3 No. 2: 189-212. Accessed July 11, 2020. https://www.mitpressjournals.org/doi/pdf/10.1162/itgg.2008.3.2.189.

Ulrich, David, and Smallwood, Norm. 2014. *Sustentabilidade da liderança: 7 disciplinas para transformar intenções em ações eficientes*. São Paulo: HSM Editora.

UN, United Nations. 2011. "Guiding Principles on Business and Human Rights". Accessed July 13, 2020. https://www.ohchr.org/documents/publications/guidingprinciplesbusinesshr_en.pdf.

UN, United Nations. 1966. "International Covenant on Economic, Social and Cultural Rights". Accessed July 11, 2020. https://treaties.un.org/Pages/ViewDetails.aspx?src=IND&mtdsg_no=IV-3&chapter=4&clang=_en.

UN, United Nations. 2015. "The Global Goals". Accessed July 13, 2020. https://www.globalgoals.org/.

UN, United Nations. 1948. "The Universal Declaration of Human Rights". Accessed July 13, 2020. https://www.un.org/en/universal-declaration-human-rights/index.html.

Vandal-Sirois, Hugo. 2013. "Translation Challenges and their Implications in Advertising: Adaptation and Multicultural Marketing". In *The Silk Road of Adaptation: Transformations across Disciplines and Cultures*, edited by Laurence Raw, 145-148. Newcastle upon Tyne: Cambridge Scholars Publishing.

Vasconcelos, Isabella Francisca Freitas Gouveia de; Alves, Mario Aquino, and Pesqueux, Yvon. 2012. "Responsabilidade social corporativa e desenvolvimento sustentável: olhares habermasianos". *Revista de Administração de Empresas*, V. 52, No. 2, (2012): 148-152. Accessed July 11, 2020. https://www.scielo.br/scielo.php?pid=S0034-75902012000200002&script=sci_arttext.

Vogel, David. 2006. *The market for virtue: the potential and limits of corporate social responsibility*. New York: Brookings Institution.

CHAPTER 12

AUDIT PERFORMANCE AND INDEPENDENCE: A CULTURAL APPROACH BETWEEN LATIN AND NORDIC COUNTRIES

ALCINA AUGUSTA DE SENA PORTUGAL DIAS

ISCAP – P.PORTO, POLYTECHNIC OF PORTO

Introduction

In order to sustain a deep analysis of audit performance and independence in the contemporary global business framework, the cultural context of business companies has to be clearly understood. Taking into account this scope of analysis, the objective of this chapter is to discuss audit, corporate governance, fraud and the independence factor related to supervision. Auditing is a technique of inspection and analysis that produces a statement of assurance about any matter. In the global market, audit is used by all the organisations around the world that have a considerable size in terms of assets and workers.

The cultural framework associated with each country, revealing different approaches and perspectives about the same issue – inherited from the past as values, mores and traditions, changed or adapted in the present – is very important for the development and understanding of any business. This chapter will undertake a comparison, under a cultural perspective, of guidelines taken from an EU country (Portugal), in contrast with the Nordic countries.[1]

---

[1] A limitation of the study is that the perspective of Denmark was not included. As a suggestion for future investigation Denmark could be included, in addition to some companies from the USA, which would be an interesting comparison. To study the auditor´s performance according to the culture of each country would be a challenge for a case study.

To reach this aim the following scheme will be considered:

1. Corporate governance as a response to the big financial scandals
2. Financial engineering and frauds
3. The problem of independence
4. The EU (Portugal)/Nordic perspective – the importance of each country's culture.

1. Corporate governance as a response to the big financial scandals

When considering corporate governance, it is expected to find a good example of good practices, meaning the real economic and financial output of an organisation described and expressed by its top management following an auditor's report. The audit report encloses the financial and nonfinancial information provided by the companies (Mirihan *et al*, 2017). Following this audit paper one finds the corporate governance report, which is a kind of reassuring letter issued by the top management of the organisation addressed to all the stakeholders transmitting to them some confidence in the company's financial transparency and future.

Corporate governance may be considered a process made up of legal, contractual and market perspectives with the goal of enabling the maximum return for the *stakeholders.* It involves the board management, the consulting staff, the auditors and the executives of the organisation (Frynas and Stephan, 2015). All these different perspectives are mixed on behalf of some important aspects such as:

- Culture and integrity
- A harmonised accounting register (IFRS, IAS, ISA).

Culture and integrity are related to each country. The specific culture and main values of the people are associated with the ethical problems that will emerge across the development of any work to be achieved *(AICPA Code of Ethics 06-08*).

A Corporate Governance report will translate the application of the International Financial Reporting Standards – IFRS and IAS International Accounting Standards (Issued by the IASB – International Accounting Standards Board, UK). The auditor analysis will be guided by the ISA – International Standards on Audit (Issued by the IFAC – International Federation of Accountants, USA).

This will enable some comparison of accounting worldwide because through these common tools one can assume a common basis for international or global decisions (Dion, 2001). The deep connection of these two entities from two different continents – Europe (IASB, UK) and America (IFAC, USA) contributes to a formal harmonisation and globalisation of accounting and auditing issues.

How and why does corporate governance emerge and what relation has it as to these entities?

After the financial scandals of the past mainly the shareholders were deeply defrauded. They were investors at the time who lost not only the money they thought duly applied in a good investment but the confidence either in the auditor or in the companies.

All the above mentioned international and representative entities like IASB, COSO and IFAC (to name a few) together created procedures, norms and schemes of supervision and control in order to reinforce the internal control of the organisations, to protect the shareholders and to regain the auditor credibility related to the financial statements' transparency.

Corporate governance was a new issue and it arose as a collection of good practices that organisations should fulfil in order to earn public faith.

Table 1 shows examples of big financial scandals such as Enron, Parmalat and Worldcom.

Table 1. Financial scandals on an International Scope

Company	Scandal	Year	Result
XEROX	Falsification of financial results on behalf of an increase on income over 5 years	2000	Fines were paid to SEC; presently Xerox is in operation
ENRON	Increase on profits: hiding more than 1 billion US DLRS debt within group companies; manipulation of Texan market; bribery in order to receive public assignments	2001/2	Bankruptcy (yet in 2008 the company was still on trial)
WORLDCOM	Increase of cash flows: registering 3.8 million DLRS as capital expenses; granting a loan of 400 million DLRS to the founder of the company	2002	Bankruptcy
MERCK	Increase on sales: registering 12.4 billion DLRS related to payments of entities that were never received	2002	Fines were paid to SEC and Merck now have a Code of Ethics
PARMALAT	Use of SPE (Special Purpose Entity) placed in fiscal 'paradise countries'	2003	Bankruptcy (the founder, Tanzi, went to trial in 2005)

As can be seen from this table, the frauds have certain mechanisms of construction and this chapter will discuss only certain types: increasing either the value of the sales or of the assets or decreasing the debt through distributing it through the affiliated companies. These types of fraud involve a kind of financial engineering associated with the aim of increasing both the profits and respective dividends. In this way new investors were invited to these fruitful companies that were distributing high dividends and more money was entering their safes. Yet this kind of financial make-up of the organisations cannot last and one day the financial engineering will be dismantled.

2. Financial Engineering and Frauds

The financial scandals were characterised by some features like those presented in Table 2. One can say that these scandals evidenced a management with a high risk (Schroeder, 2014). Yet, when someone completes a due diligence report about these companies or achieves a strict audit on these companies it is discovered that there is a big 'make-up' regarding the financial statements of the company which are covering a fraud.

The goal of these scandals was to grant high dividends to the shareholders on behalf of an increase of the assets, a decrease of debt, an accrual of income or a decrease of expenses. The final result of these changes is the increase of profits and consequently the increase of dividends. High dividends appeal more and attract more investors and in this way more money enters the organisation. How is this achieved?

The people involved in achieving this change of values in the financial statements as to the new display of profits included not only the top management of the organisation but also the employees and the auditors (Wolk *et al,* 2008). The accounting theory, among many others, like the legitimacy or the stakeholder´s theory at the time, registered a collapse (Mark, 1995; Donaldson and Preston, 1995). All the theoretical and academic efforts defending the transparency and accurateness of the financial statements of the organisations were completely destroyed after these events. At this point one may ask: what about the capability and independence of the auditor, or the ethical behaviour expected from the top management of the organisations?

Some authors (Windsor and Warming-Rasmussen, 2009) have considered that there is a connection between the rise of regulatory capitalism and the decline of auditor independence, concluding that the profession has been transformed at a defined price and this price was the loss of the public confidence and the decline of the auditor brand image. Yet, conflicts of interest are still around.

Table 2. Financial engineering and frauds profile

BALANCE SHEET **PROFIT AND LOSS ACCOUNT**

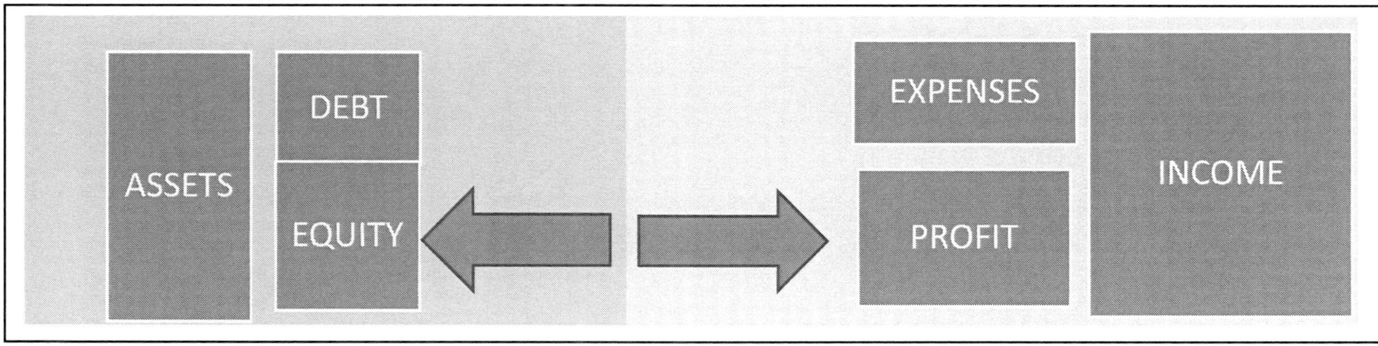

Gaffikin *et al* (2012), in a case study concerning Indonesia, considered the moral reasoning of public accountants in the development of a code of ethics. Their findings could be found and applied in any part of the world: 'It is concluded that the role of moral reasoning is an important influence on achieving ethical awareness in public accountants and financial managers. The development of a full code of ethics and an effective compliance monitoring system is essential for Indonesia if it is to play a role in the emerging global economy'. It must be added that compliance with good procedures will enable a good assurance as to the financial statements.

Rodgers and Al Fayi (2019) considered the strengths and weaknesses of three ethical pathways in a decision-making model. They described it as the Ethical Process Thinking Model where three dominant ethical pathways are considered – preference-based, rule-based and principle-based. The study's findings highlight that individuals' different perceptions and judgments, as well as information signals, can lead to different reporting lines (decision choices).

All the scholars focused on this issue agree that the ethical issue is the most important to be preserved in business.

3. Ethics and independence

3.1 An ethical issue

An individual's action is directly conditioned by the ethical climate of the company, either by those working inside or by the policies implemented therein. Mercier (2004) argues that 'the individual ethic is related to each goal of living' which is determined by personal experiences. In a business context and inside the organisation it is the result of the interaction of the behaviours of superiors and workers, thus resulting in the ethical climate of the company being influenced by the competitors. It is also influenced more indirectly by the climate of the professionals and the possible existence of regulations in the profession, as in the case of public certified accountants (auditors) who are governed by their statutes and by the deontological code. The ethical climate of business arises from the interaction between companies that participate as customers, suppliers and others (Gaffikin *et al*, 2012). Through living in society, an individual drives some of his/her learnings to the heart of the company, thus forming the ethical climate, which includes all the necessary connections to the development of the company's economic activity placed in the global market (Mirihan *et al*, 2017).

After analysing the factors that characterise unethical behaviour and the elements that determine the ethical attitude it can be concluded that 'ethics is a strategic key for the survival and profitability of the firms involved in a fierce and global competition' (Abdelhak *et al,* 2019). One could question whether this ethical issue has the same scope of analysis all around the world but it seems from a historical review that the Nordic countries are not an active player, for instance, in financial scandals. This was the reason why that we decided to examine these countries. From the literature review and according to Bondeson (2017), '… they are all relatively small countries situated in the Northern Hemisphere, with fairly homogeneous populations, well educated, and with a high standard of living. The macro-values are seen as dominated by leftism and egalitarianism. People are secularized to a high degree, but still influenced by protestant values, being often strict and moralistic but without much of a religious underpinning. To a great extent Scandinavian languages are mutually comprehensible'. The academic education and the high standard of living being at the same time strict and moralistic make the difference. This is a good path for ethics.

The importance of ethics in companies has increased with today´s relevance of corporate governance in the global market, due to its determinants (Anomaly and Brennan, 2014). The historical reference above described regarding financial scandals shows the interest in implementing rules and procedures, so that good governance practices exist for the commonwealth of the society (Bruton *et al*, 2010). It is not just a current and present concern. If we go back to the 18th century there was already evidence of this issue in the original draft of the Company of the General Commerce of Grão-Para and Maranhão in South America (Brazil).

As to the USA, the American Institute of the Certified Public Accountants[2] whose Code of Ethics (in force since 2014 and revised in June 2019) notes in its article 21 that a main issue of ethics is related to the independence factor that consists of two basic elements:

a. **Independence of mind,** allowing an individual to act with integrity, objectivity and professional scepticism
b. **Independence in appearance**, the avoidance of circumstances that would cause a reasonable misinformation including the safeguards needed to inspire some work assurance. The qualifications for performing an audit – integrity, objectivity, or professional scepticism of a firm or member – should not be compromised.

[2] Founded in the 19th century in Caroline, USA, and has more than 330,000 members.

> Instead, the member should determine whether such influences, if present, may create a threat that is not at an acceptable level, to perform the job with integrity and exercise objectivity and professional scepticism.

We are now presenting some situations or issues that may reveal a relative lack of independence as to some principles.

3.2 The independence issue

The independence issue implies some questions and eventual answers:

a. How can an auditor be independent if his/her services are subcontracted directly by the top management of the company to be audited by him/her?
b. What kind of independence does the supervision body of the listed companies – CMVM in Portugal – have when they inspect the work done by auditors for companies listed on their own portfolio? Where is the exemption and independence of this entity?
c. Sometimes companies use personal references or relations to get an auditor appointed: how independent is this?
d. At other times, big consulting companies render both non-auditing services and auditing services at the same time. They do not use the same brand name for invoicing but they belong to the scope of the same consulting group. Where is the independence factor?

These are some questions that one could pose and that arc connected to any audit, to which some improvements could be suggested, as presented in Table 3:

Table 3. Improvement suggestions

Issues	Suggestions
a. Top management/auditor	Independent contracting entity that would name auditors
b. Supervision inspection	Independent contracting entity that would inspect auditors work
c. Personal references	Rotation of auditors being compulsory after a mandate
d. Non audit/audit	An independent entity should supervise audit work as well as non-audit services

Situations a, b and d pose very difficult issues because the present supervising body – CMVM – would have to be convinced to delegate this duty to an independent entity. To be effective the government should nominate that entity. For the companies this would result in a good measure of independence once they had to use this entity to contract an auditor; besides this entity would be the one that later on would inspect the auditor's work. As to the non-audit and audit functions this entity should have the qualifications to inspect the activity of the auditors. This entity would be a supervising and inspecting body placed in the middle of the chain: between the auditors, the companies and the stock exchange commission. With the creation of this institutional entity the independence and exemption of the Portuguese Stock Exchange committee (CMVM) would be real.

As to issue c, the rotation of the auditor could be an easy task for the Order of Auditors who under a Government decision should have a supervising entity inspecting it.

These suggestions were formulated after researching what happens, for instance, in the Nordic countries. These countries, since quite a while ago, for cultural and geographical reasons some of which we have already named, have treated these issues of independence and exemption in a strict and clear way and it would be advisable to follow them for a proper benchmarking.

4. Supervision in Portugal – EU and Nordic countries

The 'state-of-the-art' of corporate governance is a kind of statutory regulation in the form of company law and other mandatory rules issued by the government or official authorities.

Self-regulation is defined and enforced by the business sector itself and informal norms and practices influence the way in which corporate governance is carried out in practice.

The main part of any corporate governance report is based upon the auditor's opinion and the objective of this chapter is to address two traits: the supervision and the independence.

In Portugal, the Stock Exchange Commission CMVM achieves the inspection of the auditor's work and opinion about the companies that are therein listed. There seems to be some lack of independence and exemption.

From the opposite perspective the Nordic region of Europe, due to the relatively strong and homogenous norms and value systems, combined with the high degree of social control typical of small communities that define and characterise these societies, reveals some features of transparency and independence that are quite interesting.

Two of these issues are going to be considered: the supervision of audit work and the audit independence across the countries Norway, Sweden and Finland.

4.1 Supervision of the Auditor's work

Across this description the names of the countries will have associated the respective entity responsible either for the supervision or for the auditor engagement.

Norway – *Finanstilsynet's (The Financial Supervisory Authority of Norway) independent government agency*

The Act on auditing and auditors (Auditors Act) supervises audit activity. Audit firms which audit annual accounts for entities subject to the statutory audit obligation must be authorised by Kredittilsynet. Authorisation is granted to firms that meet the requirements of section 3-5 of this Act. The titles "registered auditor" and "state authorized auditor" may only be used by persons who are authorized according to the provisions of this chapter'.

Finanstilsynet's (The Financial Supervisory Authority of Norway) tasks in relation to auditors comprise approval of individuals and firms in accordance with the legal requirements applying to the profession as well as their registration and supervision. It was formerly named *Kredittilsynet* (the Credit Supervisory Authority), but changed its name to *Finanstilsynet* in December 2009.

Supervision encompasses entities listed in the register of auditors, and includes checking that their activities comply with laws and regulations and are conducted in an appropriate and satisfactory manner.

Finanstilsynet is an independent government agency that is based on laws and decisions from the Parliament (Stortinget), the Government, the Ministry of Finance and on the international standards for financial supervision and regulation.

Supervision of the financial market

Through the supervision of enterprises and markets, Finanstilsynet strives to promote financial stability and to establish order in the market conditions to instil confidence that financial contracts will be honoured and services performed as intended. In addition to its preventive work, this entity is adequately prepared with experts on each field to deal with real problems that may arise. Finanstilsynet's premise is that Norwegian enterprises must be afforded competitive conditions which are in line with those enjoyed by institutions of the other EEA member states. Their duties are mainly as follows: being responsible for the supervision of banks, finance companies, mortgage companies, insurance companies, pension funds, investment firms, securities fund management, market conduct in the securities market, stock exchanges and authorised market places, settlement centres and securities registers, estate agencies, debt collection agencies, external accountants and auditors.

According to Eilifsen (1998), more than 20 years ago, the salient features of the Norwegian audit environment included:

- the government's high expectations and demand towards the auditing profession;
- a trusted and active auditing profession acting with considerable authority, especially in matters related to the conduct of an audit;
- a close interaction between the government and the profession, characterised more by caution and sensitivity to each other's position than by confrontation;
- the presence of an auditing legislation;
- a well-established and broad statutory audit requirement;
- some auditor responsibility for stewardship verification;
- the statutory auditor's responsibility for control of the auditee's tax obligations; and
- a general supportive climate for international harmonisation efforts in the auditing area.

Sweden – *Swedish Inspectorate of Auditors (SIA) is the government's expert authority*

In Sweden the supervision of auditors, dating back to 1973, became a task for the state. At the time this function was transferred to a department within the governmental authority – National Board of Trade – from the private institution Stockholm Chamber of Commerce. In 1995, the organisation took its present form. The Supervisory Board of Public Accountants (RN) was established by the Swedish Parliament in the Auditors Act of 1995, succeeded by the present Auditors Act (2001: 883), hereafter referred to as the Auditors Act.

The Swedish Inspectorate of Auditors (SIA) is the government's expert authority in matters related to auditors and auditing. In brief, its mission involves:

- securing nationwide access to qualified auditors, so ensuring that the world of trade and industry and the rest of society has access to auditors who are able to audit limited companies, banks, insurance companies, economic associations, foundations, authorities and other associations conducting financial activities, and responsibility for ensuring the appropriate development of generally accepted auditing standards and professional ethics.

To reach these goals some actions must be undertaken:

- providing an examination regime for auditors, as well as approving and authorising auditors and registering auditing firms, and
- supervising qualified auditors and registered audit firms.

The SIA's activities help to maintain a high quality of auditing and professional ethical requirements, ensuring that investors, companies, institutions and other stakeholders have access to reliable economic and strategic information needed for proper financial management and sound strategic decision-making. The ultimate purpose is to maintain trust and confidence in auditors and their work.

Finland – *The Auditing Board of the Central Chamber of Commerce examines annually the reports of auditors*

There are two categories of authorised *auditors and audit firms* in Finland defined in the Auditing Act section 2:

1) KHT auditors, authorised by the Auditing Board of the Central Chamber of Commerce of Finland; and
2) HTM auditors, authorised by Auditing Committees of regional Chambers of Commerce.

Supervision of Auditor's Annual report

The Auditing Board of the Central Chamber of Commerce examines annually the reports and documents by the authorised auditors and authorised audit firms in order to check if the auditors and the audit firms still maintain their proficiency and other qualifications required for authorisation. The objective of supervision is also to ensure that authorised auditors and authorised audit firms observe the Auditing Act and any provisions given by virtue thereof.

The Auditing Board of the State, the Auditing Board of the Central Chamber of Commerce or the Auditing Committee of a regional Chamber of Commerce have the right to obtain all documents and other records considered necessary for the supervision of the authorised auditor. They may also examine documents and other records on the premises of the authorised auditor. In addition the authorised auditor shall, without unnecessary delay, submit to the supervisory authorities any requested information or reports necessary for the supervision.

4.2 Engagement of the auditor

Norway – *Finanstilsynet related to the Minister of Finance*

The Office of the General Auditor of Norway (Norwegian: *Riksrevisjonen*) is the state auditor of the Government of Norway and directly subordinate to the Parliament of Norway. He is responsible for auditing, monitoring and advising all state economic activities, including financial audits, performance audits and corporate control.

Companies have to seek a statutory auditor to conduct an annual audit of the financial health of their organisation and the contact is the Financial Supervisory Authority of Norway – Finanstilsynet that depends on the Minister of Finance.

Sweden – *RN related to the Minister of Justice*

Revisorsnämnden (RN) - Supervisory Board of Public Accountants. RN is a governmental authority under the Ministry of Justice. RN is the government's authority for all matters concerning auditors. RN has two overall tasks; firstly, to provide the Swedish business world with highly qualified auditors and, secondly, to supervise and regulate those auditors (Dias and Álvarez-Santullano, 2016). If a registered public accounting firm is appointed as an auditor, the name of the principal responsible auditor shall be registered with Bolagsverket (the official registration of organisations).

Finland – *Auditing Board related to the Chamber of Commerce*

There are two categories of *authorised auditors and audit firm as auditor* in Finland defined in the Auditing Act section 2:

1) KHT auditors, authorised by the Auditing Board of the Central Chamber of Commerce of Finland (AB3C); and
2) HTM auditors, authorised by Auditing Committees of regional Chambers of Commerce.

In brief, the three Nordic countries considered show strict measures of supervision and engagement that depend directly on governmental entities. This fact enables an accrued value of trust to all the stakeholders.

5. Conclusion

Contemporary global business requires a cultural perspective in order to fully understand by what means does business translate cultural and intercultural characteristics. As referred in this chapter, to develop an audit there is a strict need to clearly understand the organisation of the business, which, in turn, requires a cultural approach in order to be fully understood and contextualized.

In the introduction to this chapter, it was mentioned that its goal would bc to deal with the independence issue. To reach this aim, some notorious financial scandals were named in order to prove that fraud in the financial statements showed the lack of independence of the auditor, of the employee and of the top management. As a consequence of these events, the corporate governance report emerged. When a company makes a report about corporate governance it means that there are good practices implemented that help to prevent fraud occurrence. But in order to make this corporate governance report work as a good financial warranty for stakeholders, the supervision entities, who are responsible for the maintenance of the independence issue, play an important role. There are no unique decisions that result in an organisation but there are some good practices that the international benchmarking may enable.

In this study, the Nordic countries were considered and their good practices were identified and related to the actual independence of the supervising entities. When doing so, it is well known that there are no unique decisions that can be applied to any organisation worldwide; however, there are some good practices that may be retrieved from the international benchmarking.

In Table 4, the main features found in the Nordic countries, against those already described in Portugal, are summarised.

Table 4. Main features of the Nordic countries versus Portugal (EU)

Countries	Supervision on audit depends on	Engagement of the auditor belongs to
Norway	Finanstilsynet's (The Financial Supervisory Authority of Norway) independent government agency	Finanstilsynet independent government agency related to the Minister of Finance
Sweden	Swedish Inspectorate of Auditors (SIA) is the government's expert authority	Revisorsnämnden (RN) – Supervisory Board of Public Accountants. RN is a governmental authority under the Ministry of Justice
Finland	The Auditing Board/Committees of the Central Chamber of Commerce annually examine the reports	Auditing Board/Committees of regional Chambers of Commerce
Portugal	CMVM – Portuguese Stock Commission	Organisations

As a conclusion, we may say that in Norway, Sweden and Finland, the independence issues have been considered long time ago, resulting presently in a sound defence of the shareholder (in minority or majority), thus presenting financial statements with an accrued transparency and trustfulness; therefore, one may say that this represents an added value in any business. Some authors argue that, to improve the existing corporate governance framework and to ensure high quality and uniform financial statements, the enforcement of standards should be tailored to specific cultures, or at a minimum, corporate boards need to be more culturally diversified (Chaney *et al*, 2019). Bondeson (2017) argues that there are many variables only applicable to the Nordic culture and this is the main reason for the difference with Portugal, as concerns the independence issue.

At last, we must refer that knowledge about different intercultural perspectives related to the global business enables a better understanding of the audit process work and, ultimately, this will lead to more efficiency and effectiveness in business.

References

Abdelhak, E., Elamer, A., AlHares, A. and McLaughlin, C. (2019), Auditors' ethical reasoning in developing countries: the case of Egypt, *International Journal of Ethics and Systems*, 35 (4) pp. 558–583. https://doi.org/10.1108/IJOES-02-2019-0041

AICPA Code of Ethics: https://www.aicpa.org/research/standards/codeofconduct.html

Anomaly, J. and Brennan, G. (2014), Learning Anomaly, Social Norms, The Invisible Hand, and the Law. *University of Queensland Law Journal,* 33 (2).

Bondeson, U. (2017), *Nordic Moral Climate: Value Continuities and Discontinuities in Denmark, Finland, Norway, and Sweden*, Taylor & Francis.

Bruton, G. D., Ahlstrom, D. and Li, H.-L. (2010), Institutional Theory and Entrepreneurship: Where Are We Now and Where Do We Need to Move in the Future?, *Entrepreneurship Theory and Practice,* 3 (3) pp. 421–440.

Chaney, P. K., Lodh, S. and Nandy, M. (2019), How Does Culture Impinge Upon Managers' Demeanor of Earnings Management? Evidence from Cross-Country Analysis. *International Journal of Accounting.* https://doi.org/10.1142/S1094406021500098

Committee of Sponsoring Organizations of the Treadway Commission (COSO): https://www.coso.org/Pages/default.aspx

Dias, A. A. and Álvarez-Santullano, M. (2014), Supervision on Audit and the effects of EU directive 56/2014 Case study: Portugal and Spain Global Journal of Advanced Research, 3 (11) pp. 1046–1057.

Dion, M. (2001), Corporate Citizenship and Ethics of Care: Corporate Values, Codes of Ethics and Global Governance, in J. Andriof and M. McIntosh (ed.), *Perspectives on Corporate Citizenship*, Greenleaf, pp. 118–138.

Donaldson, P. (1995), The Stakeholder Theory of the Corporation: Concepts, Evidence, and Implications *Academy of Management Review,* 20 (1) pp. 65–91.

Eilifsen, A. (1998), Auditing regulation and the statutory auditor's responsibilities in Norway, *The European Accounting Review*, 7, (4) pp. 709–722.

Financial Accounting Standards Board (FASB), USA: https://www.fasb.org/home

Frynas, G. and Stephan, S. (2015), Political Corporate Social Responsibility: Reviewing Theories and Setting New Agendas, *International Journal of Review Management*, 17 (4) pp. 483–509.

Gaffikin, M. and Lindawati, A. S. L. (2012), The Moral Reasoning of Public Accountants in the Development of a Code of Ethics: the Case of Indonesia, *Australasian Accounting, Business and Finance Journal*, 6 (1) pp. 3–28.

International Accounting Standards Board (IASB): https://www.iasplus.com/en/resources/ifrsf/iasb-ifrs-ic/iasb

International Federation of Accountants (IFAC), USA: https://www.ifac.org/

Kredittilsynet Norway. Legal authenticity remains with the official Norwegian version as published in Norsk Lovtidend – https://app.uio.no/ub/ujur/oversatte-lover/data/lov-19990115-002-eng.pdf

Mercier S. (2004). *L'éthique dans les entreprises*, La Découverte.

Miriham, Coşkun Arslan and Kisacik, H. (2017), The Corporate Sustainability Solution: Triple Bottom Line, *The Journal of Accounting and Finance,* pp. 18–34.

OECD (2014), *Risk Management and Corporate Governance*, Corporate Governance, OECD Publishing. http://dx.doi.org/10.1787/9789264208636-en, pp. 267–288.

Riahi-Belkaoui, A. (2004) *Accounting Theory*, 4th Edition, Business Press Thomson.

Rodgers, W. and Al Fayi, S. (2019), *Journal of Accounting Forum*, 43 (2) pp. 220–245.

Schroeder, H. (2014), An art and science approach to strategic risk management, *Strategic Direction*, 30 (4) pp. 28–30.

Suchman, M. C. (1995) Managing Legitimacy: Strategic and Institutional Approaches, *Academy Management Review,* 20 (3) pp. 571–610.

Swedish Inspectorate of Auditors (SIA): https://www.revisorsinspektionen.se/en/English/

The Authorisation and Supervision of Auditors and Audit Firms in Finland (2013) http://www.congreso.es/docu/docum/ddocum/dosieres/sleg/legislatura_10/spl_80/pdfs/17.pdf

Windsor C. and Warming-Rasmussen, B. (2009), The rise of regulatory capitalism and the decline of auditor independence: A critical and experimental examination of auditors' conflicts of interests, *Critical Perspectives on Accounting*, 20 (2) pp. 267–288.

Wolk, H. I., Dodd J. L. and Rozycki J. J. (2008). *Accounting Theory: Conceptual Issues in a Political and Economic Environment*, 7th edition, Sage Publications Inc.

World Business Council for Sustainable Development (WBCSD) http://www.wbcsd.org/.

World Economic Forum (2016), *The Global Risks Report 2016*, 11th edition.

CHAPTER 13

THE NEW PARADIGM OF THE CORPORATION: A COMPARATIVE APPROACH BETWEEN LAW AND BUSINESS

MARGARIDA AZEVEDO
CENTRE FOR INTERCULTURAL STUDIES (CEI)
ISCAP – P.PORTO, POLYTECHNIC OF PORTO

1. The demand for corporate purpose

Over the last few years, an important movement sustaining a change in the understanding of the corporate purpose has firmly emerged. The movement involves academics, CEOs and policy makers and rests upon the idea of purpose. It argues, contrary to Friedman's doctrine of maximization of shareholders' value as the sole intent of a company, that the purpose of a company should consider the interests of those who interact with the corporation, such as creditors, suppliers, workers, customers and society as a whole. The purpose of a company should then incorporate social concerns.

The books of Colin Mayer (2018) and Alex Edmans (2020) deal with the notion of purpose. Both authors stress the fact that the idea of purpose does not convert the company into a non-profit organization.

In the same direction, 181 American CEOs agreed on a redefinition of corporate purpose. The statements on corporate governance principles issued by the Business Roundtable since 1997 elected the interests of the shareholders as the main objective of a company. In the meeting of 19th August 2019, this group of CEOs endorsed the interests of all stakeholders and outlined a different corporate purpose. The companies should not only pursue the interests of the shareholders but should also engage in the interests of all stakeholders.

The Davos Manifesto is also part of this movement, which emphasizes the need to understand and harmonize the interests of shareholders and other stakeholders, in order to promote the long-term interest of the company[1]. This movement must not be seen as a sort of latest fashion, but rather as a fundamental change (Fleischer, 2021) in management, which raises crucial questions for Company Law. This is why the main objective of this chapter is to analyze the concept of purpose and its implications for Company Law.

2. Purpose and corporate social responsibility

As Mayer (2018) points out, corporate purpose is not altruism or corporate social responsibility. Purpose is the core of the business, its reason to exist (Mayer, 2019, p. 17). Purpose guides the activity of the company, enlightening what the company should do. Consequently, purpose is intricately linked to the company's strategy.

The purpose of a company involves the interests of all stakeholders and represents the rejection of Friedman's claim that the creation of shareholder's value is the core of the business. Consequently, corporate purpose goes beyond corporate social responsibility, becoming the cornerstone of the corporation. In the words of Mayer (2018, p. 17), "this is not corporate social responsibility (CSR) as meritorious philanthropy; it is poverty alleviation and environment protection as the core of corporate activities".

The corporation represents a solution to existing problems. By accomplishing this mission, it produces profit: doing well by doing good (2018, p. 17). The core of the company's activity is not to produce profit, but to pursue its purpose. In the same sense, Edmans (2020, pp. 27 and 29) focus on the difference between Pieconimics and corporate social responsibility. The author also regards Pieconomics as the core of the business, an idea that goes beyond corporate social responsibility. Pieconomcs consists neither of mere acts of charity nor of simple acts aimed at avoiding losses for stakeholders. Rather, it is embedded in the business. The company should actively pursue the interests of the stakeholders. Edmans (2020, p. 117) stresses that the Pieconomics primary mission is to serve society.

---

[1] Davos Manifesto 2020: The Universal Purpose of a Company in the Fourth Industrial Revolution. See:
https://www.weforum.org/agenda/2019/12/davos-manifesto-2020-the-universal-purpose-of-a-company-in-the-fourth-industrial-revolution/

Purpose is central to the business, representing its core, a fundamental idea that testifies a crucial change.

3. Purpose and stakeholder theory

Given that purpose is the core of business, it is not difficult to understand that it imposes a duty on the board of directors and senior managers to act on behalf of the enterprise, while coordinating the interests of all stakeholders (Ferrarini 2020, p. 4). Indeed, the directors have fiduciary duties towards all stakeholders, whose different interests are not subject to the bargaining of their representatives in the board. The various interests of the stakeholders must rather be synchronized by the board of directors. This approach is the one which best serves the idea of purpose as the core of the business.

4. The for-profit benefit companies

The American Benefit Corporation is a for-profit corporation that pursues a social purpose. In the same track, the Italian Corporate Law recognizes the *Società benefit,* which engages in both a social purpose and profit. However, it does not represent an independent legal form, as it can adopt any existing legal type (Fleischer, 2021, p. 23). Similarly, in France one can find the *societé a mission*, while in Germany it has been suggested the recognition of a limited liability in responsible ownership (Fleischer, 2021, p. 23).

These companies represent either a different form of corporation or a variant of an existing form. However, we claim that purpose should be a requirement for any company, implying adapted legal frameworks for all corporations. Nevertheless, as Mayer observes, the benefit companies may provide different models of organization. These models may be useful, because they should be capable of responding to the challenges arising from the corporation new paradigm.

When we consider that the purpose should be a mandatory requirement for any corporation, we are aware that the primary role of a company is to solve problems of the society, as Mayer and Edmans point out. Consequently, the purpose of the company represents a new paradigm of the corporation, which claims an adaptation of the legal rules. However, and contrary to our view, Fleischer (2021, pp. 24 and 25) maintains that the companies should be free to include purpose in their articles of association.

5. The legal challenges of purpose

Purpose is a management concept that, simultaneously, demands, from our point of view, a change in legal rules. Firstly, law should require the inclusion of purpose in the articles of the corporation. This should be binding for the management bodies of the company and its shareholders.

In the French Law, the revision of the article 1835 of the Napoleonic Code, in the context of the reform performed by the *Loi n° 2019-486 du 22 Mai 2019 relative à la croissance et la transformation des entreprises*, admits that the shareholders may introduce in the articles of the association the *raison d'être* of the company. The inclusion of *raison d'être* in the articles of the association is optional for the shareholders, but once it is incorporated in the articles of the association, it entails important legal consequences, namely for the management bodies.

The United Kingdom, as well as Portugal and other countries, have also contributed in some measure to the movement, through the recommendations contained in the Corporate Governance Codes. The importance of Soft Law must not be questioned, but the change of paradigm of the corporation requires the intervention of the Hard Law.

The French Law, by establishing the possibility of including *the raison d'être* in the articles of association, has taken a crucial step in the right direction. However, we consider that we are facing an actual change of paradigm, which demands a mandatory rule, imposing the obligation of including purpose in the articles of the association (Mayer, 2018, p. 23).

The provision of the purpose in the articles of the association raises an important question: how is the corporate purpose protected? We reject a direct state control, which would undermine economic initiative. We also deny the idea of a control by the state, because it would entitle a public body to evaluate and protect the public utility of company. This would represent a return to the old state license[2].

The protection of the purpose of the company should rather be guaranteed by Private Law mechanisms. The corporate structure should be adapted in order to promote the long-term interest of the company. On the other hand, the liability actions against the members of the management bodies and in favor of the company should be reserved to long-term investors committed

---

[2] For an historical overview, see: Fleischer, Corporate Purpose, op.cit., pp. 3 and 4.

to the mission of the corporation. Mayer emphasizes the importance of the controlling shareholders.

In continental Europe, countries like Germany, France and Portugal rely upon the notion of social interest as the criteria for the management conduct. This allows a pluralistic view of the interests that the management should promote (Fleischer, 2021, p. 19) and opens space for a reform based on the idea of social purpose.

In Germany, it is accepted by the courts and the legal doctrine that the interest of the enterprise (*Unternehmensinteresse*) incorporates the interest of the public welfare (Fleischer, 2021, p.17). French Law relies on the similar concept of *interêt social*. *Unternehmensinteresse* and *interêt social* are regarded as a gateway to other interests different from those of the shareholders (Fleischer, 2018, p. 733).

In Portugal, the article 64 of the Commercial Companies Code relies on social interest (*interesse da sociedade*) and explicitly requires the members of the management bodies to act in accordance with the long-term interests of the shareholders, considering other interests relevant for the company's interest, such as those of the employees, customers and creditors. The Portuguese law adopts the notion of social interest and unequivocally admits the relevance of interests different from those of the shareholders. Case Law and the doctrine reflect this approach.

By contrast, according to American and British laws, management appears to be intrinsically committed to the shareholders' interests, which may represent an additional difficulty. It is argued that the objective of creating long-term shareholder value is compatible with the fulfilment of the interests of other stakeholders (enlightened shareholder maximization). However, the objective of the company remains the maximization of the shareholders' value.

6. Conclusion

Purpose postulates a change in the paradigm of the corporation and demands an adequate reform of Corporate Law. In the last decades, there has been a decrease of trust, which has affected enterprises and the capital markets alike (Dias (2021, p. 732). For these reasons, the recovery of the lost confidence is crucial. It is fair to say that the social purpose embedded in the business activity is not only the right thing to do, but it also promotes the economic and the financial growth of the corporation.

We believe that the most suitable instrument to protect and enforce purpose is Private Law. The inclusion of the corporate purpose in the articles of association should be mandatory. Purpose should be protected and enforced preferentially by Private Law mechanisms. Public regulation should play only a subsidiary role, where private law mechanisms are not effective. The option for Private Law preserves economic initiative and should generally be suitable for the protection and enforcement of the corporate purpose.

The reliance on the market, in particular on the role of institutional investors, as the sole instrument to promote the change of paradigm of the corporation, may not be effective. The role of mandatory Private Law rules is crucial to enhance the fundamental change of paradigm embodied in the demand for corporate purpose.

Bibliography

Dias G.F. (2021), Sustentabilidade, grupos de interesses e propósito. Cadernos do Mercado de Valores Mobiliários sobre os 20 anos do Código de Valores Mobiliários, pp. 731-742.

Edmans, A. (2020), Grow the Pie. How Greater Companies Deliver Both Purpose and Profit. Oxford, Oxford University Press.

Ferrarini, G. (2020), An Alternative View of Corporate Purpose: Colin Mayer on Prosperity. Genoa Centre for LaW and Finance. Working Paper 10 2020.

Fleischer, H. (2018) Unternehmensinteresse und intérêt social: Schlüsselfiguren aktienrechtlichen Denkens in Deutschland und Frankreich. ZGR 2018, 703–734.

Fleischer, H. (2021), Corporate Purpose: A Management Concept and its Implications for Company Law. ECGI Working Paper Series in Law. Working Paper N° 561/2021.

Mayer, C. (2018), Prosperity, Better Business Makes Greater Good. Oxford, Oxford University Press.

CONTRIBUTORS

Junko Kobayashi is an associate professor at Kansai Gaidai University, Japan. She is the author of 15 English textbooks on intercultural communication.

Linda Viswat is professor emeritus at Otemon Gakuin University, Japan. Her research has focused on intercultural communication and learning strategies/motivation of Japanese university students.

Luísa Bravo Lamas holds a degree in Social Work, and a PhD in Educational Sciences by the University of Santiago de Compostela, focused on Citizenship Education, a theme she had already developed in her Diploma of Advanced Studies at the Universidad de Valencia, Spain. She is a researcher at the Center for Intercultural Studies of ISCAP-P.PORTO. She is an invited senior lecturer at ISCIA – Aveiro and at UMUM, Mozambique. She taught for nine years in secondary education at the Technological Course in Sociocultural Animation, and she has also been teaching in higher education in Portugal and Cape Verde, in the areas of Educational Sciences and Social Sciences. She has coordinated and supervised several internships and undergraduate dissertations.

Marco Lamas has a Post-Doc in Entrepreneurship Education, PhD in Education and Entrepreneurship, Graduate in International Relations. Currently working on another PhD in Economics and Business. Invited Senior Lecturer at ISCAP-Polytechnic of Porto and Senior Lecturer at ISLA–Polytechnic Institute of Management and Technology. Editor, reviewer and member of scientific committees in scientific journals and international conferences. He is a researcher member of the Center for Intercultural Studies and of the Center for Organizational and Social Studies, both at ISCAP, Polytechnic of Porto. Business coach certified by the European Coaching Association (ECA); certified business consultant and trainer (IEFP and CCPFC) in Entrepreneurship, Management and Strategy.

Joana Rocha is a Professor at the Medical School of Fernando Pessoa University since 2005 and a speech and language pathologist since 2001. Joana graduated at the Porto Polytechnic – Health School, has a master's degree in Speech Sciences and a PhD in Psychology by the University of Aveiro. Her research focuses on theory of mind and language development in children. She has also experience as a clinical educator, scientific reviewer (in her area of expertise), organizer of scientific conferences, adviser of academic papers/projects, and she is also a published author/co-author in national and international journals and book chapters.

Susana Vaz Freitas holds a PhD in Biomedical Engineering and a Master in Public Health. She is a speech and language pathologist in the ENT Unit of the Hospital and University Centre of Porto (CHUPorto) – Hospital Santo António, Porto, Portugal, and a senior lecturer at the Health School of Porto. She is a researcher at LIAAD – Laboratory of Artificial Intelligence and Support to Decision Making, INESCTEC, Porto. Up to date, she has edited 1 book, published more than 30 articles, and is a researcher at national and international projects. Areas of interest: Voice Assessment and Therapy; Alaryngeal Speech; Oropharyngeal Dysphagia. Scopus [h-index; =8; 2020: citations]; Scopus ID: 57210845270; ORCID: 0000-0002-0667-7632.

Rita Alegria is a Speech and Language Pathologist since 2000. Rita graduated at the Porto School of Health Technologies. She is in her final year of a PhD in Language Disorders and Development, with a specialty in Language Disorders. Rita has been a lecturer at the Medical School of University Fernando Pessoa since 2008. Her research focuses on speech therapy in an aquatic setting for patients with unilateral vocal fold paralysis or with bilateral vocal fold nodules. Additionally, her roles include that of clinical supervisor, scientific reviewer (in her area of expertise), guest lecturer at national and international conferences/workshops and is a published author/co-author in national and international journals.

Bárbara Santos holds a Master's degree in Business Management from ISCAP, the Porto Accounting and Business School of the Porto Polytechnic, and a bachelor's degree in Business Science from Fernando Pessoa University, Porto, Portugal.

Oscar Bernardes holds a PhD in Business Management from the University of Beira Interior, Portugal; a MSc in Economics and Business Management from the University of la Rioja, Spain; and a bachelor's degree in Accounting and Administration from the Polytechnic of Porto, Portugal. He is currently a professor at the University of Aveiro; at the Polytechnic of Porto's Accounting and Business School (ISCAP) and School of Engineering (ISEP); and at APNOR – the Association of Polytechnic Institutes of the Northern Region, Portugal.

Clara Sarmento holds an Aggregation in Cultural Studies by the University of Aveiro, as well as a PhD in Portuguese Culture and an MA in Anglo-American Studies by the University of Porto. She is a Tenured Full Professor at ISCAP, the Business School of the Polytechnic of Porto (P.PORTO), where she is also the Director of the Centre for Intercultural Studies and of the Master's in Intercultural Studies for Business. She is a member of the Advisory Boards of ISCAP, Porto Executive Academy, and Cambridge Scholars Publishing. Clara Sarmento was a visiting scholar at the Department of English, Brown University, USA, and has been a MA and PhD lecturer, supervisor and examiner in several universities in Portugal and abroad. Among many other international research projects, she is the director of the award winning projects StreetArtCEI and StreetArtAgainstCovid, and of E.REI, the *E-Journal of Intercultural Studies*. She is a member of COST action CA18126 Writing Urban Places. New Narratives of the European City. Clara Sarmento is the author of books, chapters, articles and conferences, as well as an editor, scientific/editorial board member, referee and project manager, in the areas of Literary, Cultural and Intercultural Studies; Feminist and Gender Studies; Culture applied to Business, Tourism and Development; Graffiti and Street Art. Her work has been recognized with: American Club of Lisbon Award for Academic Merit; CES (University of Coimbra) Award for Young Social Scientists; PRODEP III (European Commission) PhD grant; 'Best-Selling title on the study of poetry' and 'Book of the month in Social Sciences', Cambridge Scholars Publishing (UK); five times PAPRE (P.PORTO) award for papers in high quality journals; Gardners' (UK) 'Author of the Month'; Santander UNICOVID Award; Santander grants 'Best Practices in Digital Education' and 'Social Impact'; '7 Wonders of Portuguese Heritage' jury member; a regular presence on national media.

Pedro Andrade is a sociologist and researcher at the University of Minho, CECS. He taught at the Universities of Coimbra and Lisbon, on Critical Sociology of Culture, Communication, Sociological Methods, and Digital Humanities. Research about urban cultures, art communication, art/science museums, literacies, digital social networks (Web 2.0/3.0), methodologies. Coordinator of international projects, e.g.: Scientific-Technological Literacy and Public Opinion (2005, on science museums' audience) and Public Communication of Arts (2011, about art museums and their relationships with audiences, tourism, digital/virtual sociological methodology, hybrid media interaction, sociological/cultural games, social networks, virtual/augmented reality), funded by the Foundation for Science and Technology (average evaluation: Excellent). Participation in international university networks, e.g.: Virginia Commonwealth Univ., USA; project

Manifesto Art and Social Inclusion in Urban Communities (UK). Author of several books and scientific papers published in international and national journals with peer review, indexed in global bibliographic databases. Director of the first Portuguese-French scientific journal, *Atalaia-Intermundos* (1995). ORCID: https://orcid.org/0000-0003-4550-0562.

Marco António Furtado has a University Degree in Modern Languages and Literatures – English and German Studies – by the Faculty of Letters of Porto University, Portugal. He has a Master's Degree in Bilingual and Intercultural German-Portuguese Studies by Minho University, Braga, Portugal, and a PhD Degree in Interpreting Studies by Vigo University, Spain. He is currently a Senior Lecturer at the Porto Accounting and Business School (ISCAP-P.PORTO). His research work is mainly focused on Interpreting Studies. Furthermore, he is developing additional research work on Intercultural Studies, German Contemporary History and Culture, and German Culture for Business.

Laura Tallone is a senior lecturer in Translation at the Porto Accounting and Business School (ISCAP-P.PORTO). Member of the direction of ISCAP's Master's in Specialised Translation and Interpreting, researcher at the Centre for Intercultural Studies, and a member of the editorial committee of *POLISSEMA – Revista de Letras do ISCAP*. Extended background as a freelance English-Portuguese-Spanish translator and interpreter. Editor of the books *Do Signo ao Texto: Contributos Pedagógicos para a Tradução Técnica em Quatro Línguas* (De Facto, 2016) and *Do Texto ao Contexto: Novos Contributos Pedagógicos para a Tradução Técnica em Quatro Línguas* (CEI, 2020). Current research interests include the intersections between Translation and Cultural and Heritage Tourism.

Sara Cerqueira Pascoal is an Associate Professor at the Polytechnic of Porto (ISCAP- P.PORTO), Portugal, since 1997, where she teaches Rhetoric, Semiotics and Portuguese for Foreigners. She has an undergraduate degree in Modern Languages and Literatures, a Master's degree in Portuguese Culture and a PhD in Romance Languages and Cultures. She is a researcher and member of the Scientific Board of the Centre for Intercultural Studies and a researcher at the Institute for the Study of Literature and Traditions of Lisbon's Nova University. Her research interests range from Literary Geography and Geocriticism, Literary and Cultural Tourism, Rhetoric, Semiotics, Intercultural Communication and Portuguese Culture.

Rebeca Cristina López-González holds a PhD (2015, cum laude, International Mention) and a degree in Translation and Interpreting from the University of Vigo, where she has been working as a full time professor/researcher since 2011. Her teaching focuses on specialised legal and economic translation, one of her areas of research. In this field she has participated as a speaker in several conferences and published articles and book chapters such as: "Putting Touristic Destinations on the Map through Translation. How Public Institutions Provide Multilingual Visual Guides" in *Intercultural Routes Across Multicultural Spaces: From Theory to Dialogue* (2020); "Translating Culture for Touristic Purposes: A case Study" in *E-Journal of Intercultural Studies*, vol. 6 (2018) and "Translating Cultural Aspects for Tourists and Cruise Passengers: Vigo, a Case Study" in *Bulletin of the Instituto de Estudios Vigueses. Glaucopis*, vol. 22 (2017).

Alexandre Monteiro is a nautical archaeologist who specializes in post-medieval Iberian shipbuilding and who has conducted archaeological surveys and digs in Portugal, Australia, Sharjah and Oman. He has done archival and historical research regarding underwater cultural heritage of Portugal, Spain, Mozambique, Cape Verde, China, Namibia, Turks and Caicos Islands, Brazil and Uruguay. With more than 2000 hours of diving, the majority done in archaeological context, and a former Nautical Archaeologist for the Portuguese Ministry of Culture, Alexandre Monteiro teaches Maritime and Contemporary Archaeology at Lisbon NOVA University. He is also a University of Western Australia Honorary Associate Researcher, a fellow of the Portuguese Navy Academy, an expert in Nautical Archaeology for the International Council for Monuments and Sites (ICOMOS), an executive Member of the International Federation of Teaching Archaeologists and Historians (IFTAH) and a science writer and reviewer for National Geographic Magazine – Portugal.

Isabel Torres is a graduate in Languages, Literatures and Cultures (English and Spanish) by the Faculty of Arts of the University of Porto (FLUP) and holds a Masters in Intercultural Studies for Business from the Business and Accounting School of Porto (ISCAP-P.PORTO). She started her professional activity in 2019, as a translator and content writer, and is now working for a French (and vegan) project incubator, as a project manager and content writer, on a digital nomad format. Simultaneously, she has been active in social causes, she was a coordinator at the students' association of FLUP and a founding member of Alarido – Cultural Association of Vale do Ave. As part of the Erasmus generation, Isabel spent a semester in Hungary and one year in France. Isabel's personal and professional experiences have shaped her into someone who can only feel truly fulfilled in an intercultural environment.

Geisa Oliveira Daré is an attorney and a PhD student at the Postgraduate Program in Social Sciences at UNESP in Marília, Brazil. She holds a Masters in Human Rights from the University of Minho, Portugal, and a Bachelor in Law from the University Center of Bauru, Brazil. She is an associate of the research groups 'Constitution, Constitutionalism and Fundamental Rights', of the Institute of Constitutional Law and Citizenship, and 'Teaching and Extension in Human Rights and International Human Mobility', of the Federal University of Santa Maria (Migraidh/CSVM program).

Charize Hortmann is an attorney, specializing in complex lawsuits in the field of Civil Liability (TORTS) since 2011. She holds a postgraduate degree in Philosophy and Human Rights from PUC-PR (2017) and a Masters in Human Rights from the University of Minho (2020). Author of the book *Artificial Intelligence in the Labour Market* (Dialética, 2020) and ofseveral articles about environmental law, sustainability, and new technologies. Currently, she is a content professor in the civil law branch and a lawyer at the NGO Canteiros Coletivos, aiming to protect the environment in Salvador-Bahia.

Alcina Portugal Dias holds a PhD in Entrepreneurial Sciences from the University of the Basque Country, a Master in Accounting and Management from the University of Minho, and a degree in Economics from the Faculty of Economics of the University of Porto. She has been developing her entrepreneurial experience for about 30 years. Current functions: Coordinator Professor at the Accounting and Business School of the Polytechnic of Porto, and director of the Masters' Degree in Auditing, where she also lectures. She has published several articles in journals (Scopus) and international conference proceedings, as well as academic books in Germany, USA and Portugal, and fiction books in Portugal. She is a member of the editorial review board of the financial online quarterly *E-Finanse* (Poland), Emerald's *International Journal for Quality and Reliability Management*, and *Tékhne – Review of Applied Management Studies*. Her research fields go from quality management systems to risk management and auditing, always related to the company´s financial performance.

Margarida Azevedo de Almeida has an MA and a PhD in Law, specialization in Business Legal Sciences, from the Faculty of Law of the University of Coimbra, and has a Law degree from the Faculty of Law of the Catholic Portuguese University. She is an Associate Professor at the Porto Accounting and Business School. She is the author of several research studies in the field of Private Law, mainly in civil liability. Her main areas of interest include Civil Law and Company Law, under an interdisciplinary and comparative approach.